VALUES AND PRACTICE IN CHILDREN'S SERVICES

VALUES AND PRACTICE
IN CHILDREN'S SERVICES

ROGER SMITH

palgrave
macmillan

First published 2005 by
PALGRAVE MACMILLAN
Houndmills, Basingstoke, Hampshire RG21 6XS and
175 Fifth Avenue, New York, N.Y. 10010
Companies and representatives throughout the world

PALGRAVE MACMILLAN is the global academic imprint of the Palgrave Macmillan division of St. Martin's Press, LLC and of Palgrave Macmillan Ltd. Macmillan® is a registered trademark in the United States, United Kingdom and other countries. Palgrave is a registered trademark in the European Union and other countries.

ISBN 1–4039–1474–5

This book is printed on paper suitable for recycling and made from fully managed and sustained forest sources.

A catalogue record for this book is available from the British Library.

A catalog record for this book is available from the Library of Congress.

10   9   8   7   6   5   4   3   2   1
14   13   12   11   10   09   08   07   06   05

Printed in China

To
Maggie, Emma, Claire and Daniel
And to
My mum and my aunt

CONTENTS

LIST OF FIGURES AND TABLES

Figures

Tables

ACKNOWLEDGEMENTS

This book could not have come to fruition without the support and academic discipline offered by Pauline Hardiker, and the inspirational ideas of Lorraine Fox Harding.

In addition, I would like to thank all the people and agencies who gave their time and facilities to enable me to carry out my fieldwork, and to The Children's Society for letting me get on with it. I would also like to acknowledge my family, students and service users who also make it all seem worthwhile in their different ways.

INTRODUCTION: WHY DO VALUES MATTER?

Stating the problem

Applying values in practice has been acknowledged as a significant challenge. Shardlow (1998, p. 23), for example, has equated the task to 'picking up a live, large and very wet fish' out of a flowing stream. Values permeate all aspects of policy and practice in child welfare work, yet they remain nebulous and confusing. Statements of principles are to be found prominently in policy and guidance documents which are intended to provide a focus for service delivery; the beliefs and attitudes practitioners bring to their work can be identified with professional and personal values; and values are also likely to be influential in determining the perceptions and responses of those who are involved as recipients or users of services. Whilst, in some cases, values and principles may be explicit in such transactions, those which are held implicitly in the form of underlying beliefs are equally likely to be influential in determining outcomes. As Dominelli (2002, p. 15) points out, values are both integral to practice and set the 'parameters' for determining professional responsibilities and what is 'defensible' in practice. For those concerned with the provision of welfare services for children, it is therefore important to be able to reflect on and understand the part that values play in influencing all aspects of policy and practice, from strategic decisions, through management, planning and decision-making, to the critical point at which interventions are actually put into operation.

Not only do values play a central part in shaping interventions, but they are also noted to be highly problematic. Dominelli (2002) identifies a number of ways in which this is so. Firstly, the 'abstract' nature of many statements of principle, whilst enabling a measure of consensus to emerge, often renders them difficult to apply in concrete circumstances. The attempt to apply abstract ideals may only succeed in revealing a further difficulty, which is that pure values may come into conflict when contextualised. As we shall see in subsequent chapters, the task of promoting family autonomy and children's interests simultaneously may present very real professional challenges, for example. The importance of understanding the values underpinning practice is evident, but we cannot or should not (see Parton and Marshall, 1998) expect this to lead straightforwardly to solutions to all the intricate challenges of resolving central dilemmas in policy or service provision. In this book my aim is to assist in clarifying some of these issues, and providing some ideas about the strategies we can use to make concrete decisions and manage risks, in some of the problematic circumstances which permeate children's services.

In looking to provide a clear and sound basis for developing an appreciation of the relationship between values and practice, it will be helpful at this point to set out certain distinct aspects of the problem, each of which is a potential source of confusion, conflict and contradiction: definitions, expectations and orientations.

Definitions

A number of attempts have been made to provide us with a 'working definition' of values which can help those in the field of social welfare to understand what we mean by 'values', and how these provide the basis for a principled approach to service interventions. The recognition that there is 'no consensus' (Shardlow, 1998, p. 23) about the meaning of values in this context is perhaps an unpromising starting point, but it must be acknowledged that this is a problem shared in common with other terms which are fundamental and central to our understanding of the social world in general and service users' needs in particular; for example, terms such as 'race' and 'poverty', both of which continue to resist the search for a conclusive definition. Shardlow (1998) argues that, for those engaged in social work, values could be articulated at a number of different levels. A 'restricted description' could limit itself to the ethical requirements of workers' behaviour towards 'clients'. On the other hand, at the next level the relationship between the enterprise of social work and other institutions might need to be specified, in terms of organisational norms and expectations. And, at the furthest extreme, the 'social construction' of the activity itself might need to come under scrutiny, in order to understand the theoretical and ideological basis of professional values. Likewise, Dominelli (2002, p. 16) argues that it is possible to distinguish between different forms which values might take: 'personal, professional, institutional, organisational or agency, political, religious and cultural'. However, importantly, as she points out, all such value systems derive from those which 'permeate a given society at a particular historical conjuncture'. It is not possible to develop, say, a localised set of professional principles and ethics in a social and cultural vacuum. Dominelli (2002, p. 16) goes on to provide examples of 'locally specific' codes of professional ethics which consciously and deliberately incorporate specific variations in cultural norms.

In a similar vein, Clark (2000) acknowledges the persistent difficulties experienced in achieving a clear and consistent understanding of what we mean by 'values'. He argues that this is not a problem restricted to those engaging with the complexities of practice, but has confounded authorities from many fields including philosophy, sociology and psychology. For him, the significant features of values are that they concern 'weighty aspects of life' (Clark, 2000, p. 29), and they characterise morally desirable ways of acting in the social world:

> To speak of values is thus a shorthand reference for beliefs and dispositions about what is morally or otherwise good.
>
> (Clark, 2000, p. 31)

To the extent that much effort has gone into trying to analyse and articulate value statements, it might also be suggested that there is a systematic aspect to the moral precepts which guide our actions. These are considered rational judgements about the worth of particular orientations. In the field of social welfare, it might thus appear that values can be expressed in a systematic and organised fashion to set the terms for good practice. However, Clark is careful to distinguish between 'abstract' lists of expected behaviour (for example, CCETSW, 1995) and values as the 'ongoing accomplishments' of people making practical moral choices in complex social contexts. There is thus a distinction to be made between the expected values set out by policy-makers, governing bodies and service agencies, and the values demonstrated by practitioners in the course of their decisions and interventions in the field. We can, therefore, understand values as *systems of principles and beliefs* which are intended to govern our approach to practice; at the same time, however, it is important to recognise the distinction between those which are expressed in the form of external mandates or instructions, and those which are reflected in our own moral choices and professional judgements.

Banks (2001b, p. 6) agrees that the notion of 'values' is problematic. For example, 'models' of practice based on the idea of empowerment may appear to reflect commonly held values, but the implications could be quite different depending on the perspective of the practitioner concerned – who could be a 'radical feminist', a 'reformist' or even a 'conservative' (Banks, 2001b, p. 71). Values are not therefore to be found in methods or techniques, but must be located in what she terms 'perspectives' or sometimes 'explanatory theories'. This, again, seems to suggest that the search for values in pure or abstract terms is likely to be unproductive:

> a particular value position is not inherent in the model [of intervention] itself, and will depend on the broader theoretical or ideological perspective adopted.
>
> (Banks, 2001b, p. 71)

So, whilst it is possible to define values in general terms as a set of operating principles which guide the choices and actions of professionals in children's services, this does not resolve many of the dilemmas facing those who seek to put 'values' into practice.

Expectations

Despite the apparent problems with abstract 'lists' of principles (Clark, 2000) setting out expected standards of performance, there has been a proliferation of such documents in official policy and guidance. Whilst statements of ethics and standards have been long established in the field of health care (GMC, 2004, for example), they have also become more prominent in the field of social work and related services for children and young people. Indeed, 'it is often assumed that a code of ethics is a key hallmark of a profession' (Banks, 2001b, p. 89), and that without a clear and coherent set of core values, agencies and welfare services will lack credibility.

Successive attempts have been made, for example, to clarify the essential values underpinning social work (CCETSW, 1989, 1995; Banks, 2001b). Prominent amongst these are the recognition of the rights of individual service users to 'respect', 'privacy' and 'protection', allied with a commitment to the central importance of challenging discrimination and disadvantage.

The establishment of the General Social Care Council in 2001 saw a further codification of these core principles for 'Social Care Workers' (GSCC, 2002b). According to their code of practice:

Social care workers must:

- Protect the rights and promote the interests of service users and carers;
- Strive to establish and maintain the trust and confidence of service users and carers;
- Promote the independence of service users while protecting them as far as possible from danger or harm;
- Respect the rights of service users whilst seeking to ensure that their behaviour does not harm themselves or other people;
- Uphold public trust and confidence in social care services; and
- Be accountable for the quality of their work and take responsibility for maintaining and improving their knowledge and skills.

Source: GSCC (2002b).

The code elaborates the expectations of social care workers further under each of these headings, providing some substance to these broad general aspirations. In some respects, there is more detail than in previous statements of principle (CCETSW, 1989, 1995). The incorporation of the rights of carers, for example, represents a clear advance, although it also builds in an additional tension in the form of the potential conflict of interests between users and carers.

However, it is no longer the case that statements of aims and values relating to social care can be said to provide a comprehensive guide to the objectives informing welfare work with children and families in general. As the field of children's services has become more diversified, with the establishment of a variety of new initiatives, so expressions of aims and principles have also become more diffuse. The Connexions Service for young people, for example, aims to 'make a positive difference' to young people's prospects, and its work is underpinned by its own set of core values. Connexions aspires to offer a service which is based on a spirit of partnership, and which is fair, equitable and committed to achieving positive outcomes for young people (Connexions, 2002).

The principles of Sure Start (which provides support and care for parents and children up to the age of 14) refer to the aims of offering services 'for everyone', to respecting diversity, and to 'listening' to the voices of local people (Sure Start, 2003b). And, the *National Standards for Youth Justice* (Youth Justice Board, 2000) also identify a series of key operating principles which should inform practice with young people who offend. Whilst these standards tend to emphasise the responsibilities of young offenders and their parents, they also reflect a commitment to 'the rights' of young people, and a recognition of the importance of addressing other needs which may be associated with their offending (Youth Justice Board, 2000, p. 1).

There is, therefore, a variety of aspirational statements issued by governing bodies which set the tone for work in the wider field of children's services. Some of these statements are relatively unspecific, and some appear to address operational concerns rather than values or principles (for example, Connexions, 2002), but collectively they do represent a significant expansion in the range and diversity of expectations to which organisations and practitioners are subject. They also have important implications for the way in which the task of putting values into practice is undertaken. For example, the fact that these initiatives frequently overlap in their aims and scope inevitably raises concerns about the setting of priorities, and the challenge of resolving conflicting objectives. Thus, it is becoming increasingly clear that there is a potential for significant conflict between the focus on social control and individual responsibility of the youth justice services, on the one hand, and the concern to meet the welfare needs of young people through social work intervention, on the other. This complexity of overlapping and potentially competing aims and values now forms part of the terrain for those working in children's services, both within and across operational boundaries; making sense of these issues is now 'part of the load' for practitioners and operational managers.

Orientations

The third important factor which we must take into account, as part of the backdrop for the task of understanding and applying values, is the necessary recognition that we are all 'predisposed' in some way towards the work in front of us. That is, we all bring to our specific area of practice, our own sets of principles, beliefs and attitudes. It is, quite simply, not possible to act in a 'value free' or totally objective fashion, even when our work appears to be prescribed or dominated by procedures and systems. Indeed, even explicit structures and frameworks are likely to incorporate uncertainties and conflict, which must be resolved at the point of intervention. As Banks puts it:

> there is no such thing as value-free knowledge, and ... values, knowledge and skills are inseparably related.
>
> (Banks, 2001b, p. 65)

Clark agrees:

> Values are aspects or properties of the totality of human action, both individually and collectively; they cannot be detached from it except as mental abstractions.
>
> (Clark, 2000, p. 31)

Leonard (1984) illustrates this point by explaining how perceptions of childhood are historically situated, having a strong relationship to predominant forms of social organisation. Roles within the family, for instance, are observed to be crucially affected by powerful social and economic forces.

It seems that we need to consider the sources and inspirations for our own values. It is useful to draw on the concept of 'ideology' (Althusser, 1977), which helps to explain how belief systems are generated. Whilst there are some problems with the excessively deterministic nature of some of these theories, their virtue is that they locate the sources of ideas and attitudes in social structures, particularly those which exercise overarching power or authority (Gramsci, 1971). In this way, perceptions and principles which may be held by individuals in an intensely personal fashion are, at the same time, connected with broader networks of ideas and understanding which may also appear as a form of consensus, or even as 'commonsense'. What is normal, and accepted as standard practice, may therefore have its roots in structures and processes which have a pervasive effect on our thinking. The values which inform specific interventions can thus be said to derive from political influences which shape our fundamental views of the world. For Gramsci (1971), the significance of this is the transformation of ideas, which are essentially partial and selective, into belief systems which appear natural or self-evident.

Whilst earlier proponents of these arguments may have tended to suggest that power is centralised and influence is all-pervasive, Banks (2001b) notes the more recent contention that the sources of influential currents of thought may have become more diffuse in the post-modern era, reflecting a diversification of moral authority. Nevertheless, the important point is that 'hegemonic' (Gramsci, 1971) processes of this kind may be expected to operate in the field of children's services. It will be suggested here that links can be drawn between particular traditions in social and political thought and a number of specific 'value positions' in the field of child welfare (Fox Harding, 1997) which, in turn, generate distinctive approaches to policy and practice.

A framework for analysis

The preceding discussion has clarified a number of issues: definitions of values are problematic; value prescriptions tend to be abstract and contradictory; and personal values are rooted in wider social relations. This suggests that the application of values in the field of social welfare is neither simple nor straightforward. It is not possible, for instance, to achieve effective interventions simply by following standardised lists or codes of practice. The help that these offer is limited in the context of challenging dilemmas or conflicting interests; it is at this point that professional skills and judgement must be applied. It is, of course, equally important that this judgement is sensitive and well-informed; the aim of this book is to provide some guidance in that respect.

It is clear that in order to develop an effective understanding of the nature of values and the part they play in children's services, it is important to establish an effective analytical framework. The route that I have adopted here will start with a review of the potential sources of particular value positions, so that the specific impact of distinct belief systems on approaches to child welfare can be located effectively within this broader context. Values do not just appear as fully formed sets of principles which offer unproblematic practice guidance; they are derived from wider ideological traditions to be found within the fabric of society. Clarifying these influences will, in turn, provide a platform from which to develop a more detailed understanding of the interplay of these forces in the specific context of child welfare. This, in turn, will generate some ideas about the kind of strategies to be utilised in making sense of value positions, and applying these effectively in relation to identifiable challenges in the practice arena.

The structure of the book

The purpose of Chapter 1 is to develop the ideas outlined previously. It reviews previous attempts to elaborate typologies of the welfare state, notably the framework set out by George and Wilding (1976; 1985; 1994). Their initial fourfold model (rather than the subsequent sixfold version) is utilised as the basis for a discussion of similar attempts to provide classifications of 'value positions' (see, for example, Fox Harding, 1997) in child welfare. Whilst these attempts are varied and sometimes contra-dictory, they do appear to provide a practical means of contextualising particular approaches to policy and practice in children's services. Some concrete examples of the applicability of this kind of framework are provided here, in order to set the scene for subsequent chapters.

The following chapters offer a more detailed analysis of the perspectives identified, demonstrating their origins in social attitudes and political assumptions about childhood, before going on to consider the implications for specific aspects of the practice context. Chapter 2 provides an elaboration of the 'laissez-faire' or non-interventionist perspective, which argues that the welfare of children is best left to the family. State intervention should be discouraged, and should only be activated in extreme circumstances. In such cases, however, where parenting standards are shown to be 'inadequate' actions taken should be swift and decisive, with the consequence that children should be removed from parents and placed permanently elsewhere. The implications for specific methods of intervention, such as the use of adoption, are considered, particularly in the light of contemporary debates about its greater use. Chapter 3 focuses on the 'child protection' perspective, which exemplifies a much more benign view of the state and its role in safeguarding children and promoting positive parenting. From this viewpoint, the authority of the state is exercised more readily, and in order to ensure that children are not exposed to risk or danger. The implications of this for practice are explored in relation to the role of statutory bodies such as social services authorities as the guarantors of children's well-being. Parents and families are, by implication, seen more frequently as potential sources of harm to their children, and the state is accorded the moral authority to intervene, both to provide safeguards and to educate parents in their roles and responsibilities. Recent practice developments such as 'parenting programmes' are identified with this position.

Chapter 4 also focuses on a perspective which accords a positive role for the state, but it sees this as based on the spirit of partnership with parents, rather than coercion. The form of intervention to support families in this context is also seen in different terms, with a recognition of the importance of meeting material needs, and providing the resources parents require to meet their responsibilities. The interests of children and parents are seen as virtually coterminous, and models of intervention which promote children's well-being in the broadest sense are prioritised. The *Sure Start* initiative, for example, can be viewed as epitomising this approach. This chapter also reflects on the relationship between supporting families and the social inclusion agenda, noting that the consequences for the delivery of services to children may be significant (for instance, through the transfer of social work functions to the Department for Education and Skills in 2003).

Chapter 5 describes an emerging strand of thinking and practice whose influence has been growing in recent years. This can be summarised in the term 'children's rights', and it represents an increasing recognition of the distinctive voices of children themselves as primary service users. This perspective distinguishes children's interests from those of adults, whether parents or statutory bodies, and it argues that the best way to protect those interests is to strengthen the position of children. This chapter provides an account of the pioneering work of the Children's Legal Centre in promoting their rights, and it shows how this influence has come to affect statutory requirements, for example in the provision of advocacy services for children. This growing recognition of children's distinctive position is shown to have had direct consequences in terms of service and policy changes (such as the commitment to provide Children's Commissioners for England, Scotland and Northern Ireland, following the Welsh lead).

The next two chapters discuss some of the dilemmas and disagreements which arise when the distinctive strands of policy and practice come into conflict. Chapter 6 brings a practice focus to the task of resolving differences between value positions. It explores a series of challenges which are encountered when competing interests collide – for example, over parents' 'right' to administer physical punishment to their children, or the state's 'right' to carry out intrusive investigations in families where child abuse is alleged – and a number of illustrative examples are used to enable practitioners in children's services to reflect on their own perspective in such circumstances.

Chapter 7 takes a distinctive approach to the dilemmas of practice by considering the interaction of specific value perspectives and the requirement to deliver children's services in an anti-discriminatory manner. The chapter aims to provide a framework for understanding and dealing with some of the complexities of practice which need to take account of diversity and challenge oppression, but yet must retain a sense of the distinctive interests of children, families and state agencies in the service setting. The aim of Chapter 8 is to summarise the challenges for those trying to operationalise a values-based approach in children's services. It therefore concentrates on exploring a range of techniques for identifying and resolving value conflicts, in the interests of achieving best practice. The chapter considers the value of taking a 'critical' approach, and drawing on ideas of 'reflective practice' (Taylor and White, 2000), in order to understand the nature of competing perspectives. This, in turn, is used as a basis for a 'grounded' approach (Glaser and Strauss, 1967) to decision-making and intervention. It is stressed here that practitioners need to have a clear sense of their own value bases. In light of this understanding, it is argued that the specific perspectives discussed in earlier chapters provide a valid and useful framework for addressing children's needs and making choices about the nature and purposes of the services to be provided.

I will conclude with a brief and rather more speculative discussion of the contemporary political, structural and organisational climate, and the potential impact of this on the balance of power between alternative perspectives in children's services. A sense of the changing operational terrain is needed, not least because it has to be taken into account in making day-to-day professional decisions about individual circumstances and the needs of children.

VALUES IN CONTEXT

Understanding value positions

Our starting point here may appear somewhat distant from the immediate and pressing challenges of putting principles into practice on a daily basis. However, it is precisely because of this foreshortening effect that it is important to provide a sense of perspective, and to locate what might be thought of simply as 'practice values' in their wider context. Statements of professional principles, for example, cannot be divorced from broader social and political perspectives on what is or is not acceptable conduct. Despite this, the prescription of desirable values for those working in social care has sometimes foundered in the mire of abstract, but well-meaning aspirations. This is one of the challenges involved in operationalising a series of generalised statements of desirable aims which are not always entirely compatible, and which do not always appear well-grounded in their social and ideological context. The notion of 'empowerment', for example, is well-established, and rightly so, as a central principle of social work intervention with children and families. However, it has limited purchase so long as at least two key questions are not addressed. The first is the nature of the power relations, say of race or gender, which establish the context for the specific working relationship between provider and recipient of services; and the second, is the possibility of conflict with other core values, such as 'protection'. For example, the Code of Practice issued by the General Social Care Council for social care practitioners (GSCC, 2002b) simply presents this tension as a challenge for workers. The means to resolve it are not provided by the code itself.

From this observation, it can be deduced that there is a need to relate abstract statements of principle to wider debates on the nature of values in social welfare, and their applicability in specific, problematic circumstances. In order to provide an adequate grounding for addressing specific questions about this relationship, we will first explore a number of models and ideas which will help in developing a framework for relating 'values talk' to the beliefs and assumptions which permeate the context in which services are delivered. The use of models can best be understood as a form of 'ideal type' analysis, following Weber (1957). Weber introduced the methodological concept of 'ideal types' in order to provide a specific analytical tool (Worsley, 1977, p. 336). Ideal types were not intended to be a portrayal of the desirable, necessary, or even the most obvious characteristics of social phenomena. Rather, they were to identify the most significant, or even defining, qualities of institutions or movements, against which real and concrete events or structures could be evaluated:

> the constructed model of a fully rational purposive action...can be understood...with complete certainty...; as a *type* it enables [one] to understand the real action as a 'deviation' from what might be expected if those performing it had behaved in a fully rational way.
>
> (Runciman, 1978, p. 9)

This technique is useful because it supports a strategy of examining social reality in the light of idealised 'positions' which accentuate specific features of the subject matter under consideration. Thus, ideological and value perspectives can be distinguished and classified, as we shall see. This, in turn, provides a basis for exploring contrasts and convergences which may have specific practical applications.

The big picture: patterns of state welfare

The specific context of children's services is inevitably influenced by the ideas and structures which comprise the welfare state in general. The models which have been articulated in order to aid understanding of patterns of welfare delivery offer a broad canvas upon which particular approaches to the care of children can be located. The starting point for this discussion will be an examination of a number of recent exercises in developing typologies of state welfare systems. A number of influential attempts have been made to classify states, historically and comparatively, in order to distinguish between their philosophies and practices. These include the work, for example, of George and Wilding (1976; 1985; 1994) and Esping-Andersen (1990). George and Wilding (1976) have argued that specific sets of 'social values' and 'moral and political ideas' underpin the distinctive orientations towards the welfare state to be found in political debate. Initially, they developed a fourfold typology of perspectives, which represented points on a political continuum: anti-collectivism, reluctant collectivism, Fabian socialism and Marxism. Subsequently, this framework was revised and expanded to take account of changing ideas and political innovations. Thus, for example, the emerging ideas of a 'Middle Way' in social welfare (Blair, 1998) were incorporated as a variation on the theme of reluctant collectivism, and 'democratic socialism' took the place of Fabianism (George and Wilding, 1994). Other influential currents of thought were also acknowledged as playing a part in informing changes in social policy, as well, for example 'feminism' and 'greenism' (George and Wilding, 1994). The idea of a continuum, however, remains valuable as an analytical device.

The New Right

This position is associated with ideologies of the free market, competition, individualism and self-interest. In order to realise their true potential, it is argued, human beings must be at liberty to act to further their own ends. However, freedom:

> is an essentially negative state – the absence of coercion. Freedom is maximised when coercion is reduced as much as possible in society.
>
> (George and Wilding, 1985, p. 20)

The role of the state, according to this perspective, is twofold. It should act as the guarantor of individual liberty (see Gamble, 1988); and, at the same time, it should act coercively to prevent any action which might impose limits to these freedoms. The only role of the state is to act as:

> the protector of the interests of all; it ensures that they pursue their interests unmolested by others. Coercion by the State, though necessary in a few pre-defined areas becomes an instrument for liberty.
>
> (George and Wilding, 1976, p. 23)

Thus, ironically, the strong state becomes a prerequisite of individual liberty. For instance, the role of the state in setting limits to the unacceptable treatment of children could be identified as a form of guarantee of freedom and personal integrity. However, once having established the framework and the boundaries for individual self-expression and self-realisation, the state has no further proactive role under this model. Large-scale social investment or proactive social engineering are not appropriate, and may be damaging to individual enterprise and self-sufficiency. State intervention should not take the place of private provision and 'natural' formations, such as voluntary and self-help groups based around the school, the family and religious institutions. It is believed that:

> as government grows so individual responsibility is eroded...People come to believe that they have a right to have their needs met so they feel less responsibility for trying to meet them themselves.
>
> (George and Wilding, 1994, p. 31)

Significant government intervention is damaging on a number of grounds. It is socially disruptive, it is expensive, it is a source of economic inefficiency, and it intrudes upon personal freedom (George and Wilding, 1976).

Unsurprisingly, the New Right, operating within this perspective, takes a negative view of the welfare state. The only justification for intervention is to provide minimal and basic services to alleviate the worst deprivation experienced in society. This is a 'necessary evil' based on well-established principles of 'less eligibility', such that dependency should be avoided, and there should be no perverse incentives to idleness and irresponsible behaviour. To the extent that established welfare states could be seen to be over-generous in this respect, they should be pared back. There should be:

> a reduction as regards the scope of social services...a reduction in the level of financial benefits...a change in the method of administration, i.e. a movement from government to privately administered services...and thus greater guarantees of individualism and freedom.
>
> (George and Wilding, 1976, p. 38)

The role of the state should be seen as one of 'enabling' its members to provide for their own and each others' welfare, for example, by providing cash or vouchers, and by extending the range of voluntary and private providers. This 'consumerist' approach can also be associated, however, with a greater emphasis on the participation and rights of service users in determining how and by whom services are provided (George and Wilding, 1994, p. 43). Much of the rhetoric of the Thatcher governments of the 1980s reflected this minimalist and negative view of the state as an instrument in promoting social welfare; and this had a distinct influence on policy developments of that era, including a reduced role for public services, and privatisation of housing.

The 'Middle Way'

Whilst this perspective has a more positive view of state intervention, it remains distinctly unenthusiastic about it. Like the New Right, adherents of this position:

> emphasise their belief in liberty, in individualism, and in competitive private enterprise.
>
> (George and Wilding, 1976, p. 42)

On the other hand, they are able to accept that these principles must be modified by pragmatic decisions in the light of experience. Thus, in specific cases, there will be grounds for state action to deliver social benefits. It may be necessary, for example, to develop specific programmes (such as youth training initiatives or the Connexions service, perhaps) to assist the development of economic enterprise. The state, it is accepted, must sometimes intervene to steer and correct the market, which itself can be a source of inefficiency and waste, both economic and social. The free market, for example, is unable, on its own, to abolish poverty and injustice. Basic human needs cannot always be provided for by the operation of market forces. Reluctant collectivists therefore believe that there is a positive value in limited government action, particularly in the social sphere, to correct the imperfections of the market, and to make it work better – but certainly not to supplant it:

> This pragmatic response to injustice is fuelled by the belief that markets, and indeed life itself, are often unfair but that governments can, and therefore should, help to compensate for such social injustices.
>
> (George and Wilding, 1994, p. 63)

However, once difficulties are overcome, the state should withdraw. The state is expected only to act in individual cases of hardship, and it should be 'reactive' rather than 'proactive'. In the context of state welfare, this can be characterised as a philosophy of rescuing the inevitable casualties of the market system, rather than as a positive commitment to principles of universal welfare or the common good. Thus, for example, the guiding principle of intervention in families should be to help parents to meet their responsibilities rather than supplant them. The Middle Way in George and Wilding's characterisation sees a place only for limited state activity based on the need to address specific but exceptional needs. There is associated with this an acceptance of the role of 'experts', whose role is to determine when such needs are evident, and to intervene on the basis of systematic measurement and professional judgements. Intervention is based on classification and identification of need, rather than notions of rights or entitlement.

Experts have a continuing role in monitoring the efficiency of the welfare system, and drawing on technical skills to make the necessary adjustments when things go wrong – the emphasis is on a rational approach to problem-solving and effective management, rather than an ideologically driven mission of social improvement. 'One nation' Conservatism has been identified with this philosophy of welfare (Gamble, 1988), and this has been reflected in attempts to reform, rather than abolish certain key elements of public provision, such as schools and health services. Better management and closer control of the machinery of state welfare, rather than its eradication, were preoccupations of the Major government of the early 1990s, for example. It is argued by some that these are also characteristics which can be associated with the New Labour governments from 1997 onwards (Clarke *et al.*, 2000).

Democratic socialism

For those who stand at this point on the continuum, a much more positive role for the state is espoused. Rather than acting primarily as a safety net, there is a necessary role for the state in creating the right conditions for all individuals to meet their full potential. There is a sense here in which 'equality of opportunity' must be guaranteed as a cornerstone of social policy:

> The socialists argue the case for equality on four main grounds – social unity, social efficiency, social justice and individual self-realisation.
>
> (George and Wilding, 1976, p. 63)

In stark contrast to those associated with the New Right, they believe that individual rights, freedoms and fulfilment can only be assured through the active involvement of the state to create a 'level playing field'. Leaving everything to the mercy of naked competition is not in the interests of either individuals or, indeed, the economy and society:

> it is only in a more equal society that the individual has the opportunity to realise his [sic] potentialities...if equality of opportunity is to be real, it must be preceded and accompanied by equalising measures.
>
> (George and Wilding, 1976, p. 64)

Freedom and self-realisation are achieved largely as a consequence of government action, rather than being compromised by it. There is associated with this perspective a belief in the value of cooperation rather than competition, in the creation and support of solidarity within and between communities, and in a commitment to meeting human needs, for their intrinsic worth, rather than as a means towards economic objectives. To achieve these aims, the state must act extensively to secure the conditions for social benefits to be shared, particularly for those groups who are either vulnerable or discriminated against. Thus specific services and benefits must be provided for vulnerable groups, such as older people, those who are sick or disabled, and families with children. Equally, measures must be put in place to prevent and counter discrimination on grounds of race, gender, disability, age, sexuality, or for any other reason. The vision of the welfare state held by this perspective is of a benevolent, and routinely interventionist system for promoting affirmative action, in order to provide the same life chances for all. The state therefore creates the conditions for equality of opportunity, although it does not insist on equality of outcomes. Democratic socialists stop short of seeking a radical transformation of the state, and instead vest their beliefs in the creation of effective mechanisms which if properly administered can secure more equal and socially beneficial outcomes. This espousal of a benevolent and positive interventionist role for the state may be associated with much that is evident in the New Labour project to tackle social exclusion (Powell, 2000). Thus, for example, programmes such as *Sure Start* exemplify a commitment to changing the lives of families and children for the better by improving the resources available to them. There is, however, some ambiguity to this kind of initiative, in that it also carries moralising and managerial overtones which may equally be associated with the previous perspective (the 'Middle Way'; see George and Wilding, 1994; Blair and Schröder, 1999).

Radical socialism

This position is identified with a fundamental commitment to equality as the paramount principle of social welfare. For those on the radical left:

> Freedom ... without a substantial degree of economic security and equality is a hollow slogan.
>
> (George and Wilding, 1976, p. 86)

Equality and security, according to this perspective, can only be achieved by changing the economic underpinning of social relations. Redistribution on any substantial scale cannot be achieved by tinkering around with the existing institutions of capitalism. The underlying causes of inequality, exploitation and social exclusion must be tackled:

The economic base, or structure, of society influences and eventually determines the nature of other institutions...The nature of the political system, the dominant ideology, the family, the social services and other institutions are largely, though not wholly, determined by the way the production system is organised and by the level of its performance.

(George and Wilding, 1994, p. 103)

Effective social welfare provision depends on the eradication of exploitative class relations, and the ending of oppression. There is no real prospect of ameliorative reforms producing lasting and general improvements to the well-being of the population in general.

Despite their starting point, radicals of the left appear to espouse a model of the welfare state which has much in common with the ameliorative assumptions of the democratic socialists. Thus, social services should be expected to be 'universalist, redistributive, participatory and...preventive' (George and Wilding, 1994, p. 127). The achievements of the welfare state represent a series of limited achievements, in that it:

has helped to raise people's expectations in life and every step forward is a base from which further improvements and further demands for change can be made.

(George and Wilding, 1976, p. 103)

Despite their political analysis, many on the left have taken the view that appropriate forms of intervention with disadvantaged groups and vulnerable individuals have the potential to assist in the creation of the conditions for radical change (for example, Corrigan and Leonard, 1978). This has provided a rationale for practitioners who have sought to work within existing structures and yet maintain a commitment to far-reaching and fundamental transformations in social welfare. Despite this, they remain suspicious of, and hostile to those aspects of the state which are seen as oppressive and controlling (George and Wilding, 1994, p. 119).

Given its oppositional nature, the radical perspective has not been reflected directly in government policies and programmes, although it might be argued that its capacity to provide resistance and promote positive change can be demonstrated by some of the achievements of community-based activists (Holman, 1993, for example).

Alternative perspectives?

George and Wilding (1994) have most recently extended their typology of welfare philosophies to incorporate two further perspectives which, they argue, have been influential in shaping debates and developments in social welfare, namely 'greenism' and 'feminism'. It is suggested, for example that:

> Feminist analysis has added new insights to our understanding of the development of welfare states.
>
> (George and Wilding, 1994, p. 135)

The recognition of the gendered inequalities to be found in both access to resources and the distribution of caring responsibilities has had a clear impact on more recent developments in welfare reform. A range of interventions can be seen to target the interests of women (and children) quite distinctly from those of men. Thus, for example, domestic violence initiatives are now based on explicit connections between child protection and the victimisation of mothers and female carers (Mullender *et al.*, 2002).

Whilst 'Greenism' is more difficult to identify as a significant influence on the shape and structures of welfare states themselves, it is suggested that all six perspectives can be seen both as prescriptive and descriptive, acting on the one hand as ideologies of welfare, and, on the other, as explanations of change and development in the state's role in this context:

> All six ideologies are both normative and explanatory approaches to the study of the welfare state. They attempt to explain events and processes as well as make prescriptions for change to various aspects of welfare activity.
>
> (George and Wilding, 1994, p. 8)

Thus, programmes to tackle social exclusion by offering tax credits for low income families and improving provision for child care may be seen as arising at least partly from feminist analyses which emphasise the relatively disadvantaged position of women and mothers.

Making use of comparative models

The value of comparative analyses of the kind developed by George and Wilding is endorsed elsewhere. Higgins, for example, has argued that a 'comparative' analysis of developments in social welfare represents a clear advance on other approaches:

> the failure to compare has, in the past, led to inaccurate accounts of how and why social programmes have developed in different societies.
>
> (Higgins, 1981, p. 26)

She argues that assumptions of linear development in welfare provision are insufficiently flexible to account for the influence of different interests, and changing social and political trends. It is perhaps more realistic to think in terms of persistent themes and perspectives which interact and generate a more uneven pattern of change. In her view, the use of 'models of welfare' provides us with a more useful starting point for understanding the interplay of ideas and structures which create the conditions for specific interventions and outcomes.

More recently, Esping-Andersen (1990) has drawn on an extensive empirical investigation to develop welfare state models which can be found in existence in various European states. Whilst it must be accepted that none of these can be found in its purest form, he has identified a number of groupings around certain key themes. These are characterised as 'liberal' (typically found amongst Anglo-Saxon nations), 'corporatist' (Germany, France, Austria, Belgium and Italy, for example) and 'social democratic' (Scandinavia) welfare regimes (Esping-Andersen, 1999). These regimes can be distinguished according to their commitment to social investment, their view of the role and responsibilities of the state, and their approach to social engineering and redistribution. Subsequent developments of this analysis have seen the addition of further models, such as the 'rudimentary' welfare regimes sometimes associated with Southern European states (Jones Finer, 1999).

As typologies of this nature have emerged, there have been a number of attempts to establish a systematic framework for comparative analysis (Jones Finer, 1999, for example). George and Wilding (1994) themselves have provided a useful overview, and Lee and Raban (1985) have argued that most of these typologies 'merely offer variants' on a common theme.

Pinker's (1971) contribution is important not because he offers a radically different framework, but because he illustrates the methodological value of contrasting models. It is not a matter of right or wrong, in his view, but of creating a series of intelligible and defensible positions which provide the basis for dialogue and the development of more sophisticated understandings. This, it will become clear, is an important pointer for the application of a similar approach to assessment and decision-making in the context of children's services.

Applying models of welfare in this way enables us to avoid pre-judging issues, at the same time as offering a way of making complex, contradictory and changing circumstances intelligible. The fact that this kind of exercise is of value at the level of welfare state systems in general should also offer some encouragement in the task of applying similar approaches in the narrower context of services for children.

Models of welfare: children's services

Whilst the development of 'ideal types' as a fruitful basis for comparing welfare states can be identified as a promising analytical strategy on a global level, similar trends can also be observed in the field of child care and children's services (Smith, 1995). For example, Hardiker and her colleagues (1991) have formulated four strands of thought which are held to inform intervention strategies in child welfare. These are characterised as: residual, institutional, developmental and radical. These have parallels with the perspectives identified by George and Wilding. For example, the residual model is based on values of individualism, freedom and difference. The emphasis on individual needs means that conflicts of interest are inevitable, but these are determined within a strong legal and moral framework. Despite this, the state is expected only to have a limited role in welfare and child care provision; the family is relied upon to provide for its own members. Intervention is only required to address the consequences of inability or failure to provide, or where there is evidence of a substantial failure to comply with 'normal social values'. The state will act decisively and coercively when parents do not meet these basic requirements.

The 'institutional model', in common with those who see a limited but positive role for the state ('reluctant collectivists'), identifies it as having responsibility for social integration and cohesion, in order to ensure that individuals are able to act in their own interests. The state has a role in preventing damage to its vulnerable members, and in promoting commitment to the social order. It could thus be seen to have a specific responsibility for protecting children who are at risk, and promoting responsible parenting. Where parents are seen to be unable to meet their responsibilities, the provision of services to meet the welfare needs of children will be necessary, and programmes may be put in place to secure parents' compliance with rehabilitative measures. The actions of the state are less likely to be directly punitive in respect of those who are deemed to be 'failing', but the state will be prepared to exercise its reserve powers, for example, to assume responsibility for children in some cases.

Hardiker and colleagues' 'developmental' model provides for a much more central role for state provision in promoting child welfare, preventing family breakdown and securing fair treatment. Government intervention should be seen as a positive good, and as a means towards greater freedom, notably in that it guarantees an adequate standard of living. The welfare system is, therefore, a vital element in promoting a good standard of care for children within the family. Parents will not be blamed when things go wrong, and they cannot meet their responsibilities; rather, interventions will seek to empower them to act responsibly in the interests of their children, and to take control of all aspects of their lives.

Like George and Wilding, Hardiker and colleagues identify a fourth model of child welfare, which is also based on notions of radical practice and resistance. The disadvantages experienced by children are seen as the consequence of oppressive structures, so that social action, advocacy and a 'rights' perspective are necessary as a means of challenging injustice. The state is conceived as entirely negative (as in the residual model, interestingly), and therefore oppositional practice must be seen as the only effective intervention strategy. It is, however, acknowledged that maintaining a pure adversarial position such as this can be difficult to sustain, particularly in statutory practice settings, and that as a result the radical and developmental perspectives tend to converge.

Not only do these models of intervention in child care reflect distinctive ideological positions, but they also have implications for the preferred modes and levels of intervention in the service context. Hardiker and colleagues postulate four 'levels of prevention', for example, which can be linked to particular perspectives:

> In a society where a developmental model holds sway, the ideal level of prevention is primary: improve social conditions so individuals do not need to become clients. Where an institutional view of welfare is predominant, preventive efforts are placed at the secondary level: early intervention to prevent problems worsening. Under a residual value system, prevention typically takes place at the tertiary level: work with children and families in imminent danger of separation, often through court proceedings.
>
> (Hardiker *et al.*, 1991, p. 46)

Importantly, this analysis links value perspectives with practice issues and service structures. In addition, it highlights an important consideration which is that these intervention strategies are likely to be found running in parallel, and the tensions between them are likely to be significant. This framework demonstrates that it is unwise simply to assume that modes of intervention routinely follow the model adopted; rather, it illustrates the importance of the dynamic interplay between beliefs and practices.

A number of other attempts have been made to develop typologies of intervention in child welfare. Frost and Stein (1989) and Smith (1991), for example, have both formulated threefold frameworks. Frost and Stein use terminology which focuses on the nature of intervention with children, using a continuum comprising: 'child savers', 'child welfare' and 'child liberators'. They argue that these positions are not necessarily clear cut, and that there is evidence of fluidity, with the 'child welfare' position encompassing those who favour more control by 'agencies and experts' as well as others who would emphasise children's participation more strongly. They argue that the issue of power and control is pivotal, and that the key question is the extent to which children and young people are seen as similar to, or different from, adults. It is this judgement (by adults) which determines the way in which adult (and state) power is exercised over children. For them, the nature of children's services is:

> closely linked to the broader social, economic, political and ideological context in which it is located.
>
> (Frost and Stein, 1989, p. 128)

As a result, they argue, it is impossible for either commentators or practitioners to assume a position of neutrality in determining their own orientation to service delivery. They do not accept, for example, that intervention can be determined on the basis of finding an acceptable 'balance' between competing arguments. This is an important point since the idea of balance is often utilised as an organising principle in the practice setting; but it may be neither achievable nor desirable where it masks unequal power relations, or cements inequalities into place.

Smith (1991) developed a framework for the analysis of the Children Act 1989, utilising the three elements of 'welfare', 'protection' and 'rights'. These strands are identifiable with particular provisions of the act, notably Part III (welfare), Parts IV and V (protection), and Sections 1, 26 and 40 (rights). Clearly, however, the expression of these three policy objectives as parallel strands of legislation creates tensions, with the likelihood that there will be conflicting demands at the level of policy and in practice. There would, in his view, be better prospects for an integrated approach to service delivery if certain minimum standards could be guaranteed to *all* children, over and above the specific requirements of child care legislation (Smith, 1991, p. 480).

The most comprehensive attempt to develop a framework for understanding child welfare based on 'ideal types' has been undertaken by Fox Harding (1991a,b; 1997). Perhaps to a greater extent than the other typologies referred to, she also provides a basis for bridging the divide between ideologies of welfare and children's services. This is demonstrated by the terms used to characterise the four 'value positions' identified: 'laissez-faire', 'state paternalism', 'birth family defender' and 'children's rights'. Whilst Fox Harding acknowledges that there are uncertainties and overlaps between the four positions, she argues that they do represent quite distinct orientations towards policy and practice in relation to children. This is illustrated by reference to specific historical and international developments.

Laissez-faire

The 'laissez-faire' approach is based on a belief that it is important not to intervene in the 'natural' processes of the family. Like the minimalist position identified by Hardiker and colleagues, this position is associated with a belief in 'minimum coercive intervention' which maintains respect for the dignity and freedoms of family members, and sends strong messages about the importance of appropriate standards of care for children. Restrictions on the freedom of parents and the exercise of powers to intervene should only be used on very rare occasions by the state in order to enforce these standards. Where intervention is required, it should be decisive and definitive, for instance involving the rapid removal of the child from unacceptable parental care, the cessation of family links, and the immediate substitution of an alternative family. Fox Harding links this authoritarian approach to intervention with wider ideological perspectives such as patriarchy, whereby there is an implicit belief in the presence of a strong father figure at the head of a well-organised, morally sound and efficiently run family unit. Harris and Timms (1993), however, take issue with her over this point, arguing that there is no necessary association of the laissez-faire perspective with a particular male-dominated set of gender relations.

The laissez-faire model of child welfare is not simply a theoretical abstraction, but can be identified as having significant influence at different points in history, such as the Victorian era, and under the New Right Conservative government of 1979–97. As Fox Harding acknowledges, the laissez-faire position is subject to criticism on at least two grounds; the negative view of state intervention and its association with a specific gendered model of family life.

State paternalist

State paternalism can be equated to the model of welfare associated with the reluctant collectivists or the 'Middle Way'. The state's role should be limited, but authoritative, guaranteeing freedom and security for its citizens, but not encouraging a spirit of dependency or loss of individual enterprise. This perspective is characterised by a belief in the need for strong and effective state intervention to protect children, particularly where they are at risk of harm, or where parents are unable to maintain adequate standards of care, for whatever reason. The view of the state associated with this position is 'neutral and wise'. Considerable belief is placed in the abilities of 'experts', and the reliability of intervention mechanisms, where well-judged and appropriate interventions will prevent the mistreatment of children, restore failing families, and provide good quality alternative care for children if necessary. State paternalism appears as a dominant strand in child welfare provision in the expansionary era of the late 1960s and 1970s, when the numbers of children in state care increased significantly. As Fox Harding observes, this perspective can be criticised for appearing overbearing and overconfident, placing too great an emphasis on the authority of experts, and giving too little recognition to the perspectives of families and children themselves. In addition, the fact that intervention is not always reliable and effective is not acknowledged clearly enough.

Birth family defender

Fox Harding's third child care perspective is termed 'birth family defender', which can usually be interpreted as implying a belief in a positive role for state intervention to promote the well-being of families. Adequate levels of support, both financial and in respect of other forms of family assistance, are sufficient, according to this view, to enable families to thrive independently. Children's upbringing is best promoted in this way, based on the notion of partnership between service providers and parents. Even where specific needs are identified, intervention should be supportive. Where it is necessary, for example, to provide alternative accommodation for the child away from the family home, this should be pursued as a temporary and voluntary arrangement, with the aim of improving family functioning rather than as a route towards permanent alternative care. However, within this perspective, Fox Harding (1997) identifies two distinct strands; those who place a greater emphasis on promoting the rights of families, and those who emphasise the importance of state investment in welfare services to support children in their families. The establishment of the post-war welfare state and, indeed, aspects of the New Labour strategy can be associated with this model of intervention. If this value position is to be subject to criticism, it may be for tending to idealise the birth family, and perhaps to hold an over-optimistic view of the capacity and willingness of the welfare state to commit resources to family support. The 'birth family defender' perspective could also be criticised for making unproven assumptions about the efficacy of measures intended to prevent the maltreatment of children, according to Fox Harding. This may be associated with the 'rule of optimism' identified amongst social care professionals by Dingwall *et al.* (1983), and an over-reliance on a small number of favourable studies, according to Morgan (1995).

Children's rights

Fox Harding also identifies a fourth value position, that of a belief in 'children's rights'. In her view, the emergence of this perspective is more recent than the others, and it has therefore been less influential in shaping services for children. The adoption of the UN Convention on the Rights of the Child in 1989 may herald a change of emphasis, however. This perspective is distinctive in that it promotes a radical agenda of rights for children, on the one hand, and societal responsibilities towards them, on the other. It is argued, for example, that adult systems of law and welfare have worked against children's best interests on occasion, in spite of their good intentions. Rights to determine the nature and content of interventions should rest with children themselves, rather than being administered indirectly, through the agency of adults, however sympathetic and however close their relationship. By assigning power to children in this way, many of the disadvantages and injustices they experience could be overcome. Fox Harding notes that some proponents of this perspective take a rather more moderate view, suggesting that the rights to which children should be entitled are necessarily partial, and are acquired or 'grown into', rather than held universally and unequivocally from birth. She suggests that some examples of a children's rights perspective in practice can be identified, notably in Norway with the establishment of a Children's Commissioner. As she observes, there are also a number of cogent criticisms of the children's rights perspective, which must be considered. For instance, in emphasising the rights of children, it appears not to take account of the obverse, their responsibilities, and how the concomitant of acquiring adult entitlements might be also acquiring adult obligations such as earning a living. In addition, the pure children's rights position appears to underestimate the extent to which life experience itself may be a necessary prerequisite for the exercise of informed choice (see King and Trowell, 1992, for example). It is also unclear whether proponents of children's rights also believe that they should continue to receive 'special treatment', in the sense of protection from exploitation by way of child labour or additional benefit entitlements, such as Child Benefit. Fox Harding (1997) argues that the uniformly negative view of the welfare state held by this perspective in its pure form is unsustainable, given that some aspects of state provision clearly work in children's favour.

Positional analyses: acknowledging complexity

The preceding attempts to develop typologies of child welfare perspectives appear to share some common elements, but they also generate some interesting points of divergence (Figure 1.1). It could be suggested, however, in common with the models of welfare considered previously, that the different characterisations could be identified as sharing points on a continuum.

Whilst neither Frost and Stein (1989) nor Smith (1991) identify a non-interventionist position, in other respects there is a considerable degree of similarity between the positions identified. Even where there appear to be differences of emphasis, some common ground can be identified. For instance, the oppositional 'Radical/Conflict' orientation suggested by Hardiker *et al.* (1991) shares a commitment to advocacy and challenge with the 'rights' perspectives suggested by the other authors. In this sense, their characterisations might be seen as mutually validating.

However, it has been suggested, not least by Fox Harding (1997) herself, that it would be unwise to accept the distinctions between perspectives as definitive and unproblematic. As she acknowledges, there are clear areas of convergence between some, if not all, in certain respects. At a fundamental level, for example, all share a concern with the welfare and development of children, and all are concerned with the role of the state in contributing to that – albeit leading to very different conclusions. Three perspectives are viewed as sharing a positive view of the family, whereas for supporters of 'children's rights' living arrangements are to be determined by reference to the child's wishes. Some perspectives appear to share a common hostility to the proactive state (laissez-faire; children's rights), whilst the others appear to take a positive view of its role in actively intervening in the lives of families. Equally, there appear to be differences in the way in which family problems and child

(1) Residual	Institutional	Developmental	Radical/Conflict
(2)	Child saver	Child welfare	Child liberation
(3)	Protection	Welfare	Rights
(4) Laissez-faire	State paternalism	Birth family defender	Children's rights

Figure 1.1   Child care perspectives

Source: (1) Hardiker *et al.*, (1991); (2) Frost and Stein (1989); (3) Smith (1991); (4) Fox Harding (1997)

maltreatment are accounted for. Both the laissez-faire and state paternalist positions attribute disadvantage and mistreatment to poor parenting, whilst for birth family defenders and children's rights proponents, it is social and structural factors which are more important.

In a sense, these observations anticipate some of the criticisms which can be made of an approach to understanding child welfare based on a positional analysis of the kind considered here. By its very nature, this kind of portrayal tends to overemphasise the differences between perspectives, and creates dichotomies which may not exist so clearly in the complexities encountered in practice. It may be felt that the implicit pressure to make definitive judgements about the subject of analysis is too rigid, and fails to allow for a working compromise to be achieved. The suggestion has been made in respect of Fox Harding's work that it may only provide a partial basis for understanding:

> Though the process of ideal type analysis, of which [Fox] Harding's book is an example, is an established mode of Western scientific enquiry which can identify the strands in a complex set of interrelations and lead to a synthesis, it can also deceive us into believing that the strands exist as isolated phenomena, not as indissoluble parts of a shifting and restless whole. When the analysis patently fails to end in synthesis it can illumine neither form nor content....It is a unidimensional account of a multifaceted phenomenon.
>
> (Harris and Timms, 1993, p. 37)

In other words, in trying to establish neat categories for complex and diverse social realities, essential interconnections and dynamics between the elements of the whole may go unnoticed, leading to arbitrary and incomplete judgements. The argument that ideal type analysis can lead to arbitrary judgements, and attempts to 'force' social phenomena into categories, has also been made elsewhere. Johnson and his colleagues have pointed to the risk of such an approach being reduced to mere 'story-telling'. They argue that, in the formulation of ideal types:

> value-selection and abstraction create one-sided models of social events which can provide useful tools of analysis, but...these should not be mistaken for reality.
>
> (Johnson *et al.*, 1984, p. 85)

The choice of categories and theoretical concepts to form the basis of any given analytical framework may simply be a matter of the individual preferences of the investigator.

This leads to a key problem for ideal type analysis as a means of understanding social phenomena and then acting on the basis of our understanding. If the categories developed rely on the judgement of their author, how can we use them subsequently to account for what we find?

> A problem relating to the use of the ideal types of action is how they can be used in the *explanation* of a course of action. In effect, how does [one] adjudicate between competing plausible accounts of the 'real' meaning of a course of action?
>
> (Johnson *et al.*, 1984, p. 89)

Similarly, in relation to the models of welfare identified earlier, Lee and Raban (1985) take issue with the idea of a continuum, which, it is suggested, provides only a one-dimensional framework. Similar criticisms are made of Fox Harding by Dominelli (2004).

Lee and Raban argue that flexibility must be built into the way in which the welfare state is understood – a two-dimensional strategy is equally plausible, in their view (Figure 1.2). For example, the anti-state perspectives held on both left and right can more easily be contrasted with interventionist perspectives in this way.

The sense in which we must acknowledge common interests between perspectives can also be extended to our understanding of developments in child welfare. For example, the progressive reduction in the use of institutional care for children during the 1980s could be accounted for in terms of a non-interventionist political climate (laissez-faire), an emerging commitment to children's rights, a recognition of the fact that many children were not safe in children's homes (state paternalism), or a move towards a strategy of supporting children in their own families. In other words, this trend could be explained according to any or all of the value positions identified.

EQUALITY

Radical socialism   Democratic socialism

ANTI-STATE   PRO-STATE

New Right   'The Middle Way'

INEQUALITY

Figure 1.2   Models of welfare: a two-dimensional framework
Source: Adapted from Lee and Raban, 1985, p. 24.

More substantive criticisms could be offered of the positional approach to child welfare set out here. For example, it might be suggested that it represents a form of abstraction which does not take sufficient account of the fundamental dynamics which impact on children's lives and create oppressive experiences for them (Dominelli, 2004). In assuming that differing perspectives are equally valid, such an approach appears to overlook their underlying shortcomings. The influences of factors such as class, gender, racism and misuse of power may be given less weight than they should be (see Humphries and Truman, 1994). Such factors may carry substantial explanatory force, and may therefore be of crucial importance in informing interventions. We should perhaps be reminded, too, that Frost and Stein (1989), in advancing their own continuum of child welfare perspectives, suggest that it is neither possible nor acceptable for those involved in children's services to avoid making a choice as to their own preferred philosophy. An approach based on value positions must therefore not fall into the trap of generating a spurious impression of neutrality in relation to fundamental questions of rights and social justice.

The value of value positions

It is recognised that criticisms can be made of the use of abstract constructs to account for developments in child welfare. However, it will be suggested here that they can provide an effective framework for both analysis and practice. The key starting point for this is the recognition that the value of abstract models lies not in their pure and distinct identities, but in the way in which they can contribute to our appreciation of dynamics and change. Fox Harding (1997), who is more sophisticated than her critics recognise, readily acknowledges the linkages and interactions between the idealised positions she sets out. These constructs are simply intended to be used as a starting point for more detailed and thorough analysis. For example, the adoption of a two-dimensional approach, along the lines suggested by Lee and Raban (1985), illustrates some significant lines of convergence and divergence (Figure 1.3).

Utilising this kind of matrix, we are able to consider areas where distinctions may blur, alliances may form, and the impact of other 'variables' may be incorporated. The issue of racism, for example, raises significant questions for a strategy which relies simply on promoting children's rights, without an accompanying programme of enhanced support services for families. Otherwise, notional rights will not be supported by substantive improvements in provision.

ROUTINE STATE INTERVENTION

State paternalism   Birth parent defender

SOCIAL   EMPOWERMENT
CONTROL

Laissez-faire   Children's rights

LIMITED STATE INTERVENTION

Figure 1.3   Values in children's services (1)

The matrix approach offers a further degree of flexibility in that the axes can be changed to accommodate other dimensions (Figure 1.4).

Thus, it may be the case that what appear to be straightforward and reasonable assumptions about the importance of the integrity of the family may overlook the child's interests. Where the child wishes to be cared for away from the family, counter pressures may yet be found to operate. However, children placed in local authority accommodation may be reluctant to accept rehabilitation as a goal, at least in the short-term. In one study of young people accommodated by social services departments:

> Several teenagers refused to visit their families in spite of their social workers' encouragement to renew contact.
>
> (Triseliotis *et al.*, 1995, p. 220)

CHILD-CENTRED

State paternalism   Children's rights

SOCIAL   EMPOWERMENT
CONTROL

Laissez-faire   Birth parent defender

FAMILY-CENTRED

Figure 1.4   Values in children's services (2)

CHILD-CENTRED

State paternalism   Children's rights

ROUTINE   LIMITED
STATE   STATE
INTERVENTION   INTERVENTION

Birth parent defender   Laissez-faire

FAMILY-CENTRED

Figure 1.5   Values in children's services (3)

In addition, young people were often not consulted about their wishes in these circumstances, perhaps because of prevailing beliefs about their best interests being met through reunification with the family (Figure 1.5).

The congruence of arguments for limited state intervention was particularly noticeable in the late 1970s and early 1980s in the UK, when observers from both 'left' and 'right' argued that too many children were being drawn into the care system. A consensus emerged that the emphasis should be on promoting the rights of children and parents to resist excessive state interference in their lives (Taylor *et al.*, 1979; Morris *et al.*, 1980; Morris and Giller, 1983).

Convergence and conflict: the relationship between values and action

This kind of framework allows us to explore possible 'affinities' and 'antagonisms' between the differing perspectives (Kalberg, 1994). Simplistic assumptions about the 'child-centredness' of state paternalist interventions, for instance, might account for the long-standing failure to recognise children's rights in care settings (Utting, 1997). There is thus a demonstrable value in the adoption of an ideal type analysis in the context of children's services. We are offered a framework which can help us to classify and operationalise the beliefs and principles which underpin the delivery of welfare services to families, children and young people. Whilst there are possible reservations about the rigidity of the categories offered, and the dangers of forcing the facts to fit preconceived ideas, there are also real benefits to be gained. Of particular importance will be the ability to explore the relationship between values and action in order to provide a basis for our own judgements about service delivery and specific interventions.

The following chapters will provide a more detailed account of the perspectives identified here. Taking each in turn, the links between legal and policy frameworks and practice orientations will be explored, in order to demonstrate the way in which each position can be associated with particular strands of activity in children's services. It will become clear that these diverse influences remain significant in driving practice developments, and this will further illustrate the need for those in the field to be aware of, and work with, the competing demands which may arise.

KEEPING IT IN THE FAMILY: 'LAISSEZ-FAIRE' AND MINIMAL INTERVENTION

Ideology and family values

The first perspective to be considered in detail will be that identified with a residualist position, where it is believed that the family is largely sacrosanct, and the state has no role routinely to interfere in its day-to-day functioning. Parents should be free to exercise their rights and responsibilities towards children without feeling that they are under scrutiny or direction from outside. As we have seen, this viewpoint also has certain implications for the nature of intervention (Hardiker *et al.*, 1991; Fox Harding, 1997), which we will explore more fully in due course.

For the moment, however, it is important to spell out the ideological and political underpinnings of this orientation towards the family, particularly in light of its persistent and powerful influence on social attitudes and assumptions. As Gamble (1988) puts it, this position can be characterised in terms of the 'free economy and the strong state'. According to this argument, it is the responsibility of the state solely to create the preconditions for the exercise of personal freedom, not only in terms of economic activity, but also in the personal sphere. He argues that this line of thinking was prevalent under the right wing Conservative government of the 1980s, which held the belief that people are happiest, and perform at their best when they are free to conduct their own affairs, both in the sphere of business and the market, and in their family and personal lives. The state, therefore, should always seek not to intervene. Unnecessary meddling in people's lives can do real damage, by debilitating people and families capable of providing for themselves. Such arguments are associated with fears that too active and generous a role for the state would lead to the creation of a dependency culture, and the emergence of an 'underclass' (Murray, 1996a). Instead, the state must concentrate on its policing role in terms of maintaining the boundaries of acceptable behaviour, and acting swiftly to ensure that infringements are dealt with. It acts as the guardian of economic rectitude and public morality, and must therefore be seen to act effectively where these standards are breached. Minford (1991), for example, argues that the state should only maintain a minimal 'safety net' approach to welfare provision, relying largely on 'private charitable interests' and 'informal social insurance', and that at the same time, it should act to 'compel' parents to care for their children.

The family should be seen as the proper site of children's care, and personal and moral development according to this view. Morgan (1992), for instance, questions the increasing role of the state or non-family members in providing day care for young children.

Mount (1982) argues that the family has been identified as a consistent phenomenon over the ages and across different societies, and must have a fundamental function which transcends historical and political change:

> The family is a subversive organisation ... Only the family has continued throughout history and still continues to undermine the State. The family is the enduring permanent enemy of all hierarchies, churches and ideologies.
> (Mount, 1982, p. 1)

The family is not, for him, a transient or socially determined institution, but remains a constant force to provide nurture, well-being and a sense of fulfilment to its members:

> it is difficult to resist the conclusion that a way of living which is both so intense and so enduring must somehow come naturally to us, that it is part of being human.
> (Mount, 1982, p. 256)

Furthermore, the specific form of the family is also not accidental:

> the family as we know it today – small, two-generation, based on choice and affection ... – is neither a novelty nor the product of unique historical forces.
> (Mount, 1982, p. 153)

These arguments from the political right seem to interpret the upbringing of children within the specific form of the nuclear family as natural, inevitable, and impossible to improve upon.

It is interesting to note that such opinions were to a large extent reflected in political circles, notably in the era of the Thatcher government

(Fitzgerald, 1987). A series of significant pronouncements were made by leading figures at this time. Margaret Thatcher herself, speaking to the Conservative Party Conference stated that:

> it is time to change the approach to what government can do for people and to what people can do for themselves: time to shake off the self-doubt induced by decades of dependence on the State as master not as servant...
>
> (quoted in Fitzgerald, 1987, p. 49)

Patrick Jenkin, who became Secretary of State for Health and Social Security in the first Thatcher government, expressed his priorities clearly when stating that 'the most important social work is mother-hood' (quoted in Fitzgerald, 1987, p. 49), and Margaret Thatcher herself was also famously heard to remark that:

> there is no such thing as society. There are individual men and women, there are families. And no government can do anything except through people and people must look after themselves first
>
> (*Woman's Own*, 31 Oct. 1987)

Fox Harding (1997) reminds us that, like the family itself perhaps, such beliefs about the role of the state in relation to child care are not restricted in time and place. She illustrates this specifically with reference to Victorian England, and the United States of the 1970s and 1980s. She also makes the connection with patriarchal attitudes, suggesting that these are most clearly evidenced in Victorian times, but that they can be seen to persist into the modern day. According to such beliefs, the preferred family form is structured according to gender, with a strong male authority figure at its head. Whilst in government, Patrick Jenkin himself stated that mothers should not have equal rights to work as fathers (Fitzgerald, 1987). However, as already noted, Harris and Timms (1993) argue that there is no necessary connection between patriarchal attitudes and a 'laissez-faire' philosophy of the family.

Indeed, despite the association of non-interventionist views with right wing ideology, the family has been recognised as a source of strength and solidarity by writers on the left. Barrett and McIntosh (1982) argue that the family offers certain features which effectively insulate it from hostile external forces, including stability for children, a sense of identity and protection. These arguments are balanced, however, by a recognition that the family can also be a site of oppression and abuse for women and children.

Minimalist ideology and child welfare practices

The theoretical and political arguments for minimal intervention in family life are paralleled by a number of contributions in the field of child care and social work. Notably, Goldstein *et al.* (1973; 1980) set out a detailed prescription for the state's minimal role in relation to parents:

> Considering what a child loses when he [*sic*] passes, even temporarily, from the personal authority of parents to the impersonal authority of the law, what grounds for placing a family under state scrutiny are reasonable? What can justify overcoming the presumption in law that parents are free to determine what is 'best' for their children...
>
> (Goldstein *et al.*, 1980, p. 3)

The state, in their view, must have clear cut and substantial grounds for taking steps to question or, in some cases, remove the rights of parents to care for their children. This leads to a preference for 'minimum state intervention' in the child's interests. They believe that the nature of the ties and interactions between the child and parental figures is 'all-important' in securing a healthy 'line of development'. This is most likely to be found in the birth family. 'Family integrity' is 'fundamental' to providing a safe and secure basis for the child's upbringing. However, once the state is found to be justified in taking action to protect children, it must then make the child's interests the 'paramount' consideration. Goldstein and colleagues' preference in such cases is for the replacement of failing family relationships with alternative families because of the importance of the family setting in offering positive psychological resources to the child.

> As much as anything else [the child] needs to be accepted, valued and wanted as a member of the family unit consisting of adults as well as other children.
>
> (Goldstein *et al.*, 1973, p. 14)

In stressing the importance of the family as a developmental setting for children, the authors do not ignore the possibility of things going wrong, and children being put at risk of harm. In this event, family autonomy can become a positive threat to the child's well-being. Despite this, state intrusion is not necessarily to be commended in such cases. Goldstein and colleagues argue that, by intervening, the state may 'make a bad situation worse'. It must, therefore, only take action where it can demonstrate that this will lead to a better outcome for the child.

The grounds for intervention must be specified to set boundaries to the state's activities, and to ensure precision about the objectives of intervention. They are critical of 'vague and subjective' definitions of risk, concluding that it is only in verifiable cases of physical and sexual abuse that the grounds for intervention can be made out. They are sceptical about the use of definitions associated with emotional abuse and neglect:

> neither concept should be used as a ground for modifying or terminating parent–child relationships.
>
> (Goldstein *et al.*, 1980, p. 77)

It is only where there is serious and tangible evidence of 'gross failures' of parental care that action should be taken, not least because the state has repeatedly failed to provide satisfactory solutions, in their view.

A very high threshold for intervention, however, requires decisive action when it is breached. Goldstein and his colleagues argue that the state may intervene 'too little' as well as 'too much'. Children are thus returned to abusive family settings, where they suffer further harm – they cite Maria Colwell as an example of this. The foster care setting is cited as one site where these conflicting patterns of over and under involvement are detrimental to the child:

> By failing to keep families together, by failing to restrict foster care to children who have a real chance of being returned to their absent parents in a 'short time', and by failing to regard longtime foster parents as autonomous, the authorities prevent feelings of security from developing in either child or adult.
>
> (Goldstein *et al.*, 1980, p. 135)

The preference is for a secure, permanent alternative family setting, ideally an adoptive placement, because 'temporary' arrangements perpetuate uncertainty and insecurity for the child. On this basis, for example, Maria Colwell's foster carers would have been encouraged to pursue adoption, rather than returning her to her birth mother (Goldstein *et al.*, 1980, p. 183).

In summary, then, the minimum intervention strategy proposed by Goldstein and his colleagues involves: a presumption in favour of family autonomy; no routine state involvement; high thresholds for intervention; explicit and determinate grounds for intervention; quick and decisive intervention when justified, based on the child's psychological needs; and permanent alternative family settings as the preferred long-term solution.

Others, too, have argued along similar lines, drawing on beliefs in the importance of family life, as well as making critical observations about the efficacy of state interventions. Brewer and Lait (1980) argue that social work has been unable to demonstrate a sufficient degree of expertise and certainty to justify routine interventions in the family simply 'on suspicion'. This view coincides with that of Geach (1983), who suggests that some aspects of the intervention process represent real threats to 'civil liberties' (p. 50), and result in families becoming unfairly labelled as 'inadequate'. He argues that infringements of the rights of parents can only be justified where there is clear evidence that they contribute to saving a child from death or serious harm, and that this should set a very clear limit to the role and practices of state agencies. Howitt's (1992) analysis of 'child abuse errors' pursues a similar line of argument. He argues that a growing belief in the damaging nature of the '(patriarchal) family' has contributed to a greater readiness to intrude in this private arena. By contrast, he states:

> the *nuclear* family is a relatively safe environment in terms of sexual abuse.
> (Howitt, 1992, p. 62)

Like Goldstein *et al.*, he believes that the activities of state agencies in responding to abuse may also, in themselves, be damaging. The presumption must therefore be against intervening, unless it can be demonstrated to be beneficial to do so. These ideas do not preclude the state from an active role in protecting children, but they share a common view that this must be undertaken sparingly, and only when clear and substantial grounds for intervention are demonstrated.

Minimum intervention: the policy context

It does appear that there is a recurrent strand of 'laissez-faire' thinking in policy debates about the family. Both Hardiker *et al.* (1991) and Fox Harding (1997), for example, argue that the Thatcher governments of the 1980s and early 1990s could be characterised as 'residualist', and therefore inclined to discourage certain types of intervention. According to Hardiker and colleagues, we might expect this to be reflected in a withdrawal of resources from the 'primary' and 'secondary' levels of provision, where preventive services might be offered, and a concentration on a limited range of reactive interventions designed to respond to extreme cases of harm or family breakdown. On the other hand, inconsistencies are identified, and Fox Harding observes that the kind of practices associated with a residualist perspective were not always found to be dominant in this era. For example, the opportunity to narrow the grounds for intervention, or to introduce more stringent time limits for decision-making, was not taken, even with the introduction of the Children Act 1989. The Act's implementation did, however, appear to lead to a short-term reduction in the number of statutory interventions, especially in the use of emergency protective measures (Smith, 1995).

Despite this somewhat confused picture, certain key events do appear to have acted as triggers for the re-emergence of 'pro-family, anti-state' campaigns. For example, the Cleveland controversy in the late 1980s provided a focal point for resistance against apparently unwarranted intrusion by child protection agencies. Parton (1991) contrasts the 'Cleveland affair' with other child protection inquiries, in that it revolved around the issue of 'too heavy-handed' intrusion into the family, rather than the provision of 'too little, too late'. The chain of events in Cleveland in 1987 involved the rapid diagnosis of a substantial number of cases of child sexual abuse by two paediatricians (Drs Higgs and Wyatt), and the consequential removal of many of these children from home by way of Place of Safety Orders (as defined by Section 28 of the Children and Young Persons Act, 1969). The immediate consequence of this development was the establishment of a campaign by parents of the children concerned, supported by a church minister and local MPs. This quickly transformed the issue into one of state vs family, in a way which appeared to elide children's interests unquestionably with those of their parents. One MP, for example, equated the activities of the social services department with the SS and according to Parton (1991), the media played a significant role in 'publicly defining the agenda'. As he points out, this contributed to a number of clear themes emerging:

> First, the image of the authoritarian state which was out of control and unwarrantably and insensitively interfering in the lives of families – both children and parents. Second that the parents – by implication all of them – were innocent [of child sexual abuse]. Third, that various state agencies and professionals were not in unison.
>
> (Parton, 1991, p. 81)

The latter theme provided, if it were needed, confirmation of the incompetence of the state agencies, who could not agree even amongst themselves on the extent or nature of the problem.

The subsequent public inquiry into the events in Cleveland conspicuously avoided trying to determine the exact number of children involved where initial suspicions of child sexual abuse were justified, preferring to focus on the procedural issues, and the apparent failures of the state agencies concerned (Butler-Sloss, 1988). As Parton (1991, p. 114) observes, this meant that the accusations made by the 'pro-family' lobby were able to continue to dominate debate on the issue. As a result, it was possible for the government to conclude that the approach taken was insufficiently 'balanced', as between the need to protect children and the preservation of the rights of parents.

There are some indications that both the Children Act 1989 and subsequent practice in child care were influenced by the 'Cleveland affair'. Whilst stressing its commitment to the principles of protecting children, the government also gave considerable emphasis to the desirable limits to intervention. Like Goldstein and colleagues (1980), for example, ministers stressed that the positive value of taking action must be demonstrated. Orders should not be made simply as 'insurance' (Smith, 1995). The Lord Chancellor stated that he wanted to reverse the prevailing practice prior to the Children Act, so that:

> care orders will result in [the child's] needs being better met or at least better catered for, and ... intervention will not do more harm than good.
> (Lord Chancellor, House of Lords Hansard, 19.12.88, Col. 1165)

Perhaps as a consequence, a number of trends were identified following the implementation of the Children Act which were consistent with the minimalist position. By March 1992, the number of children in the care of local authorities had fallen by 5000 compared to the pre-implementation total 12 months earlier. In addition, there had been a reduction of 6700 (16 per cent) in the numbers on child protection registers; and the first year of the Act's operation saw the making of 2300 Emergency Protection Orders (EPOs) compared to 5000 Place of Safety Orders in the year to 31 March 1991. The first annual report by the government on the Act also appeared to emphasise a 'laissez-faire' message:

> central to the philosophy of the Act is the belief that children are best looked after within the family with both parents playing a full part and without resort to legal proceedings... The Act, while requiring any compulsory intervention in a child's life to be authorised by a court, seeks to discourage unnecessary court intervention in family life...
> (Department of Health and Welsh Office, 1993, p. 3)

Thus, it may be considered that practices and outcomes in children's services were influenced by the ideological perspective of the Conservative administration of the time.

Whilst the residualist perspective has been associated with a particular period of 'New Right' government, it is also important to consider the extent to which the philosophy of family autonomy and self-determination remains an influential factor even in a context of political change and policy innovation. There are, indeed, some aspects of New Labour policy which demonstrate some consistency with themes highlighted by its predecessor. The incoming 1997 government took active steps to demonstrate its commitment to 'the family' (Home Office, 1998). Ministers stressed that they did not wish to 'interfere' in family life, although they did appear to adopt more interventionist rhetoric than the Conservatives (Straw, 1998, p. 2). Setting out the principles underpinning New Labour's family policy, the consultation document, *Supporting Families*, stated:

> governments have to be wary about intervening in areas of private life and intimate emotion. We in Government need to approach family policy with a strong dose of humility. We must not preach...
>
> (Home Office, 1998, p. 4)

Additionally, the paramountcy of children's interests was emphasised, and the primacy of parents' role in raising children acknowledged. However, the need for direct intervention in extreme circumstances was also identified as a key principle. The document provided further evidence of the new government's views on family life in its endorsement of marriage as an institution. Whilst acknowledging the fact that 'many lone parents bring up their children successfully', and that cohabitation can be seen as a committed basis for family life, the preferred family form still seemed to be a stable and lasting marriage:

> marriage does provide a strong foundation for stability for the care of children...[I]t makes sense for the Government to do what it can to strengthen marriage.
>
> (Home Office, 1998, p. 31)

Perhaps the recognition of the virtues of marriage as well as the reassurances of a 'hands off' approach reflect a defensive stance against those who might accuse Labour of 'nannying' and being hostile to traditional family forms. On the other hand, there is some evidence that *Supporting Families* did represent genuinely held views. Frank Field, for instance, was influential in linking notions of parental responsibility with concerns about the consequences of moral failure and welfare dependency (Newman, 2001, p. 150). Failure to accept the responsibilities of citizenship could be expected to lead to serious consequences. In the specific context of *Supporting Families*, teenage parenthood was highlighted as an area of particular concern. The consultation document seemed to take a wholly negative view of young parents:

> Unwanted and under-age pregnancies, whether planned or unplanned, have a high personal, social and economic cost and can blight the life chances of younger teenagers.
>
> (Home Office, 1998, p. 44)

The Home Secretary, Jack Straw, speaking at the conference held to launch *Supporting Families*, argued that, in such circumstances, it would be reasonable to consider adoption. Teenage mothers without 'the necessary skills to look after their children' should be willing to consider having their babies adopted (BBC Radio 4, 26 Jan. 1999). This would be preferable to allowing the baby to 'suffer in its first year because the mother...was unable to cope'. He added that adoption provided evidence of better outcomes than placements in care. In this respect, the government appeared to be setting out an argument consistent with the principles elaborated by Goldstein and colleagues (1980). Where the standard of parenting is demonstrably inadequate, children should be removed as soon as possible, and placed in an alternative permanent family setting. It became clear subsequently that this was not mere rhetoric on the part of New Labour, but that adoption would become a central plank of its child care reforms (Cabinet Office, 2000). The Prime Minister himself lent his name to the policy review of adoption services, strongly reiterating pro-family arguments:

> It is hard to overstate the importance of a stable and loving family life for children. That is why I want more children to benefit from adoption. We know that adoption works for children. Over the years, many thousands of children in the care of Local Authorities have benefited from the generosity and commitment of adoptive families...
>
> But we also know that many children wait in care for far too long...Too often in the past adoption has been seen as a last resort...the Government should take a new approach to adoption, putting the child's needs at the centre of the process...
>
> (Blair, 2000, p. 3)

He promised a White Paper and a new drive to promote adoption as a positive choice for children needing permanent care, to which we shall return in due course.

The legislative framework: 'no order' and permanence

In considering the legislation and guidance which reflects a laissez-faire or residualist approach to children's services, it may appear that we are faced with two potentially contradictory imperatives: the requirement to avoid intervening wherever possible, on the one hand; and the expectation of decisive action and permanent solutions, on the other. However, this is not inconsistent with the underlying assumptions of this position, whereby the 'strong state' establishes the moral and legal framework within which families are free to exercise self-determination, whilst also setting clear and explicit boundaries of acceptable behaviour.

The Children Act 1989 and 'no order'

As we have seen, parliamentary debates surrounding the Children Act were influenced by the contemporary furore about events in Cleveland, and this helped to ensure that the Act itself reflected government aspirations to discourage excessive interventions. However, we are reminded by a number of authors that the Act cannot be read as purely representing a single ideological preference. Fox Harding (1991a) argues that the laissez-faire perspective does not figure strongly in the Act, and that all four of the value positions she identifies can be found to a greater or lesser extent embedded in it. Freeman (1992), on the other hand, agrees that each of the value positions can be found in the text of the legislation, but argues that its broader political intentions should not be overlooked as a result. He sees it as essentially a vehicle for promulgating the laissez-faire philosophy of the government of the time. We should be cautious about making assumptions that particular outcomes will flow straightforwardly from the wording of legislation, regulations or guidance. Implementation remains a politically loaded process, too.

Freeman relates his argument to the underlying principle of minimum intervention, as propounded by Goldstein and colleagues (1980). He points out that in a broader context of equality and social justice, such a philosophy may be applied in such a way as to produce 'fair' outcomes. But, he asks, can this be achieved in a world of 'structured inequalities'? The apparently neutral orientation of the Children Act may simply act to compound unfairness, rather than compensate for it. The legislation must be understood in the context of its application, rather than simply as a shopping list of worthy intentions. Thus, we must look not to Part III of the Act which promises much in the way of support and assistance for families 'in need', but rather to those parts which chime with a minimalist perspective. The real significance of the Children Act, for Freeman, lies in Section 1(5), which creates a presumption against action by courts or statutory agencies to intrude in the lives of families:

> Where a court is considering whether or not to make one or more orders under this Act with respect to a child, it shall not make the order or any of the orders unless it considers that doing so would be better for the child than making no order at all.
>
> (Children Act 1989, Section 1(5))

This, in Freeman's opinion, is bound to have an impact on the whole machinery of intervention in relation to the family. Local authorities will be less willing to initiate action, lawyers less enthusiastic about seeking court orders, and courts themselves more reluctant to make orders. As Allen (1998) points out, the practical consequences of this can be seen in the explicit requirement for agency intervention plans for children to be detailed and coherent at the point where court action is taken. The 'no order' principle is linked in Freeman's view with the principle of parental responsibility, set out in Section 3, which emphasises the continuing obligations of parents towards their children, which they retain in all circumstances short of adoption. For Freeman, the symbolic messages here are of considerable importance, although they offer no guarantees that behaviour change will follow:

> There is no reason to suppose that giving parents greater freedom will guarantee that the standard of care will improve ... [The Act] seems to take it for granted that parents will naturally behave with responsibility. The legislation would have been largely otiose if that were true.
>
> (Freeman, 1992, p. 187)

Other features of the Act are taken to indicate further support for the principle of non-interference in parents' exercise of their caring role. For example, the requirement that authorities do not accommodate children if anyone with parental responsibility is ready and able to do so (Children Act 1989, Section 20(7)), and the additional provision that anyone with parental responsibility can remove an 'accommodated' child at any time (Section 20(8)), are cited as examples of the unacceptable logical consequences of pushing the concept of enhanced parental freedoms too far. As Freeman observes, this provision appears to allow for the removal of a child from a settled placement by a parent who has no regular contact or established relationship with the child. Ball (1990), too, has been critical of the 'ideological' impetus behind some aspects of the Children Act, also highlighting the provision for parents to be able to remove children from accommodation at any time as an example of this. Eekelaar (1991) agrees that the Act represents a clear shift in the balance of power between state and families. His view is that the concept of 'parental responsibility' is 'nakedly ideological' (Eekelaar, 1991, p. 45). The Act is based on a belief that:

> given freedom from state regulation, parents will *naturally* care for their offspring…It may be asked whether the historical record justifies such a view.
>
> (Eekelaar, 1991, p. 50)

My own conclusion on the impact of the legal concept of 'parental responsibility' was somewhat similar (Smith, 1990a). This conclusion was further supported by the incorporation at various points in the Act of increased protection for parents against unjustified state intervention, such as the power to apply for the discharge of an EPO (Section 45(8)). We might conclude, then, that there are grounds for identifying the laissez-faire perspective as having a strong and influential place at the core of the Children Act.

The search for permanence: adoption law

Whilst the Children Act appears to set limits to state interference in family life, and to promote a particular view of parental autonomy, we must turn to the legislation on adoption to identify the statutory basis for decisive intervention consequent on 'gross failures' of parental care (Goldstein *et al.*, 1980).

In pursuit of the agenda to make adoption more widely available, the government took a number of steps to this end, including the White Paper noted previously, and culminating in the Adoption and Children Act 2002, with full implementation planned for 2004.

The Quality Protects initiative (Department of Health, 1998b) had set the initial agenda for these developments, specifying as its first objective:

> To ensure that children are securely attached to carers capable of providing safe and effective care for the duration of childhood.
>
> (Department of Health, 1998b, Annex. 1)

The concern was that if the quality of parental care should fall below a 'threshold of safety and effectiveness such that children are at risk of significant harm' they may need to be placed with other carers. In order to achieve this end, a number of 'sub-objectives' were also identified within the Quality Protects framework, including the 'maximisation' of the use of adoption as a route towards permanent alternative care, and a reduction in waiting times, prior to long-term placements in adoption or foster care. These practice objectives were later supplemented by the publication of a detailed set of Adoption Standards (Department of Health, 2001b). As Tunstill (2003) points out, however, the target-led nature of Quality Protects and the associated Adoption Standards appear to foreshorten the process of providing substitute families, apparently at the expense of birth family support:

> So, in reality therefore, there is no procedural mechanism, such as a 'Set of Standards for Family Support', to put into practice the stated emphasis on the importance of the birth family, nor even a single standard within the Adoption Framework, to ensure that every possible effort has been made to enable the child to grow up in her/his birth family.
>
> (Tunstill, 2003, p. 99)

The White Paper, *Adoption: A New Approach* (Department of Health, 2000a), with a Prime Ministerial foreword, gave a new flavour to the changed agenda. The strategy set out by this document could be seen as a modification of the Children Act's aspirations to support children in birth families, as Tunstill argues. Where children are 'unable to live with their birth parents', for example, then a 'fresh start' and a 'loving family' should be sought for them. The emphasis throughout is on 'permanence', avoidance of 'delay' and an alternative 'long-term family life'. There should be an increase of 40 per cent in the number of looked-after children adopted by 2004–2005, and each child looked after for a continuous period of six months should have a 'plan for permanence'.

The Adoption and Children Act 2002 gives legislative substance to these aspirations, and should be seen primarily as an enabling piece of legislation, which will over time create a more comprehensive service to promote and support adoption. It may also change the way in which adoption is seen, so that it becomes less a residual option in child care, and more a central element in the range of alternative placements. According to the explanatory notes:

> The Act changes the process of adoption itself...The Act makes the welfare of the child the paramount consideration for courts and adoption agencies in all decisions relating to adoption, including whether to dispense with a birth parent's consent to adoption.
>
> (Explanatory Notes to the Adoption and Children Act 2002, par. 8)

The emphasis on the paramountcy of the child's interests (as opposed to giving them 'first' consideration, as previously) aligns the legislation with the framework established by Goldstein and colleagues (1980). This also brings it into line with the Children Act 1989, although courts are additionally required to consider the child's welfare 'throughout his [*sic*] life, in recognition of the lifelong implications of adoption'. The legislation also requires that 'decisions are taken earlier' than under previous legislation (the Adoption Act 1976), whilst consideration must also be given to the ability of the child's 'relatives' to maintain a stable relationship and provide a secure home. Taking a long-term view may, of course, serve to highlight the fragility of such relationships. The impact of these provisions taken together may be to shift the balance in favour of 'longtime caretakers':

> when 'temporary' placements become long-term, for whatever reason, the familial bonds that develop between the child and his caretakers must not be shattered by state action on behalf of absent parents or because of agency policies.
>
> (Goldstein *et al.*, 1980, p. 51)

Thus, the changing legislative framework for adoption appears to represent a move towards a greater emphasis on certainty and permanence, which, in turn, is likely to mean a greater reliance on alternative family placements for children who are 'looked after'. Jones (2003) is particularly critical of this apparent shift of priorities, arguing that the value of 'permanence' in planning for children has not been demonstrated, but that the consequence of this may well be a further neglect of preventative services, and a failure to recognise the complex nature of children's needs:

> So, birth parents may be forced to relinquish their children if they are unable to guarantee permanency in terms of the material conditions and care provided; yet permanency in terms of a sense of belonging may be sustained.
>
> (Jones, 2003, p. 174)

'The dog that didn't bark': minimal intervention in practice

Like Sherlock Holmes' dog that didn't bark, it may seem that the 'residualist' position in children's services can best be identified by the absence of intervention, rather than by its presence. On the other hand, as we have seen, a number of strands of activity would seem integral to this perspective. For instance, it is possible to identify an advocacy function, whereby those who might feel victimised by state intrusion can resist and maintain the integrity of their family life. In addition, it is implicit in the laissez-faire position that irrefutable evidence of parental incapacity may lead to action being taken when it is in children's best interests to secure alternative, long-term placements away from birth families.

Defending families: Parents Against INjustice (PAIN)

One organisation, in particular, has typified the approach based on supporting and advocating parents and families subject to what they feel is unwarranted state intrusion, usually in the context of allegations of abuse – Parents Against INjustice (PAIN). PAIN was formed in 1985 by Sue Amphlett, who herself had been the subject of investigation for alleged physical abuse of her child; and the organisation continued to operate until 1999, when its funding ran out.[1] PAIN was founded to represent parents who were 'innocent of child abuse or neglect', but still found themselves the objects of investigation and statutory processes. It became recognised as the national charity which would represent the interests of parents and other carers who believed themselves to be wrongly suspected of abusing their children (*The Guardian*, 12 Jan. 2000).

The aims of the organisation were both to provide a helpline service to others in the same position and to act as a campaigning body, promoting the rights of 'parents, children and families'. Sue Amphlett gave evidence to the Cleveland Inquiry, pressing for a recognition of the importance of 'preserving family life' (Parton, 1991, p. 95), and arguing for proper procedural arrangements to ensure parents' perspectives were included in investigations.

In terms of its practice, PAIN sought to provide information, support and sometimes advocacy to those who wished to challenge the way in which they were being investigated by social work agencies. The aim of this intervention would be to reassert the presumption against removing children from the family, whilst recognising the paramountcy of the child's interests (Smith, 1995). PAIN emphasised, too, the principle of partnership. Recognising the sensitivity of its role, the organisation sought to promote improved understanding between agencies and parents:

> PAIN aims to promote and preserve family life by enabling its members to work in partnership with professionals and practitioners in cases of alleged abuse or neglect.
>
> (PAIN, 1993)

The aim of intervention would be to support 'parents, carers and children ... to make their own views known', without prejudging case outcomes. The belief was that enabling people to represent their own interests, and encouraging agencies to be less confrontational, should result in clearer mutual understanding, the correction of mistakes, and fewer unnecessary removals of children from their families. PAIN also drew attention to the relatively large number of child protection investigations which did not lead to any further action, and were in fact unsubstantiated (Gibbons *et al.*, 1995), arguing that the experience of being investigated in itself may be unsettling, traumatic and damaging to family relationships.

While Fox Harding (1997) associates PAIN with the 'birth family defender' position, the argument here is that the organisation was more concerned to resist unwarranted interference in the family, and could thus be better classified as 'non-interventionist'. For example, concerns were identified by the organisation as to the possible impact of 'system abuse'. PAIN's role in supporting families who were affected in this way led to a recognition of the importance of the 'secondary' consequences of child abuse investigations, regardless of whether or not allegations are substantiated:

> We at PAIN know that the problems of such children and their families ... are not recognised by the vast majority of child care workers.
>
> (Amphlett, 1992, p. 26)

PAIN's approach was based on the principle of putting parents and other family members in a better position to respond to the pressures arising directly and indirectly from a child abuse investigation, and thereby also to challenge bad practice. At least partly as a consequence of PAIN's work, the importance of providing independent support for families in these circumstances came to be acknowledged, and greater recognition of the importance of including parents, for example in case conferences, has ensued.

Seeking permanence

The other side of the coin to advocacy against unjustified intrusion is, in practice terms, decisive intervention to remove children from harmful situations and provide long-term alternative placements. Thus, according to Goldstein and colleagues, where clear and robust criteria of parental failure can be shown to have been realised, and it is demonstrably in the child's best interests to intervene, an alternative placement must be found which is 'unconditional and final' (Goldstein *et al.*, 1973, p. 101). The principle of 'permanence', in the sense of making a 'clean break', is thus associated with the position of minimum state intervention;

although Fox Harding (1997) also links it with the 'state paternalist' perspective because it emphasises psychological rather than biological parenting.

In practical terms, the notion of decisive intervention becomes associated with measures to establish secure and lasting substitute family relationships. Support emerged for this kind of strategy during the 1970s, when the tragic failure of attempts to reinsert Maria Colwell into her birth family coincided with influential studies which found that many children were 'drifting' in supposedly short-term residential care awaiting rehabilitation (for example, Rowe and Lambert, 1973). Thus, despite evidence that a large proportion of children in care would stay there, there appeared to be substantial delays in finding alternative family placements for them:

> it is difficult not to feel that in a number of cases earlier decision could have been reached through more attention to family diagnosis, better assessment of the child's needs and more emphasis on planning in the early days after admission to care.
>
> (Rowe and Lambert, 1973, p. 94)

Adoption, it was argued, would be more successful than fostering, not least because it offered greater security to children. Thoburn and colleagues (1986) argue that this change of emphasis was given recognition in policy terms by the Children Act 1975, which appeared to signal increasing support for the use of adoption to provide long-term security for children, rather than primarily as a vehicle for meeting the needs of childless adults.

Parker (1999) explicitly links this development to the influence of the 'permanency' movement. The adoption of children in care was encouraged by the 1975 Act, and by the Adoption Act 1976, and local authorities began to provide more extensive adoption services. As a result, the profile of adoptions also changed, with adoptions from care of older children displacing baby adoptions over the ensuing period (rising from 7 to 40 per cent of all adoptions between 1975 and the 1990s; Parker, 1999, p. 3). These changes in the characteristics of adopted children were also mirrored by the development of new forms of practice:

> Adoption came to be acknowledged in official and professional circles primarily as a means of meeting the needs of certain children rather than as a solution to the problem of unmarried motherhood or to the needs of infertile couples.
>
> (Parker, 1999, p. 5)

As a result, the emphasis shifted to comprehensive assessment of children's needs, and detailed and painstaking 'matching' with adoptive families. The prioritising of children's interests also led to a recognition of the need to avoid 'drift', and a readiness to consider terminating contact with birth parents (Thoburn *et al.*, 1986, p. 9). An increasing number of adoptions, too, were found to be contested (Parker, 1999). The adversarial nature of the process, and the concern for long-term stability certainly appear to have encouraged social work practitioners to consider terminating contact in some cases (Thoburn *et al.*, 1986).

It could be argued, too, that other aspects of the adoptive process came to be influenced by the underlying assumptions about permanence. For example, the continuing debate over trans-racial adoption (Gupta, 2003) appears to have been influenced by some of these ideas. As a result, it is suggested, certain preoccupations may have obscured other important considerations:

> while it is clearly in all children's interests that appropriate placements are made with minimum delay, there is a risk that children's long-term needs for a positive identity and self-esteem may be compromised by rushed and inappropriate placements.
>
> (Gupta, 2003, p. 212)

As well as the potential oversight of 'socio-genealogical connectedness' (Owusu-Bempah and Howitt, 2000), ideas of a 'clean break' approach to adoption have affected other aspects of provision. The emphasis on assessment and matching may have been associated with a relatively lower priority being accorded to post-adoption support services. The assumption that all that is needed is the creation of a 'new' family may be too simplistic (Forrest, 2003).

The emergence of new challenges in the context of adoption practice also helps to illustrate some of the limitations of the non-interventionist perspective. The assumption that the failure of birth families can be dealt with by a decisive and permanent intervention overlooks the continuities and connections which already exist in children's lives, whatever their ages.

Jones (2003), for example, describes permanence as a 'fiction'. It is a 'social work construct' which idealises complex processes and multi-faceted needs of children, in her opinion. Thus children will remain connected to their histories, their culture and to prior relationships following adoption. They will need to make sense of these and some may remain important to them:

children may have strong mutually loving relationships with their adoptive family yet at the same time, retain the feeling of being permanently connected to their birth family. It is not in the designs of children to go along with adults who would seek to create permanent families through adoption as if the child had no connection to any other family.

(Jones, 2003, p. 175)

It is also a matter of concern that a preoccupation with the idea of adoption as a guarantee of permanence and security may 'divert energy and resources' away from the provision of preventive services for birth families. Ryburn (1996) concurs, arguing that the very simplicity and low cost of adoption may compound distortions in service provision and slow decision-making processes.

On the other hand, some of the provisions signalled by the Adoption and Children Act 2002 appear to take account of the need for flexibility. The introduction of specific adoption support services, and the inclusion of 'special guardianship', for example, both appear to indicate a readiness to provide for the needs of children, in the light of their continually changing relationships with adoptive parents and birth families. It is also the case that the legislation attempts to broaden the pool of potential adopters by taking a more positive approach to cohabiting and same-sex couples. This suggests a readiness to move away from a preoccupation with the idealised form of the married two-parent family, and at the very least a modification of some of the traditionalist assumptions associated with the laissez-faire perspective. The pure form of any particular perspective will be hard to find replicated precisely in the complex sphere of practice, and in this respect, developments in adoption are no exception.

State authority and residual intervention: some limitations

In considering the practice context of the perspective associated with a limited but authoritarian role for state intervention, we can also identify some of its potential flaws. Thus, whilst it is clear that there is a need to avoid unjustified and intrusive action to regulate family life, the underlying assumptions which provide the rationale for such intervention are problematic. It is not sufficient simply to reduce the role of the state to a minimum, since this appears to be associated with fixed beliefs about what unsuitability means in the context of specific families. This, in turn, may result in precipitate actions which do not reflect the tangled realities of children's lives. Tunstill summarises the challenge helpfully:

It ought...to be possible for adoption and family support to survive and indeed thrive within the same child care continuum. This will only be the case if strenuous effort is made to avoid the apparently easy option of premature adoptions.

(Tunstill, 2003, p. 103)

In addition, the association of the minimal state perspective with an idealised model of the family (and its association with 'patriarchy') also serves to limit its applicability to the changing nature of family ties and personal relationships. As children become more mobile in the sense of accumulating a series of increasingly complex and multi-faceted relationships with other family members and carers, it becomes increasingly difficult to sustain a one-dimensional model based on a preferred model of family life, whatever the advantages of this may be.

CHILD PROTECTION AND THE AUTHORITATIVE STATE

Authority and intervention

Unlike the minimalist, laissez-faire view of the state, the 'institutional model' (Hardiker *et al.*, 1991) sees it as having a legitimate role in intervening in the social order. The state is seen as having a positive role in 'correcting' the organisational and individual malfunctions which are an inevitable feature of any social system. The purpose of intervention is not to transform living conditions or institutional structures, but to maintain order and to sustain the conditions for effective economic and social functioning. As George and Wilding (1994) put it, this view of the 'Middle Way' state sees it as reflecting the interests of all sections of the community, based on a substantial level of consensus about how society should be organised, and how services should be delivered:

> The social and political order are accepted as serving the interests of all sections of society. The state exercises its power and authority in a legitimate, even handed way on behalf of individual and sectional interests . . .
> (Hardiker *et al.*, 1991, p. 23)

This suggests that the state and its institutions are essentially benevolent, in contrast to the minimalist perspective. Intervention can be assumed to be motivated by the aim of protecting vulnerable groups, preventing harm and ameliorating unsatisfactory circumstances. As George and Wilding (1994) put it, there is a strand within Conservative thinking which sees it as the obligation of the state to 'make good market imperfections'. Social improvement is a legitimate aim, and the welfare state has a positive role in 'binding the community together' (Patten, quoted in George and Wilding, 1994, p. 53). The state thus has a legitimate role in supporting the family, but not supplanting parents' roles or undermining its independence. The state should create the conditions for the exercise of family responsibilities, such as caring for vulnerable members or nurturing children.

Despite this relatively optimistic view of the state and its institutions, the role identified for it is still relatively limited, and active intervention can only be justified where it will clearly enhance the interests of those affected. Its focus will be on individual problems, the 'failure' of particular families, and the consequences of inefficient allocation of social benefits. Associated with this view, consequentially, are assumptions that it is possible to identify or to diagnose those components of the social system which are malfunctioning, and to repair them accordingly. Authors such as Bauman (1992), Giddens (1991) and Beck (1992) link this perception, in turn, to a high level of confidence in the perfectibility of knowledge and the effectiveness of scientific techniques to carry out such diagnostic and corrective functions (see Chapter 6).

The growing influence of a belief in the value of science represents a move on from assumptions about the 'natural' or 'God-given' nature of social phenomena (Parton, 1996, p. 7). The development and application of thoroughgoing scientific understanding potentially offers a route by which the apparent vagaries of human existence can be brought under control, according to this line of reasoning. The assumption of expertise and certainty is of particular importance in this context, and, according to Hardiker and colleagues (1991), this provides the justification for the development of a particular orientation to social work:

> Here, then, lies the role for social work in providing a service that has the necessary specialist skills both to understand and to intervene to remedy a wide range of social problems on the basis of professional assessments of need.
>
> (Hardiker *et al.*, 1991, p. 24)

Both in practical and conceptual terms, the role of the social worker becomes one of identifying, assessing and intervening with problems located at the level of individuals or family 'systems', and a preoccupation with correcting these identified shortcomings, rather than any 'fundamental adjustments of the social environment' (Hardiker *et al.*, 1991, p. 25).

The role of the experts in child protection

The broad perspective on the role and responsibilities of social work represented here can also be associated with the emergence of a particular orientation towards intervention with children. The 'discovery' of child abuse by Henry Kempe in the early 1960s was perhaps an important moment in this context (Jones *et al.*, 1987). As Hendrick (1994) notes, the way in which the problem of harm to children was formulated lent itself to an individualised and medicalised frame of reference:

> When child abuse was 'discovered' it was as an individualistic *disease* rather than as a sociological and political malaise. The reverend Arthur Morton, Director of the NSPCC, described it in 1972 as a 'contagious disease which must be notified'.
>
> (Hendrick, 1994, p. 254)

Intervention based on these assumptions quickly took on distinctive characteristics (Baher *et al.*, 1976). Notions of 'diagnosis' and 'treatment' informed intervention strategies, with a particular emphasis on the nature of parent–child interactions, and the extent to which parents could be expected to meet children's needs, and there was clear evidence of a judgemental approach on the part of professional practitioners. Parton (1991) argues that this orientation towards the problem of child abuse became a dominant influence, informing major child protection inquiries throughout the 1980s, for example. The location of the causes of child abuse within a model of family pathology led inevitably to a focus on the question of 'what type of individual or family would harm their children?' (Parton, 1991, p. 58). As a consequence, the primary focus of both research and professional assessments would be on the individual and family factors likely to be associated with child abuse, and, in turn, the nature of interventions which might be found to treat these effectively, and to prevent any reoccurrence. Authoritative lists of indicators of risk might be drawn up (Jones *et al.*, 1987; Parton, 1991), which could be used to frame judgements about the likelihood of harm. Accordingly:

> the ability to identify and predict abuse and therefore prevent *it* before *it* happens was central to what all those involved in the child abuse system should be doing.
>
> (Parton, 1991, p. 62)

Shortcomings in the provision of statutory services to protect children and deal with the consequences of harm to them could be attributed to lack of knowledge, inadequate training or poor practice, rather than any fundamental structural flaws or social problems (Parton, 1991, p. 63).

That this kind of assumption is deeply embedded in the understandings of child protection systems and practices is demonstrated again in more recent inquiries, including that into the death of Victoria Climbie (Laming, 2003). It is argued that better professional practice, better and more focused supervision and management, and better run organisations are the core requirements for enhancing the quality of the safeguards offered to protect children.

Intervention, tutelage and better parenting

The 'authoritative' model of state welfare can also be associated with a particular view as to the nature of intervention in families to promote children's well-being. This originates with the assumptions already discussed which attribute expertise and certainty to state agencies and professional bodies. A consequence of this is a particular 'correctional' orientation to the provision of services, which is based on the idea that parents can be trained to protect their children, and to provide more supportive forms of care for them. Donzelot (1979) argues that this kind of tutelary role is a central characteristic of the modern state. What is represented in state intervention is a process of 'government through the family'. Thus, compliance with social norms of acceptable behaviour could be achieved by the exercise of the state's authority, and the delivery of expert services. This gives rise, in his view, to a 'climate of paternalistic philanthropy' (Donzelot, 1979, p. 163) where the receipt of practical support or financial assistance depends on a degree of compliance with certain behavioural expectations, which might be associated with 'good parenting'. Similar preoccupations are to be found in the emphasis on prescriptive forms of treatment and the conditional nature of crucial decisions in the specific context of child protection work. Thus:

> The professional worker is seen as the expert, providing or withholding resources according to the degree of client compliance with the treatment programme.
>
> (Hardiker *et al.*, 1991, p. 25)

Considerable emphasis in intervention is likely to be focused on reducing the level of risk indicated, programmes designed to correct parental shortcomings, and intensive supervision to ensure compliance. As Fox Harding (1997) also observes, the concern with managing and controlling risk also implies a readiness to remove children from the care of parents where other measures are seen as insufficient to guarantee children's safety. The expertise vested in the state allows its agents (child welfare professionals) to make the judgement that parents are irretrievably unable to ensure their children's welfare, and then take action accordingly:

> In summary, in the paternalist and child protection value perspective, those birth parents who do not bring up their children 'well' cannot expect to keep them ... state power should be readily and extensively used ...
>
> (Fox Harding, 1997, p. 42)

As she ironically observes, the legitimacy of this form of intervention relies on a considerable degree of faith in the capacity of the state to act appropriately and benevolently to safeguard and promote children's welfare.

In common with the laissez-faire perspective, then, the child protectionist position bases the authority for its intervention on evidence of families' failure to care satisfactorily for their children. However, thresholds for intervention appear lower for those prioritising the safeguarding of children (Hardiker *et al.*, 1991), being based on evidence of risk, rather than operating only at crisis point or in the context of complete family breakdown. This, in turn, means that rehabilitative and preventive services can be offered in order to enable families to remain intact, and to promote the future security of children in this setting.

The context of intervention, then, is one of relative optimism, both about the potential for promoting parental competence, and about the capacity of the state to provide the means for achieving this. On the other hand, this also means that the expectation will be of a role for the state which may involve either suspending or removing parental responsibility, or being highly directive as to the manner in which this is exercised. Whilst parents who do not provide evidence of 'good enough' care for their children do not necessarily risk losing them, they do incur the likelihood of investigation, close supervision and surveillance by professionalised state agencies under such circumstances. The notional paramountcy of children's interests does provide the rationale for superseding the role of parents, where specific risks are identified, and imposing specific requirements as to the way in which they conduct the care of their children:

> parental rights are not valued highly in this approach; it is the parental *duty* to care properly for the child which is prominent ...
>
> (Fox Harding, 1997, p. 40)

Of course, the extent to which the state can exercise any kind of prescriptive role depends on achieving the legitimacy to do so, both in general terms and in the specific service context. As Parton (1996, p. 12) observes, this may be increasingly difficult to achieve in the context of growing 'diversity, uncertainty, fragmentation, ambiguity and change'.

The policy context: the 'nanny state' and the machinery of child protection

The view of the benevolent and expert state which informs this perspective is associated with specific themes in policy debates. In particular, there is a preoccupation with the protection of children and the improvement of the machinery to achieve this, on the one hand; and there is a concern to ensure that the nature and quality of parenting is improved, on the other.

In relation to child protection, the era of the welfare state has witnessed a high degree of 'political, public and professional interest' in this subject, originating, it is argued, with the Maria Colwell case (Parton, 1991, p. 52). There have been a substantial number of similar inquiries since (for example, Blom-Cooper, 1985; Kenward, 2002), culminating in the Victoria Climbie report (Laming, 2003). The fact that these reports are usually concerned with child deaths, and attract substantial media attention, ensures that their conclusions and the accompanying interpretations are likely to have a strong influence on policy and practice. It is therefore important to try to understand the extent to which they reveal common themes and point towards similar conclusions. A number of consistent elements do appear to emerge, contributing to the construction of a unified discourse about improving the safeguarding of children. These can be seen in terms of parental/carer failure, operational failure, practitioner incompetence and managerial solutions.

Parental/carer failure

Clearly, in cases involving the death of a child, there is likely to be a concern with the quality of parenting. Child protection inquiries typically find copious evidence of shortcomings in this area, which should have been apparent to statutory agencies. Thus, the Maria Colwell inquiry (Secretary of State for Social Services, 1974) details a pattern of incidents giving cause for concern. Maria was cared for by relatives when her mother was unable to care for her, but was eventually returned to live with her mother by the local authority. Her mother was found to be 'insensitive' towards Maria's needs when visited by a social worker in July 1970, and appeared not to be concerned with her best interests on another occasion in October of that year. By the Summer of the following year, when plans to return her to her mother (and stepfather) were well under way, and she was staying with her mother on a short-term basis, she was reported to have run away, and as a result to be 'slapped' by her mother. Further evidence of physical mistreatment was recorded in the period leading up to her eventual death, reportedly at the hands of her stepfather.

Similarly, the inquiry into the death of Jasmine Beckford (Blom-Cooper, 1985) found a prolonged pattern of inadequate care and mistreatment. Her mother was reported to be suffering from depression, while her stepfather was convicted of assaulting her at the age of 18 months. Like Maria Colwell, she was fostered but then returned to her mother and stepfather. And equally, there emerged a pattern of inappropriate parental behaviour subsequently. According to the inquiry report, there was evidence of parental disharmony, poor school attendance and further physical harm over the two-year period leading to Jasmine's death in 1984.

Although the context was different, in that she was living with her father's aunt under a private fostering arrangement, the pattern of poor quality care is repeated according to the inquiry into Victoria Climbie's death (Laming, 2003). Verbal abuse, lack of affection, oppressive behaviour and a history of repeated physical injuries is reported to have been observed, generating an overall picture of persistent mistreatment by carers. Other more recent cases are also found to have been characterised by violence and an excessively punitive attitude from parents and carers. Ainlee Labonte who died of 'chronic abuse and neglect' at the age of 2½ was found to have been 'strapped in a chair facing the wall, "because she had been flicking food around" ' (Kenward, 2002, p. 33), during a social worker's visit to the family.

In all these examples, over many years, inquiry reports have generated a picture of persistent and blameworthy failure on the part of those with direct responsibility for the children's care and development.

Operational failure

Associated with the evidence of carers' inadequacies, there also appears to be a common concern with agency failure. Thus, even though the reports span nearly thirty years, there are some remarkable similarities in their conclusions about the mistakes and oversights of those responsible for protecting the children concerned. Routine systems and standard procedures within and between agencies seem to have broken down in each case. Thus, in Maria Colwell's case, no-one responded to a phone call from a member of the public to report that she was being mistreated (Goldstein *et al.*, 1980, p. 167). The inquiry into the death of Jasmine Beckford also found evidence of system failure:

> had the system set up by Brent Education Department since 1977 operated as it should have done, Social Services would have been alerted. Another aspect of fault in the education services was the failure to recognise the significance of the irregular attendance....
>
> (Blom-Cooper, 1985, p. 292)

Again, in the case of Victoria Climbie, the inquiry concluded that there had been a 'gross failure of the system' (Laming, 2003, p. 3). For example, a duty system was in place in Ealing Social Services which: 'was almost totally reliant on the memory of one manager' (Laming, 2003, p. 44), and thus liable to break down at any time. The overall conclusion was that the responsible agencies 'were under-funded, inadequately staffed and poorly led' (Laming, 2003, p. 3). These concerns are further underlined by the evidence from a much larger sample of 'serious case reviews' (Sinclair and Bullock, 2002, p. 40) that agency shortcomings, such as 'inadequate information sharing' and 'a lack of inter-agency working' remain as major flaws in the arrangements to protect children at risk of serious harm.

Practitioner failure

The shortcomings of practitioners also appear as a common strand in child protection inquiries over the years. According to Parton (1991), such failures are attributed to lack of knowledge, reluctance to exercise statutory powers, and an over-optimistic view of the capacity of parents and carers to safeguard children (see also, Dingwall *et al.*, 1983). Maria Colwell's social worker, for example, is reported as consistently taking a positive view of her demeanour, even when the evidence was ambiguous or unclear. On one occasion, after she had run away and subsequently shown a considerable amount of distress, the view was taken that Maria had 'calmed down quite well' and was 'bright and chatty'. The report into Jasmine Beckford's case equally criticises the failure of social workers to be systematic, or to take account of available evidence. The combination of warning signs in the case should, in the author's view, have precluded any consideration of removing Jasmine (and her sister) from the child protection register:

all these would have led any reasonable bunch of social workers to question what they were about to do.

(Blom-Cooper, 1985, p. 118)

Equally, whilst the Victoria Climbie inquiry is at pains to avoid singling out social work practitioners for blame, the tone is clear – the report suggests that there was 'plenty of evidence' that limited resources were being misused (Laming, 2003, p. 3), and it reports the social worker in the case making the same kind of assumptions as her predecessor almost thirty years previously. Without meeting Victoria:

> she formed the impression that Victoria was happy and seemed like the 'little ray of sunshine' described by the nurses.
>
> (Laming, 2003, p. 31)

Similarly, failure to recognise the severity of the situation and to follow agreed procedures in cases of non-accidental injury were found to be factors in the circumstances leading to the death of Chelsea Brown in 1999 (*The Guardian*, 2001).

Managerial solutions

Not only do child protection inquiries seem to focus on common areas of concern, but they also look towards a similar range of solutions. These are predominantly managerial, and revolve around improving systems, knowledge and practice. Once again, the power of the prevailing discourse is evident (see Parton, 1991). In the case of Maria Colwell, there are calls for more robust supervision arrangements for practitioners, for better sharing of information, and a better sense of shared responsibility. Of course, these recommendations did lead to changes, and to the promotion of effective inter-agency arrangements to protect children (Department of Health and Social Security, 1976, for example). Despite this, similar proposals were aired at the culmination of the Jasmine Beckford inquiry (Blom-Cooper, 1985). For example, the duties of health and local authorities to cooperate 'should be made more explicit' (Blom-Cooper, 1985, p. 299). In addition, research to improve the ability to predict risks of abuse was recommended, and the practice knowledge of social workers should be improved, according to the report. Once again, the recommendations of the Victoria Climbie report represent, if anything, a further refinement of these ideas. The policy guidance for child protection should develop a 'common language' between agencies; social workers should have a clearer understanding of 'best practice'; effective inter-agency training should be mandatory;

and monitoring and management arrangements should be strengthened (Laming, 2003, pp. 373–374).

The preoccupation with managerial solutions becomes even more obvious in the light of broader overviews (Sinclair and Bullock, 2002). Perennial concerns with the need to improve inter-agency working and information sharing have led to elaborate proposals for an 'information hub' (Chief Secretary to the Treasury, 2003, p. 54), coordinating knowledge about all children in an area, in order to identify early signs of risk of harm.

The influence of the state paternalist/child protection perspective in framing these contributions to policy development is clear. The emphasis is on improving the ability of the state and its agencies to intervene to safeguard children, by improving expertise, ironing out systems failures, and improving the reliability of the procedures in place.

Better parenting?

The concern within this perspective to improve the reliability and effectiveness of child protection is paralleled by a belief that there is a role for the state in promoting better parenting. This is reflected within particular policy initiatives, notably those of the New Labour government, which has taken a proactive view of its role in intervening in family life. The incoming government issued *Supporting Families*, claiming that:

> This is the first time any government has published a consultation paper on the family.
>
> (Straw, 1998, p. 2)

Although Lord Joseph of the 1970–74 Conservative government would probably have taken issue with this (Department of Health and Social Security, 1974b), it is indicative of a positive belief in the role of government in relation to the family. The document is couched primarily in terms of supporting families, but it is peppered with references to the aim of improving the standards of parenting. Parents are encouraged to accept:

> that asking for help is seen as a sign of responsible parenting.
>
> (Home Office, 1998, p. 10)

In this context, it is suggested that parents require 'a great deal of help', proposing a more extensive role for health visitors, for example, in *preventing* problems arising. Parents could be encouraged to participate in 'toddler training' groups, and even 'teenage years groups' to learn how to handle children's behaviour.

It is not just a matter of providing appropriate help, however. Parents are also to be educated in their responsibilities to ensure children attend school and behave properly (Home Office, 1998, p. 15). In addition, a more strongly interventionist role for the state is envisaged at just the point where things go wrong in families. Where parents are demonstrably not meeting their responsibilities, either to control or to protect their children, then the state is held to have a legitimate role to step in. This is perhaps most apparent in the approach to teenage pregnancy and parenthood, which seems to make the assumption that this should be treated as a tragedy, where negative consequences are almost inevitable:

> Unwanted and under-age pregnancies, whether planned or unplanned, can have a high personal, social and economic cost and can blight the life chances of younger teenagers.
>
> (Home Office, 1998, p. 44)

Such a grim prognosis prompted the government to commission the Social Exclusion Unit to investigate teenage pregnancy, and subsequently, to establish the Teenage Pregnancy Unit. The conclusion to be drawn is that there remains a strong element of government thinking which accepts the legitimacy of intervening in family life to ensure that adequate standards of parenting and child rearing are met, despite the assurances of minimum intervention offered by documents such as *Supporting Families* (Home Office, 1998).

These tendencies are evident in specific 'policy streams'; however, the extent to which they are able to influence ideas about practice depends on their perceived legitimacy, both in general terms and in the specific context of family failure. Legitimation is achieved in part, by the establishment of a particular orientation towards practice, focusing on individuals and families:

> Much of the legislation governing child care practice is focused on the needs/best interests of the individual child...The implication...is that the targets for change are likely to be seen as either the family unit as a whole or individual members of that unit.
>
> (Hardiker *et al.*, 1991, p. 40)

Concerns with structural change are accorded less priority according to this analysis. This creates a kind of circularity, whereby evidence of individual problems provides the justification for focusing intervention at this level, irrespective of other external influences.

Protecting children: the legislative framework

In common with the wider policy context, there appear to be two strands of law and guidance which give substance to the protectionist/ paternalist position. These are, broadly, those aspects concerned with safeguarding children and more recent developments which legitimise and prioritise intervention to change parental attitudes and conduct. This is contrasted with strategies which emphasise improved services and support for families, and are less concerned with prescribing behaviour (see Chapter 4).

The first UK legislation explicitly concerned with preventing harm to children was the Prevention of Cruelty to Children Act 1889, coinciding with the establishment of the National Society for the Prevention of Cruelty to Children (NSPCC) (Hendrick, 1994). This also coincided with a particular era in which the state paternalist perspective became increasingly influential, and where there was a 'reshaping of public opinion away from the view that the family was inviolate' (Hendrick, 1994, p. 59). In any case, from that point onwards, there has remained a legal commitment to the protection of children, where they are at risk of harm. Currently, of course, this is given substance primarily by the Children Act 1989.

The Act was introduced following the Cleveland Inquiry, which prompted concerns about speculative and apparently 'arbitrary exercise of power by the employees of a local authority' (D. Mellor, Minister of State, House of Commons Standing Committee B, 25.6.89, Col. 277). Despite this, counter pressures were felt as a result of the series of child death inquiries also published in the 1980s (Noyes, 1991). As a result, the legislation concentrated on clarifying and more closely specifying the circumstances in which child protection procedures could be invoked. This approach could be seen to apply in both Parts of the Act with specific relevance to the protection of children (Parts IV and V). For example, an EPO could only be sought in precisely defined circumstances, that is, where the child 'is suffering, or is likely to suffer, significant harm' or that 'access to the child is required as a matter of urgency' (Section 44). This was intended to counter the apparently indiscriminate use of the EPO's predecessor, the Place of Safety Order (see Parton, 1991, p. 37). Notwithstanding this, where the case for an EPO is made, the 'applicant', usually the local authority acquires substantial power in relation to the child, including the acquisition of parental responsibility, and the ability to determine the child's placement. In view of this, the use of the EPO is constrained by a series of safeguards, such as its limited duration (eight or exceptionally fifteen days; Section 45), and the power of parents to challenge orders (Section 45). In addition, provision was made for the use of the Child Assessment Order (Section 43) where the situation is less urgent, in order to avoid the use of the draconian powers of the EPO wherever possible.

As Parton (1991) has observed, the emphasis on precision, calculability of risk and specific criteria for intervention also infused those aspects of the legislation relating to the investigation of possible harm to the child and subsequent interventions. Thus, a clear progression is marked out, whereby the 'duty to investigate' (Section 47) is only incurred by the local authority where a child is already under protection, or where there is 'reasonable cause to suspect that' a child is suffering, or is likely to, suffer significant harm. The enquiries themselves are directed towards determining whether or not this is the case, and only when this threshold is reached can specific orders (such as Care or Supervision Orders; Section 31) be sought. The threshold itself is also more closely defined, in terms of 'ill-treatment or the impairment of health or development', in order to limit the possibility of orders being made on spurious or insubstantial grounds. This attempt to specify precisely the evidential grounds for the making of orders can be related to the belief, outlined previously, that the state is able to formulate and apply rules of scientific accuracy in the context of child care. The detailed framework for the delivery of child protection services is set out in the government guidance, *Working Together to Safeguard Children* (Department of Health *et al.*, 1999). Published initially in 1988, *Working Together* was revised to underpin the Children Act (Department of Health, 1991c), and has continued to form the basis for work to safeguard children, in its various forms. It attempts, for example, to provide more detailed elaboration of what is meant by 'harm' to children, and how that can be judged. It distinguishes between categories of abuse and neglect ('physical abuse', 'sexual abuse', 'emotional abuse' and 'neglect'), and it sets out a framework for the conduct of investigations by social services and partner agencies.

Working Together seeks to make clear the importance of making links between the protection of children, their wider needs and the provision of other services. For example, it acknowledges the influence on children's lives of experiences such as domestic violence and racism, and it draws attention to the potential victimisation of disabled children. Agencies and practitioners are reminded to:

promote access to a range of services for children in need without inap-
propriately triggering child protection processes; [and] consider the wider
needs of children and families involved in child protection processes,
whether or not concerns about abuse and/or neglect are substantiated ...

(Department of Health *et al.*, 1999, p. 11)

However, the preoccupation with 'significant harm' remains central to
the document, somewhat belying these aspirations, and those of its
companion volume concerned with the assessment of children's needs:

safeguarding children should not be seen as a separate activity from
promoting their welfare. They are two sides of the same coin. Promoting
welfare has a wider, more positive, action centred approach embedded in
a philosophy of creating opportunities to enable children to have opti-
mum life chances in adulthood, as well as ensuring they are growing up
in circumstances consistent with the provision of safe and effective care.

(Department of Health *et al.*, 2000, p. 5)

Despite this, the practical implications of *Working Together* are somewhat narrower. In common with the broader protectionist perspective,
the guidance appears preoccupied with a 'case management' approach
(Parton, 2002; Smith, 2002). This is reflected both in its views of the
structural arrangements to safeguard children, and in its detailed prescriptions for practice. The broad remit of the Area Child Protection
Committee (ACPC) is set out by the document to include awareness
raising and promotional activity, but its specific duties reflect a preoccupation with the 'relevant population' of children likely to suffer significant harm. The protocols for ACPCs (Department of Health *et al.*,
1999, p. 36):

exclusively concern the conduct and management of specific features of the
child protection system such as case conferences, joint assessment procedures
and decisions to add children's names to the child protection register.

(Smith, 2002, p. 253)

The centrepiece of *Working Together* is a lengthy chapter on the procedural aspects of 'handling individual cases', which originates with the
exhortation to be 'alert to children's welfare':

Everybody who works with children, parents and other adults in contact
with children should be able to recognise, and know how to act upon,
indicators that a child's welfare or safety may be at risk.

(Department of Health *et al.*, 1999, p. 39)

From this starting point, the document sets out recommended procedures for referrals to social services, initial assessment and intervention
to protect children. It is made clear that where concerns are immediate
or where children's safety requires it, action may be taken without
reference to parents, and that the basis for action will be a 'strategy discussion' including social services, the police and 'other agencies as
appropriate' (Department of Health *et al.*, 1999, p. 46). Where child protection concerns are substantiated following an investigation, a child
protection conference will be convened in order to determine whether
to include the child's name on the child protection register, and draw
up a 'child protection plan' (Department of Health *et al.*, 1999, p. 55).
Decisions at this point should be determined by reference to expert
opinion. For example:

> The conference should consider the following question when determin-
> ing whether to register a child:
> * **Is the child at continuing risk of significant harm**?
>   The test should be that either:
> * the child can be shown to have suffered ill-treatment or impairment of
>   health or development as a result of physical, emotional, or sexual
>   abuse or neglect, and *professional judgement* [my emphasis] is that
>   further ill-treatment or impairment are likely; *or*
> * *professional judgement* [my emphasis], substantiated by the findings of
>   enquiries in this individual case or by research evidence, is that the
>   child is likely to suffer ill-treatment or the impairment of health or
>   development as a result of physical, emotional, or sexual abuse or
>   neglect ...
>
> (Department of Health *et al.*, 1999, p. 55)

It is important to note that, as the process unfolds, there is a progressive
diminution of parents' role, in that their participation, their judgement,
their decision-making power and their 'parental responsibility' are
superseded by those of professionals and statutory agencies. This is not
necessarily a critical point, but it illustrates a key, but problematic, fault
line between family (parental) autonomy and the powers of the state to
assert its expertise, to claim authority and to intervene.

Controlling parents: a new agenda?

In addition to the legislative tradition surrounding the protection of
children, originating in the nineteenth century, as we have seen, a
more recent development appears to have been the state's ascription of
powers to itself to intervene in a directive fashion in relation to parents'

performance of their roles. This has been particularly evident with the emergence of concerns about ensuring that parents exercise due responsibility in controlling their children's behaviour. The clearest evidence of this development is represented by the parenting order, which was incorporated initially in the Crime and Disorder Act 1998 (Section 8). The parenting order was intended to consist of two elements: a requirement on parents to attend counselling or guidance sessions to receive help in 'dealing with their child'; and a second, discretionary arm, which could impose requirements on parents to exercise specific controls over their child, for example school attendance or compliance with a curfew. The parenting order could run for up to 12 months, and it could be imposed in any criminal proceedings relating to a child, where an anti-social behaviour or child safety order is imposed, or where parents have failed to ensure a child's attendance at school (Home Office, 2000). Whilst the guidance on the parenting order claimed significant research support for its aims (Home Office, 2000, p. 6), it represented a significant new incursion into the terrain of the family. It seemed, however, that evidence of parental failure could be taken to legitimise such intrusions – consistent with the broader state paternalist ideology, as we have seen.

It is ironic, perhaps, that the initial focus of parenting orders has not been on the protection of children, but rather the control of their behaviour. The powers offered by the Children Act to impose requirements on parents under the terms of a supervision order (Section 35; Schedule 3) are little used, and, significantly depend on the consent of those to whom they are applied.

Despite this, the legislative framework clearly provides for the assumption of parents' responsibilities by statutory agencies, or the mandating of parents to carry out their obligations to their children as laid down by the state. The exercise of control and authority is inextricably linked to the notion of expertise and professionalism which legitimises the erosion of parental autonomy and the imposition of statutory powers (Donzelot, 1979). These may be intended either to promote the protection of children or to control their behaviour, but they stem from similar assumptions and share the same roots.

Protecting children and preventing abuse: the shape of practice

As in the previous chapter, the aim here will be to link the preceding contextual material to the practice setting, where the protectionist perspective is manifested. The history and practices of the NSPCC will help to illustrate the role of a particular organisation whose work has always prioritised the prevention of child cruelty. Subsequently, an outline of the specific practice strategies associated with this perspective will also be presented.

The NSPCC: working to protect children

As a voluntary organisation, the NSPCC is unique in taking a strong role in investigating and responding to specific forms of maltreatment of children. As such, it is the only non-statutory body accorded legal authority in relation to the carrying out of child protection functions (Children Act 1989, Section 31). It is also named as a core member of the ACPCs (Department of Health *et al.*, 1999, p. 35).

This central role is consistent with the history and development of the NSPCC. It was founded in 1889, amid growing awareness of the problem of child cruelty in the United Kingdom, and it was awarded a Royal Charter in 1895 (Jones *et al.*, 1987). It has sought to promote public awareness and legislative change, as well as developing a strong practice base. Its early emphasis was on establishing a network of 'inspectors', who were given legal powers to remove children from abusive homes. The society also sought to establish a range of services to support families and improve the quality of parenting. It was only with the 'discovery' of child abuse, at a later stage, that the NSPCC moved more actively into the field of care and treatment for children who had been victimised (Baher *et al.*, 1976). In 1968, the 'Battered Child Research Team' was established, with the aim of identifying the prevalence of child physical abuse, and testing out possible 'treatment models'. Subsequent work has focused on enhancing and broadening these intervention techniques (Dale *et al.*, 1986; Jones *et al.*, 1987). The NSPCC has come to be identified with a particular perspective on child protection, which is concerned with the development of expertise in identification, diagnosis and effective intervention. It was associated, for example, with the campaign for the establishment of child abuse (now child protection) registers, which came to fruition initially in the 1970s (DHSS, 1974a; 1976). Other practice innovations have included the establishment of 'Special Units':

> providing a mixture of direct casework to families, consultation on case management to other agencies, central administrative and coordinating services and teaching.
>
> (Jones *et al.*, 1987, p. 48)

Subsequently, this specialist approach was developed to include over 180 teams and projects (NSPCC, 2002) providing:

a range of investigation, treatment, training, consultation and case-conferencing services in collaboration with local authorities.

(NSPCC, 2000)

Expertise was developed in identifying the signs of abuse (Jones *et al.*, 1987); assessment and treatment of 'dangerous families' (Dale *et al.*, 1986); listening to and empowering children (Cloke and Davies, 1995); and the implementation of particular intervention techniques, such as 'brief focused casework' (Macdonald, 2002). In addition to intervening to protect children and prevent the recurrence of abuse, the NSPCC is 'continuously developing new ways of working with parents' (NSPCC, 2002). These are intended to 'help parents and carers to understand children's needs, improve parenting skills, and cope with pressures that might otherwise cause them to harm their children' (NSPCC, 2002). One such project uses video techniques to help parents to identify ways of improving their parenting skills 'in action'.

These priorities have been found to be reflected in the views and practices of NSPCC staff (Smith, 1995). One such example is of a 'Therapist', who describes using a range of techniques to intervene with a mother to promote her ability to protect her own child, including assertiveness training and practical assistance. By combining these interventions with regular use of assessment questionnaires, the 'cycle of abuse' could be broken, in the Therapist's view. Whilst, in this instance, there was some discomfort with the power of the professional, which should not usurp the child's role in 'leading the intervention' (Smith, 1995, p. 243), there is also a clear sense in which the NSPCC is identified with a particular form of expertise. The methods of intervention espoused by the society rely on professional authority and the body of specialist knowledge and skills it has built up:

> When the NSPCC is contacted because a child is at risk of harm, our first step is to look at the child's personal situation and assess the likelihood of abuse occurring.
>
> (NSPCC, 2002)

Where abuse is identified, therapeutic work, counselling or family support are the preferred means of intervention. This approach might mean, for example, that the kind of service offered by an NSPCC family centre would be more focused, and possibly more directive, than that offered by other organisations (Holman, 1988; Cannan, 1992; Smith, 1996).

Despite this, it is important to avoid caricaturing the work of the NSPCC. Whilst it has retained its preoccupation on the identification and treatment of abuse, it has also acknowledged the relevance of wider social factors. The 'FULL STOP' campaign launched in March 1999 has sought to promote improved services to support families and the quality of care for children in general, and its approach has not been restricted to core child protection services. Nevertheless, it seems justifiable to associate the organisation with the 'state paternalist/child protection' perspective. There appears to be a distinctive emphasis on the use of interventions based on professional judgements of abuse and parental difficulties, which are concerned with the application of specific methods to 'put things right'. The NSPCC remains associated with therapeutic and behavioural interventions.

The practice of child protection

The distinctive role and practices of the NSPCC find their echo in the conduct of child protection practice in general. Parton, for example, argues that:

> the emergence of child protection as a central activity for social workers underlines the centrality of social workers in providing social assessments of 'risk' and 'dangerousness'.
>
> (Parton, 1996, p. 11)

The starting point, then, for interventions to safeguard children, is the investigative work to identify and assess the level of risk, or the 'likelihood' of 'significant harm'. As Corby (2000) notes the methods involved have emerged and built up over several decades. They are characterised, for example, by a lengthy association of different disciplines, including medical and legal perspectives. The medical profession has been influential in developing checklists of physical signs which may be taken as indicative of abuse (physical or sexual) or neglect (Polnay, 2001). For example, the shape, number, age and location of injuries, as well as the degree of force needed to cause them, can all help to contribute towards the conclusion that a particular instance of physical harm is 'suspicious' (Besharov, 1990). In addition to 'medical' indicators, a number of other factors may be taken into account, introducing a 'social' dimension. These may relate to: a history of family violence, or mental illness or socio-economic problems, for example.

Corby (1996) acknowledges that the predictive value of such indicators is relatively unreliable, but he still commends the use of a 'systematic' approach to risk assessment. This assumption lies behind attempts to rationalise assessment of risk (*and* need) in children's services (Department of Health, 2000b; Department of Health *et al.*, 2000; Horwath, 2001; Ward and Rose, 2002). Assessments should follow a standard format. They should be 'carefully planned', based on 'effective inter-agency cooperation', and they should seek to deliver a common body of information (Adcock, 2001). Identification of risk factors should not simply be routinised, but there should be a process of putting professional meaning to what is observed. This will enable practitioners to understand risk factors within the specific context, and to use this analysis as the basis for planned intervention. These processes will need to be adapted to specific contexts, such as the needs of black children (Dutt and Phillips, 2000; Banks, 2001a) or disabled children (Marchant and Jones, 2000).

Where an assessment substantiates a likely risk of significant harm, the interventions which follow will be likely to emphasise 'control and protective functions' (Hardiker *et al.*, 1991, p. 40). The authoritative role of the state and its agencies is likely to come to the fore:

> It follows that many interventions...will occur within a statutory framework...or that there will be a high probability of statutory action unless the family situation can be sufficiently improved.
>
> (Hardiker *et al.*, 1991, p. 40)

The kind of programmes that are put in place are likely to emphasise behavioural change and a prevention of further abuse, with a substantial concentration on the quality of parenting; although as Corby observes, this may lead to an emphasis on mothers' parenting potential, whereas 'males may be responsible for half of all physical abuse' (Corby, 1996, p. 18). Nevertheless, Macdonald (2002) identifies a number of strategies which concentrate on 'parent training'. These include behavioural and cognitive-behavioural methods which:

> have much to offer in dealing with the problems that need to be tackled if abuse and neglect are to be prevented from recurring.
>
> (Macdonald, 2002, p. 223)

Other forms of intervention which seek to address abusive situations include 'ecobehavioural' and family therapy, 'social network' interventions, play therapy and groupwork. Macdonald (2002) concludes, however, that despite the evidence of effectiveness for some of these, they are not widely practised in the UK. In her view, the preoccupation with the legal and administrative processes to prevent abuse and neglect has to some extent inhibited the development of effective remedial services.

Parenting programmes

One growth area, which coincides with the policy concerns of government, is the development of parenting programmes. Some of these are directed at improved family functioning and prevention of harm to children, whilst others focus on behavioural control (see Ghate and Ramella, 2002). Parent training programmes fundamentally:

> aim to enhance parents' abilities to manage their children's behaviour, to reduce conflict and confrontation while increasing compliance, cooperation and pleasant interaction ...
>
> (Macdonald, 2002, p. 219)

One national evaluation of parenting programmes has identified a number of common strands in practice:

> The work with parents typically addressed:
> - Dealing with conflict and challenging behaviour by young people
> - Constructive supervision and monitoring of young people
> - Setting and maintaining boundaries and ground rules for young people
> - Communication and negotiation skills
> - Family conflict in general
>
> (Ghate and Ramella, 2002, p. i)

Programmes typically offered a combination of groupwork interventions and individual help and advice, and by the time parents left they reported positive improvements, such as improved communication, improved supervision of children, reduced conflict, better relationships, more influence over children and better ability to 'cope with parenting in general' (Ghate and Ramella, 2002, p. ii). Macdonald (2002, p. 221) also identifies specific elements of programmes which may enhance parents' abilities to manage their own anger, including cognitive restructuring, problem-solving skills and relaxation.

It may seem that there is little evidence of continuity between this kind of approach and the heavily 'treatment'-oriented interventions developed during the 1970s (see Jones *et al.*, 1987). Parton (1996), for example, argues that there has been a move away from notions of 'treatment' to a preoccupation with managing behaviour in order to control risk. In this sense, the shift of emphasis from therapeutic models to those which emphasise behavioural techniques may represent a significant break with social work traditions, in his view. However, it seems equally plausible that this can be represented more as a 'reframing' of the discourses of child protection and state paternalism. Notions of professionalism and expertise have had to be adjusted to changing circumstances and the emergence of the 'postmodern' era, but they still retain an influential and significant role, according to Hopkins (1996). The overarching preoccupation of this perspective with changing parental behaviour and, at the same time, protecting (and, sometimes, controlling) children, through the use of professional expertise and technical skills, remains constant.

4

WORKING IN PARTNERSHIP? THE STATE AND FAMILY SUPPORT

A positive relationship

Whilst the focus on the quality of parenting and the nature of family life might suggest some common ground with other viewpoints, the position based on principles of supporting families ('defence of the birth family', in Fox Harding's terms [1997]) takes a much more positive view of the state's potential role in promoting and supporting the family in meeting children's needs. This originates in a distinctive view of the state itself, which emphasises its capacity to facilitate social functioning and improve the quality of life in general. The state is seen as a benign force, being proactive, enabling and egalitarian. These assumptions are associated with the ideas and policies which gave rise to the welfare state, and particularly its more ambitious manifestations. George and Wilding (1994), for example, make the connection between the development of the welfare state and 'democratic socialism'. This, in turn, is characterised by a set of core principles including universalism, redistribution of wealth, altruism and social integration. As they put it: 'Equality, liberty and fraternity have been its underlying values...' (George and Wilding, 1994, p. 97). This perspective is distinguished carefully from more radical positions , being associated with the aim of ameliorating rather than replacing existing social structures. As Clarke and his colleagues have put it, the aim is to achieve 'fairer distribution' rather than 'challenging capitalism as an economic system' (Clarke *et al.*, 1987, p. 176).

Hardiker and colleagues describe this as a 'developmental model of welfare' (1991, p. 25), which sees society as basically 'consensual'. As a result, government is able to act proactively and disinterestedly to promote the well-being of all members of society and particularly those who are disadvantaged:

The role of the state in promoting the conditions for *a more just and equal society* is central to the developmental model. Government should adopt a proactive stance and engage in positive planning and purposeful action in furtherance of greater freedom and equality for all sections of society . . .

(Hardiker *et al.*, 1991, p. 26)

This can and should be achieved even though it will be at the expense of wealthier and more powerful members of society. The consequence of this should be the provision of universal and high quality services, and guaranteed minimum standards of living. As they put it, 'there is an emphasis on *both needs and rights*' (Hardiker *et al.*, 1991, p. 26).

Underlying this argument, there is an assumption that government and state agencies themselves are capable of operating in a way which is able to control vested interests, counter the effects of inequality, and provide services which are of universal social benefit. Titmuss (1973), for example, provides a powerful argument for the beneficent role of the state in establishing, organising and maintaining the supply of social goods in the face of the distortions of the market. His analysis of blood distribution systems illustrates the capacity of government and social policy to harness good intentions for general benefit:

It is the responsibility of the state, acting sometimes through the processes we have called 'social policy', to reduce or eliminate or control the forces of market coercions which place men [*sic*] in situations in which they have less freedom . . .

(Titmuss, 1973, p. 273)

Within this perspective, however, distinctive strands can be identified. George and Wilding (1994, p. 91) suggest that there are three different views about the role of the market, for example: 'bureaucratic centralism, social democracy and market socialism'. According to the principles of bureaucratic centralism, government should take a strong role in the ownership and administration of the means of production, particularly those which constitute the social and economic infrastructure. On the other hand, proponents of social democracy are more relaxed, seeing the government as having a kind of reserve power, but no need to commit itself to an extensive programme of nationalisation. According to some, following the advent of the welfare state, capitalism:

had been so transformed that socialism should no longer be essentially concerned with nationalisation and public ownership. Instead, its core business should be social equality.

(Timmins, 1995, p. 216)

The third variation on this theme is characterised as 'market socialism', whereby different forms of ownership, and different forms of social organisation should coexist. The emphasis should be on empowerment, and a 'democratisation' of social policy (George and Wilding, 1994, p. 94).

In terms of service delivery, too, this appears to have certain consequences. There is a shift from a concern with bringing about personal change to 'achieving social change' (Hardiker *et al.*, 1991, p. 27). Social work intervention focuses on representing the interests of disadvantaged groups, in order to achieve 'positive discrimination'. Empowerment has meaning at a personal as well as a structural level:

> It is an approach which sees personal change occurring through the greater sense of self worth and self confidence that arises from successful participation in self help and mutual support initiatives...
>
> (Hardiker *et al.*, 1991, p. 27)

In this sense, more generalised notions of 'social justice' can be equated with individual rights and expectations of fair and equal treatment.

It has been suggested that this orientation has increasingly become a central feature of policy debates, with an emphasis on consumer interests, 'customer contracts' and effective mechanisms of complaint and redress. However, this can be equated to a relative de-emphasising of one key tenet of the social democratic approach in favour of another. Thus, there is relatively less weight given to strategies to achieve collective ownership and material equality, and rather more to principles of participation, rights and accountability. The aim would appear to be one of equalising *power* rather than *resources*:

> the greater emphasis placed ... on participation and consumer satisfaction at the expense of professionalism in welfare services will probably create a less inegalitarian ethos in the provision and receipt of services.
>
> (George and Wilding, 1994, p. 101)

On the other hand, given the differential access to resources and influence, there might be some doubt as to whether this aim could be achieved in isolation. Despite this a positive and emancipatory role for the state remains integral to this perspective.

'Putting families first'

Naturally, the identification of an active, supportive and positive role for the state will have implications for attitudes to intervention with families. The notion of 'partnership' is particularly important here, suggesting a contractual arrangement between equals, rather than a coercive or antagonistic relationship.

As Fox Harding (1997) puts it, there is (as in the laissez-faire model) a clear emphasis on the strengths of the birth family, which (unlike the laissez-faire perspective) parallels a belief in the positive virtues of the state:

> The original, biological family is perceived as being of unique value and as being, for the vast majority of children, the optimum context for their growth, upbringing and development.
>
> (Fox Harding, 1997, p. 71)

This echoes the conclusions drawn by Bowlby (1953), whose research has retained a significant influence. He showed that the impact of separation of a young child from a maternal figure could be extremely damaging, in terms of undermining attachments, creating insecurity and inhibiting development. Winnicott (1986), too, develops a strong psychoanalytical argument for the value of parenting, and mothering, in particular. He argues, for example, that 'mothering' is a natural attribute, and that it is important that this should not be subject to impositions or constraints from outside experts. The role of professionals is to promote and encourage the nurturing relationship, rather than impose preconceptions.

The argument about the importance of 'natural' bonds can also be extended to the important area of cultural and ethnic identity, according to Fox Harding (1997). This recognition has become of considerable importance in influencing debates about both family support, and appropriate placement of children in care (see, for example, Barn, 1993). It is argued that awareness and understanding of one's origins is important in developing a sense of identity and self-worth, for example (Banks, 2001a, p. 142). Evidence that black children are over-represented in care, whilst black families are not gaining access to appropriate family support services might offer dual grounds for concern, in this context (Dutt and Phillips, 2000, p. 40).

The assumption that the bonds between parent and child are 'natural' and positive implies that where these fail, the reasons must lie outside the family. Where children's needs are not being met, this must be attributable to factors beyond their parents' control. These factors are likely to be related to family circumstances. Thus, there is considerable emphasis placed on the impact of inadequate services, social deprivation and victimisation. Holman (1988) has argued consistently that family problems can be linked almost extensively to the experience of poverty and living in disadvantaged communities. This assumption has become influential in shaping government's analysis:

> Too many children live in poverty. Poor housing, social exclusion and lack of opportunity are at the root of many serious family problems.
>
> (Home Office, 1998, p. 40)

A range of factors can be identified as giving rise to social exclusion, which are largely outside the individual's or the family's control:

> The key risk factors include: low income; family conflict; being in care; school problems; being an ex-prisoner; being from an ethnic minority; living in a deprived neighbourhood...; mental health problems, age and disability.
>
> (Social Exclusion Unit, 2001, p. 11)

'Sarah' is one such person:

> Sarah is a 27 year old from south London living in a temporary bedsit with her two year old daughter. Her own unsettled childhood and adolescence was spent in foster homes and children's homes after she suffered physical abuse and she has not attended school since she was 14. She now suffers from mental health problems as well as having difficulties with drugs and alcohol. Her daughter's father is in prison serving a life sentence for murder and she too has a conviction for assault. Sarah is now pregnant for a second time and although she thinks the relationship with her new partner is stable she is uncertain about how she will cope in the future.
>
> (Social Exclusion Unit, 2001, p. 11)

Despite the efforts taken to avoid casting blame or making assumptions of inadequacy, Holman (1988) argues that children have been taken into care unnecessarily, simply because of the difficulties experienced by their parents.

The consequence of these arguments is twofold. First, in common with the laissez-faire position, the rights of families against unwarranted state coercion should be maintained. But, importantly, this should be accompanied by a significantly proactive programme of state intervention to promote family integrity and the well-being of children.

In summary, this perspective is based on a positive view of the desired relationship between families and the state. The assumption is that the 'natural' place for children is with their birth families; and a wide view is taken of this term, so that the role of relatives such as grandparents is also emphasised. Children should be brought up by their (birth) parents wherever possible, but other forms of 'kinship care' are also viewed positively (Broad, 2001); it is the responsibility of the state to support and encourage families in this role.

In order to achieve these aims, the state must meet its responsibilities to provide both universal services (health, education and income maintenance, for example) and preventive services (child care, family centres, counselling and advocacy). Failure to provide this platform (or safety net) will be counter-productive, not just in the sense of undermining families, but also in leading to a greater incidence of social problems:

> Where universal approaches founder or fail, the possibility exists that the selective policies which fall within the remit of social services might increase in importance and, indeed, in punitiveness.
>
> (Tunstill, 2000, p. 83)

Family values and 'looked after children'

Not only is there evidence of a move towards a more partnership-oriented form of intervention with families, but some of the same trends have become evident in the context of work with children within the care system. Associated with the Children Act, but also influenced by key research evidence (for example, Stein and Carey, 1986), renewed emphasis was placed on creating a family-like living environment for children looked after by local authorities. The Department of Health took the lead in stressing the importance of providing services for children in care settings which replicated the experience of the great majority of children living with their families:

> it is no longer enough to look narrowly at the needs of an individual child, for the child's welfare has to be understood in the context of a web of relationships ...
>
> (Department of Health, 1991a, p. 77)

Factors such as secure and settled relationships, friendships, non-institutional settings, choice and control over home environment and family involvement have become increasingly significant in the planning and delivery of services for children looked after by statutory agencies.

These ideas have had a number of impacts. For instance, it might be argued that the trend towards an increasing reliance on foster care as the preferred placement option reflects the aim of recreating a family-like setting for children in the care system (Department of Health, 1995b;

2000a). By 2001, fostering accounted for 65 per cent of all placements of accommodated children in England (Department of Health, 2001a). Interestingly, this has been paralleled by a growing use of 'kinship care' (Broad, 2001).

Alongside these changing patterns in the placement arrangements for looked-after children, there have been a number of policy initiatives designed to emphasise the importance of providing care services in a way which reflect the 'normal' expectations of children living in families (Parker *et al.*, 1991; Ward, 1995). The major *Looking After Children* initiative sponsored by the Department of Health explicitly sought to link assessment of outcomes for looked-after children to the question 'What do good parents want for their children?' (Jackson, 1995, p. 13). The assessment materials developed in parallel with this project are also constructed in order to judge plans and services for children against global indicators of well-being and achievement, for instance in health, emotional and behavioural development and educational attainment (Parker *et al.*, 1991). Interestingly, too, these materials were tested with a 'community group' of families (Moyers and Mason, 1995), in order to provide benchmarks for 'good enough parenting' which should be expected of providers of services for children looked after away from home.

The needs of and services for children accommodated by local authorities are thus to be judged according to a series of criteria which are held to be equally applicable to the child population in general. Their aspirations and expectations should be the same as those living with their families, according to this viewpoint. Success or failure in service provision should be judged according to the extent to which children achieve a range of socially desirable objectives. The Quality Protects programme set out such targets as key elements of the government's social inclusion strategy for looked-after children:

Objective: To ensure that *children looked after* gain maximum life chance benefits from educational opportunities, health care and social care.

Sub-objectives:
To bring the overall performance of *children looked after*, for a year or more, in National Curriculum tests closer into line with local children generally.
(Department of Health, 1999)

This provision sets the expectations for children living in care in the same context as children in general, although the Quality Protects' targets themselves are more modest than those for the population as a whole. Nevertheless, this should be seen as part of a 'normalisation' agenda.

Associated with this initiative there has also been a move to stress the 'corporate parenting' responsibilities of local authorities, including education as well as social services departments (Department of Health and Department for Education and Employment, 2000).

It is possible to draw the conclusion, then, that the 'family support' perspective has established a significant degree of influence on the shape and purposes of services for children for whom the parental role has actually been taken up by a statutory agency, alongside, or in place of, parents themselves.

Supporting families: the bigger picture

It is important to draw attention here to wider changes in provision of services for children and families, since this has a clear bearing on the specific context for statutory intervention. As we have seen, factors associated with social exclusion are linked with adverse outcomes for individual children, and it is therefore important to consider the possible relevance of broader policy initiatives in this respect. This widening of scope for the 'refocusing' debate is associated with the change of government in 1997, and the move away from individualised models of child protection and family support (Parton, 2002). This follows from the underlying assumptions of the family support perspective, as we have seen, that the problems of parents and children stem not from their own deficiencies, but from poor services and inadequate levels of provision.

There is no doubt that the developing government agenda of promoting social inclusion can be seen, in one sense, as a significant contribution to preventing family problems and poor outcomes for children. This is one of the explicit aims of both *Supporting Families* (Home Office, 1998) and *Preventing Social Exclusion* (Social Exclusion Unit, 2001). According to the former:

> All families face pressure in their everyday life and all families want some measure of support. But a small proportion of families encounter more serious problems and need particular help and assistance.
>
> (Home Office, 1998, p. 40)

The significance of this language is that it points towards a 'targeted' approach *within* a global framework of help to families and children. Thus, the government aims to provide more intensive and specialist programmes in those areas and to those groups which are identified as particularly vulnerable. The ensuing strategy involves a combination of area-based initiatives such as the Neighbourhood Renewal Programme, with projects which aim to address specific groups, such as poor families, young mothers, disaffected teenagers and those 'middle-age' children 'who are showing early signs of difficulty' (Children and Young People's Unit, 2001a, p. 8).

Specific examples of this kind of approach include *Sure Start* and the *Children's Fund*. *Sure Start* was initiated in 1999, in order to provide a UK equivalent to the 'Headstart' programme from the United States, which had demonstrated considerable success with pre-school children. The initial focus was explicitly on improving life chances for young children in disadvantaged areas, but by 2004 there were planned to be 522 *Sure Start* programmes, and the overall budget was planned to rise to £1.5 billion by 2005 (Sure Start, 2003a). Within each programme, a range of services is on offer, including home visits, befriending, mentoring, information services, health care, learning and child care opportunities, and parent education. In broad terms, the objectives are to improve health, education and development for children. It is suggested that *Sure Start* has begun to improve access to services for children in need (Aldgate and Statham, 2001, p. 146).

The *Children's Fund*, likewise, is a national programme, targeted at specific areas, with the aim of preventing 'poverty and disadvantage' for those aged 5–13. The budget for this programme has been set at £450 million, and local partnerships are expected to provide services such as 'mentoring', counselling and out-of-school activities (SEU, 2001).

These broad-based preventive services are identified as being complementary to statutory services provided through more traditional routes, such as Social Services Departments, with a strong emphasis on collaboration and partnership. The aim is to:

> ensure that Government and its partners in the statutory, voluntary and community sectors design and deliver children and young people's services effectively...
>
> (Children and Young People's Unit, 2001a, p. 8)

It is likely that the realisation of this aspiration towards 'joined up' service delivery will be variable on the ground, but in policy terms it is clear that there is a wide-ranging strategy in place to 'refocus' the way in which children's needs are addressed, going well beyond the confines of statutory agencies. This, in turn, has significant implications for the way in which partnerships are developed, and services are integrated. There may well be a need to rethink professional roles and identities, where, for example, much of the social work task now appears to be organised and delivered outside the boundaries of local statutory agencies. Expectations of greater flexibility, inter-professional training, and the ability to 'work effectively across organisational boundaries' (Laming, 2003) are all likely to follow from a more diffuse service delivery context, where professional expertise depends, in part, on the ability to link broader understandings of need with circumstances of immediate and significant risk of harm to individual children (Department of Health *et al.*, 2000).

It is perhaps worth noting here that this emphasis on diversity of provision represents both a widening of potential sources of intervention, and an effective diminution of the role of social services departments, which are barely mentioned in *Supporting Families* (Home Office, 1998). This trend has been further escalated with the establishment of Children's Trusts, and the explicit promotion of inter-agency working in the Green Paper *Every Child Matters* (Chief Secretary to the Treasury, 2003).

Meeting children's needs: the legislative framework

The Children Act 1989 was the culmination of a period of intense debate about the appropriate balance between different aspects of intervention in the sphere of child welfare. The impetus for the legislation was generated by the House of Commons Social Services Committee which published what became known as the 'Short Report' in 1984. This appeared to demonstrate a cross-party consensus behind the view that excessive reliance was being placed on statutory intervention to protect children, and too little was being offered by way of support for families. Whilst some of its arguments could be seen as somewhat paternalistic (or patronising), there was no doubting the political will to improve the quality of assistance offered to prevent family breakdown:

> Family aides or 'homemakers' can pass on some of the simple and practical domestic skills such as buying, cooking, washing and budgeting.... The value of such help cannot be overemphasised: its prompt provision could avert a number of receptions into care.
> (House of Commons Social Services Committee, 1984, p. xxv)

Successive publications, emerging from departmental and governmental sources further developed proposals to improve support for families (DHSS, 1985a; DHSS *et al.*, 1987; Secretary of State for Social Services, 1987). The idea of 'partnership' emerged from this period, perhaps surprisingly given the overt laissez-faire rhetoric of the government of the time. Support for parents was linked with an enabling role for government:

> The interests of children are best served by their remaining with their families and the interests of parents are best served by allowing them to undertake their natural and legal responsibility to care for their own children.
>
> (DHSS, 1985a, p. 4)

The subsequent Review of Child Care Law (DHSS *et al.*, 1987) and the White Paper on children's services (Secretary of State for Social Services, 1987) retained this broad direction, with the emphasis on parental rights and enabling parents to meet their responsibilities as opposed to precipitate intervention to remove children (Stevenson, 1989).

The Children Act 1989, as a consequence, was drafted to contain both additional safeguards for parents, and much more explicit reference to family support services than had previously been the case. The Act seeks to avoid the use of language which implied pejorative assumptions about parents, and it clearly promotes notions of partnership.

From the outset, the Act draws attention to the importance of considering the role of parents when making decisions about children's upbringing (Section 1 (3) (f)). It establishes the principle of 'parental responsibility' (Section 2), which empowers parents 'to take most decisions in the child's life' (Department of Health, 1989, p. 9). The exercise of parental responsibility can only be modified in very specific circumstances, such as where a care order is in force (Section 33 (3) (b)).

The continuing nature of parental responsibility importantly provides the basis for the principle of partnership which underpins the delivery of services to meet children's needs (Part III of the Act). Section 17 is crucial in this respect, as it sets out the terms for local authority intervention:

> (1) It shall be the general duty of every local authority (in addition to the other duties imposed on them by this Part) –
>
> > (a) to safeguard and promote the welfare of children within their area who are in need; and
> > (b) so far as is consistent with that duty, to promote the upbringing of such children by their families, by providing a range and level of services appropriate to those children's needs.
>
> (Section 17, Children Act 1989)

This achieves two things which are of central importance to the overall approach taken. The first is to link the idea of protecting children ('safeguarding' them) with the principle of meeting their needs. In other words, these two aims are presented as indissoluble.

And secondly, it is made clear that the principal route to achieve these ends is through the provision of support to families to enable them to care effectively for children, as far as possible. Part III goes on, for the first time in legislation, to specify some of the specific forms of provision which might be made available to assist families in this respect. Section 18 imposes a duty on local authorities to provide day care for 'children in need within their area'; and Section 20 likewise requires authorities to provide accommodation for a child, where it may be required:

> as a result of:
>
> (a) there being no person who has parental responsibility for him;
> (b) his being lost or abandoned; or
> (c) the person who has been caring for him being prevented (whether or not permanently, and for whatever reason) from providing him with suitable accommodation or care.
>
> (Section 20(1), Children Act 1989)

Schedule 2 to the Act sets out other forms of provision which local authorities are expected to make available to children, such as 'inclusive' services for children with disabilities, practical help for families and family centres.

The two principles, of partnership with parents and an integrated approach to needs and protection, flow through from this to the detailed requirements for those practitioners engaged in assessing and planning for children. Thus, the *Framework for the Assessment of Children in Need and their Families* (Department of Health *et al.*, 2000) sets out to demonstrate how to adopt an intervention strategy which maintains these principles:

> An understanding of a child must be located within the context of the child's family ... and of the community and culture in which he or she is growing up.
>
> (Department of Health *et al.*, 2000, p. 11)

Even where there are concerns about the possibility of harm, or hostility is encountered, the aim of establishing a working relationship with the family should be pursued:

> However resistant the family or difficult the circumstances, it remains important to continue to try to find ways of engaging the family in the assessment process.
>
> (Department of Health *et al.*, 2000, p. 13)

The *Framework* is notable also for stressing the importance of seeing children and their needs against a wider backdrop of social and environmental factors, in order, once again, to avoid the risk of focusing exclusively on family problems and the apparent shortcomings of parents in isolation. This also leads to a recognition that assessment is not simply about identifying problems, but about supporting the provision of services for families. Therefore, it is important that assessment is not seen:

> as an end in itself but a process which will lead to an improvement in the well-being or outcomes for a child or young person.
>
> (Department of Health *et al.*, 2000, p. 53)

For practitioners in statutory settings, the approach to intervention with children and families is set in the context of: a requirement to work collaboratively with parents and family members; the need to integrate assessments of risk and need; and the objective of providing services which enable families to meet the needs of children. Despite this (see Chapter 6), some of these objectives are contradictory, and it is important to avoid over-simplistic assumptions about the commonality of parents' and children's interests.

New Labour, new services?

Interestingly, when we move on to consider the changing context for the delivery of services to children and families, much of what is provided appears to have bypassed the agencies (particularly Social Services Departments) responsible for identifying and then responding to the needs of individual children. As we have observed, the Children Act 1989 provides extensive powers to local authorities to develop services directed towards 'children in need'. However, it seems that much of government strategy in this respect has fallen outside this framework.

The role of the local authority has, in effect, been redefined as one of coordination and strategic planning, but with a reduced role in terms of direct responsibility for addressing needs. It is the responsibility of local government to establish a 'Children and Young People's Strategic Partnership' for each local authority area, to provide the focal point for multi-agency and multi-sector service planning and delivery (Social Services Inspectorate, 2002). These partnerships will be expected to include the 'voluntary and community sectors' with explicit mechanisms for involving children, young people and their families in the planning process. The delivery of specific services, such as Sure Start, Connexions and the Children's Fund should be located within this strategic framework. The approach to providing support to vulnerable families and children is thus redefined, with 'children in need' as a 'subset' of this larger group (Social Services Inspectorate, 2002, p. 23).

The reordering of government thinking about support for families and children also implies a revised approach to intervention and service delivery. This is highlighted, for example, in the context of *Sure Start*, where centralised aims and objectives must be adapted to local circumstances, in order to provide services which are accessible and appropriate for particular groups and communities. Thus, in one locality with which the author is familiar, the provision of stair-gates to promote child safety and reduce parental stress represents a creative adaptation of an externally determined service target (Sure Start, 2003a).

The aim appears to be to try to create mechanisms which bridge the gap between overarching programmes of structural improvement and localised, specific, 'targeted' services. The government has sought to drive change:

> on two levels. Targeted support services need to be strengthened so that vulnerable children are better supported. And mainstream services need to be improved so that all children are better served.
>
> (Children and Young People's Unit, 2001b, p. 5)

This appears to be a further variation on the theme of 'refocusing'. Government has accepted that there are structural reasons for the emergence of childhood problems, which originate outside the family, and these must therefore be addressed in a systematic and coherent manner, but without stigmatising the individuals concerned. The approach which follows from this is one which tries to supersede specific statutory or operational divides:

> By encompassing all vulnerable children, and focusing on outcomes they can achieve, the planning framework seeks to overcome the obstructions to action that arise from different legislative bases.
>
> (Social Services Inspectorate, 2002, p. 23)

Government establishes the terms for service delivery, puts in place the funding mechanisms, and specifies the desired targets and outcome indicators, whilst the onus is placed on local cross-sectoral and inter-professional partnerships to secure these aims. The emerging challenge for the providers of family support services is to relate these broad objectives to local needs and personal circumstances.

Supporting families in practice: Family Rights Group

The aim of developing effective partnerships to assist families finds its reflection in practice in a number of ways. As with other value positions, organisations can be found which can be identified with the family support perspective. In addition, there are specific aspects of professional practice which can be seen to reflect this orientation, such as the development of strategies which destigmatise families and actively promote partnership working. This can be seen to apply both at the point of assessment and planning, and also in the implementation of interventions, through the use of mechanisms such as Family Group Conferences.

One organisation which appears to be closely linked to this perspective is the Family Rights Group (FRG), established in 1974, which has built up and maintained a clear identity based on assisting families to engage effectively with statutory service providers. Unlike PAIN, FRG tends to emphasise a positive role for the state as service provider, and therefore encourages parents to engage with local agencies, and secure access to suitable provision, rather than simply resist unjustified intrusion. The positive view of the state's *potential* role is highlighted in FRG mission statements:

> Our belief, supported by research is that most children are best looked after within their own family. Where it is not possible for children to live with their own family, there should be a presumption in favour of some form of contact with the child's family and network, appropriate to the situation.

> (FRG, 2003)

As a result of its underlying philosophy, FRG has tried to develop a multi-faceted approach to its work:

> In order to achieve our aims FRG provides an advice and advocacy service; undertakes policy and research projects; runs training courses and conferences; and campaigns for changes in legislation, policy and practice.

> (FRG, 2003)

For the organisation itself, the dual task of promoting 'respectful' treatment of families, and securing access to appropriate resources, has meant adopting a twin-track approach, Individual casework and advocacy has been supplemented by a promotional and lobbying role, which has attempted to encourage the provision of more and better quality child care and family support services. Poverty and inadequate resources are held to be at the heart of parents' problems in providing adequate care for their children (FRG, 2003).

The history of FRG's casework reveals a commitment to act on behalf of service users to promote services which meet individual and family needs and are non-discriminatory:

> Examples...include a Muslim child who, when placed with a Christian church-going family, began going to church herself; a Church of England child placed with a Catholic family and taken to church with the family...We have often been disappointed with the unsympathetic response that we have encountered from social services departments...
>
> (FRG, 1987)

These cases illustrate a failure to recognise or engage with children's family circumstances and cultural origins in providing services.

It is its casework experience which has informed FRG's campaigning role. The orientation of the organisation to child protection work has been shaped by its view of the family as the source of nurture and security, rather than a place of threat and danger. FRG would argue that it is not justifiable to exclude parents from key decisions, or even from involvement with their children, solely because the child may be at risk of suffering significant harm – even where they have been unable to prevent this occurring in the past:

> The protection of children results from the efforts and skills of parents as well as of professionals. An essential element of the professional task is to encourage and bolster the parents' skills in this direction.
>
> (FRG, 1986, p. 4)

Family Rights Group now argues strongly for the use of Family Group Conferences to secure constructive parental involvement, even where there are 'care or protection' issues (FRG, 2003).

Like NSPCC, interestingly, FRG also ascribes a positive role to professional agencies and practitioners in protecting children and promoting their well-being, despite the organisation's concerns about poor practice which is sometimes encountered. However, the agency role is seen as being one of enabling and assisting families, rather than of exerting authority and control over them. This means that families must be enabled to participate in and, if possible, take the lead in procedures and planning for their assistance and the security of their children; they must also be empowered to question and challenge decisions with which they disagree:

FRG believes that services to families will be improved if families have an influence on deciding and planning what services are offered to them. Many who need the help of social services tell us they feel nobody asks or cares what they think.

(FRG, 2003)

If effective cooperation is not achieved FRG fears that child protection work will become increasingly institutionalised and alienating to families. This, it is emphasised, will create particular difficulties for black and minority ethnic families because abstract and universalised procedures are unable to address the nature of their distinctive circumstances and aspirations (FRG *et al.*, 2003). In order to develop effective partnership, says FRG, then effort must be put into providing preventive services, which should complement the child protection function, rather than being seen as opposed or irrelevant to it. Thus:

FRG believes that all families should have access to relevant support services so that wherever possible children can remain looked after within their own family. We seek and promote the full participation by families in the planning and evaluation of services...

(FRG, 2004)

The principles of partnership and family support should therefore inform child protection processes, rather than being seen as conflicting with them. Not only should the balance of service provision be shifted, but the very operation of child protection procedures should be more inclusive, in FRG's view. The norm should be to seek active parental involvement, and parents should only be excluded where there is a clear and immediate risk to the child. Parents can be expected to have most knowledge of the child and her/his interests, although not always (FRG, 2003), and in most cases spend more time with her/him than anyone else – excluding parents (and other family members) from participation in assessment, planning and decision-making is hard to understand in the light of this. There should be:

A duty on local authorities to support families' plans unless these would place the child in danger.

(FRG, 2003)

These arguments are supported by the empirical evidence showing the effectiveness of interventions such as Family Group Conferences in achieving effective working partnerships between families and professionals 'without putting…vulnerable or abused' children at risk (Gilligan, 2001, p. 85).

Promoting partnership: assessment, planning and intervention

The lessons from FRG's experience have, to a considerable extent, been incorporated in more recent accounts of best practice in working with children and families (Department of Health *et al.*, 2000; Children and Young People's Unit, 2001b). For example, approaches to identifying the needs of children should be based on principles of partnership, an integrated approach and a holistic understanding of need. Thus, parents should be involved from the start:

> It is important to agree an assessment plan with the child and family, so that all parties understand who is doing what, when, and how the various assessments will be used…
>
> (Department of Health *et al.*, 2000, p. 7)

Although assessments are also likely to be carried out in difficult circumstances, this does not alter the underlying importance of establishing effective working relationships. Where children may be at risk, this is all the more important, and should be pursued wherever possible:

> Use of mediation may be helpful in assisting professionals and family members to work together. The quality of the early or initial contact will affect later working relationships…
>
> (Department of Health *et al.*, 2000, p. 13)

The partnership approach is also important because it helps to maintain a focus on family strengths as well as problems. This ensures that an over-emphasis on what is going wrong is avoided, and there is an opportunity to consider the needs of the child alongside any potential risks to her/his safety. Assessment and intervention should be informed by the recognition of the value of an integrated approach, which ensures that both the processes and the thinking behind assessments are informed by a dual perspective. The use of the same wording in Sections 17 and 47 of the Children Act helps to cement this in place. Where, in Section 47, the local authority has a responsibility to investigate possible cases of significant harm, in order to 'enable them to decide whether they should take any action to *safeguard or promote* the child's welfare', Section 17 imposes the duty to provide services, likewise, 'to *safeguard and promote* the welfare of children within their area who are in need'. Thus, inquiries undertaken under either section should address the dual concerns of protecting children *and* meeting their needs.

This, combined with the broader recognition of the structural nature of many aspects of need, underpins the further development of a 'holistic' framework for understanding risk and need, and arranging appropriate service responses. Government guidance identifies three elements: the child's developmental needs, parenting capacity, and family and environmental factors (Department of Health *et al.*, 2000, p. 89):

> The interaction or the influence of these dimensions on each other requires careful exploration during assessment, with the ultimate aim being to understand how they affect the child or children in the family.
>
> (Department of Health *et al.*, 2000, p. 17)

Such holistic analyses might also be informed by other frameworks, which help to identify the different 'levels' of children's experience and circumstances, and the way in which both external and internal dynamics can impact on the family (Figure 4.1).

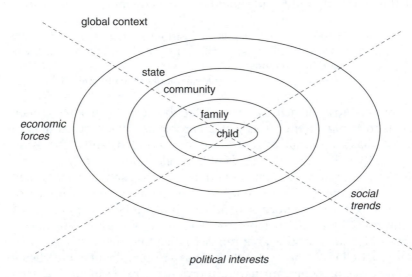

Figure 4.1   The child in the world

Source: Smith (2004)

Partnership in practice

In practical terms, the family support perspective can also be identified with specific approaches to promoting partnership, which go beyond and build upon principles of professional good practice. For example, Family Group Conferences give substance to the principle of involving families in decision-making and planning interventions. The essence of this approach is that the family is given the core role in determining how children's needs and risks will be addressed. At the outset, independent elements are introduced into the process, in order to ensure that power imbalances are recognised:

> an independent and culturally attuned co-ordinator begins the process of preparation and planning.
>
> (Gilligan, 2001, p. 84)

This ensures that the family is able to determine who should be invited to take part, widening the definition of whose input is seen as relevant. The coordinator chairs the initial meeting, where information is shared between family members and professionals, but no decisions are taken. Subsequently:

> the family is given private time to address the issues and come up with a plan (including contingency and review arrangements). The co-ordinator and professionals then come back in to hear the plan. If the plan is satisfactory from the professionals' perspective, it will be agreed...
>
> (Gilligan, 2001, p. 85)

This does not entail the professional practitioners abdicating their assigned roles, but does indicate a shift in the way in which decision-making processes are shaped, and who 'sets the agenda'. It is reported that this process is largely effective, as well. One study is reported to have found that of 80 Family Group Conferences, 74 produced agreements which were accepted by both professionals and families involved. Of these, three-quarters were out into effect and remained in place:

> Families were positive about FGCs and three-quarters said they would choose to be involved in another.
>
> (Gilligan, 2001, p. 85)

It is also likely to be the case that the needs defined by children and families themselves are more wide-ranging and less tied to specific concerns than those identified by professionals. Resultant service inputs may be shaped more towards the families' own perceptions and priorities:

> there is an increased use of family placements, ... family plans are no more costly than professional plans, but are different in content.
>
> (Morris, 2002, p. 132)

This appears to prefigure a much more extensive re-orientation of services, perhaps along the lines heralded by the emergence of Sure Start and the Children's Fund:

> Poverty, economic deprivation and social exclusion impact the skills and resources that families can develop to participate, with many families only able to gain help on an individualistic, crisis management basis. With professional input repeatedly confined to acute need, the possibility of empowering effective service user participation to achieve best outcomes for children remains the critical issue . . .
>
> (Morris, 2002, p. 135)

Thus, not only do families need to be in the lead when decisions are made, but they also need to be able to gain access to services which are compatible with their aspirations, and which improve their own capacity to care for and protect children. Professional and service responses must be guided by these aspirations, rather than cutting across them.

RIGHTS AND EMPOWERMENT IN CHILDREN'S SERVICES

Rights, resistance and the user perspective

The fourth perspective which we shall consider differs somewhat from the others, in two specific respects. It is more diffuse, sharing a general sense of 'opposition' to the improper imposition of state power, on the one hand; and it is less well-established, on the other. For some, for example, there is a sense in which this position is best characterised by its rejection of other views, rather than a positive orientation towards a particular form of state intervention. For Hardiker and colleagues (1991) the radical position is determined by its rejection of existing state structures which are 'dominated by' and serve the interests of powerful vested interests. The objective of practitioners and activists taking this perspective is not to specify in precise terms the nature of any alternative social structure or pattern of service delivery, but simply to secure transitional change:

> the nature of this new society is not specified, nor need it be . . . , since the objective is to work towards social transformation through the creation of the conditions conducive to major social change.
>
> (Hardiker *et al.*, 1991, p. 28)

According to this perspective, the welfare state as it has developed, is not, and cannot be a force for good in general, even if it provides individual gains from time to time. The services provided by the state are organised and delivered in a way which primarily serves the underlying interests of the dominant classes, and any benefits delivered to recipients are contingent and incidental. At best, the welfare state itself is a source of contradictions, in that its development represents the outcome of struggle and challenge on the part of disadvantaged groups, which have resulted in partial concessions:

> the welfare state is a contradictory social formation. It involves concessions to the working class and hence it is to be welcomed; but it also involves protection and support for the capitalist class and hence it is unacceptable.
>
> (George and Wilding, 1994, p. 114)

The welfare state, therefore, is both a source of potential, but limited, help to those who have particular needs, and it promotes a sense of dependence which only perpetuates inequality. By the very act of providing social benefits on its terms:

> the welfare state has served to mask the most oppressive and unjust aspects of the existing order whilst reinforcing class, gender and racial inequalities.
>
> (Hardiker *et al.*, 1991 p. 29)

The consequence of this has been that the impact of structural and economic pressures has also been experienced unequally. Certain groups have become marginalised, and are particularly exposed to oppressive and discriminatory practices. These include women, ethnic minorities, people with disabilities and children.

Whilst the processes which operate to oppress these groups may differ, and in some cases overlap, the implications for them as 'beneficiaries' of state welfare are similar. In order to represent their interests fairly and fully, the model for intervention must be oppositional, collective and user-led – an 'adversary' model (Corrigan and Leonard, 1978; Hardiker *et al.*, 1991). Whilst the origins of this thinking lie in the 1970s, more recent developments have seen an increasing emphasis on the position and perspective of people who use welfare services.

The emergence of this strand of thought and action has perhaps most clearly been demonstrated in the context of disability, where 'rights' emerged as a counterpoint to experiences of oppressive attitudes and practices in and beyond service settings. As Oliver (1990) puts it, it is the specific social order which is responsible for the construction of a particular view of service users as vulnerable, dependent and in some way inadequate. As a result, they are believed to be in need of help or guidance to provide compensation for their disadvantages. A further consequence of this is that service providers and delivery systems tend to operate in a way which confirms this sense of dependency. Services are provided according to a 'medical model' which objectifies recipients and does not see them as active participants in the process. They are to be offered 'treatment', rather than to be engaged in a process of dialogue and empowerment:

> many disabled people are forced into the position of passive recipients of . . . unwanted gifts or inappropriate services.
>
> (Oliver, 1990, p. 93)

In response to this, however, people with disabilities have developed and sought to put into action an alternative perspective, based on the rights, capabilities and potential held by individuals and groups of people. The disability movement emerged as a 'new social movement' (Oliver, 1990), which rejected imposed definitions of problems and their solutions, reframing 'needs' in the form of 'entitlements', and 'developing its own service provision, sometimes in conflict and sometimes in cooperation with state professionals' (Oliver, 1990, p. 129). Subsequent developments have seen the rights of service users more powerfully articulated by other groups, too (Croft and Beresford, 2002). It is argued that service users' priorities can be summarised in terms of: 'autonomy, participation and inclusion' (Croft and Beresford, 2002, p. 389). The objective is to secure services which are genuinely user-led. In order to achieve this aim, a number of prerequisites can be identified, such as:

> support for service users to be able to participate on equal terms; equity in the treatment of service users, regardless of age, class, 'race', disability, sexual identity and gender;
>
> recognition of diversity, such as people's different ways of communicating – non-verbally, in pictures, by signing or in minority ethnic languages.
>
> (Croft and Beresford, 2002, p. 390)

Services should promote independence, rather than maintaining people in dependent states, enable users to exercise choice and autonomy, and promote social inclusion as opposed to specialist provision which stigmatises and isolates participants. The contrast between rights and needs is particularly highlighted, because it represents the difference between a person's own definition of the 'problem', and a definition imposed from outside, based on limited understanding. According to Beresford (2000), it is important to reconcile rights and needs from the user perspective:

This gives equal priority to:
establishing and securing people's common and shared civil and human rights and
meeting their different self-defined needs in the way they, ensured full knowledge, support and choice, prefer.

(Beresford, 2000)

Children and their rights

The influence of user-led rights movements has also progressively involved children and families. The organisation *Shaping Our Lives*, an 'independent, user-controlled network' has developed a role as a powerful lobby for service users regardless of their specific characteristics. In the light of continuing concerns about their treatment, both within and outside the care system (Utting, 1997; Laming, 2003), children's rights have inevitably come to the fore as one of the organisation's priorities. Beresford (2003) draws attention to the practical consequences of these concerns in relation to the Victoria Climbie Inquiry (Laming, 2003). The distinction is made between 'proceduralism' and paper commitments to listening to children, and more thorough-going rights to participate in and ultimately control decisions made on their behalf. Rights are delivered through the prioritisation of user-led consultations, independent advocacy and quintessentially changing 'organisational attitudes, cultures and understandings' (Beresford, 2003).

Despite these developments, it might be felt that the relatively late addition of children to the list of service user interests who should have control over decisions about their lives is not accidental. It reflects, perhaps, an underlying sense of unease about the extent to which children can be seen as 'competent' to participate in crucial decisions about their upbringing. As Wyness (2000) puts it, there are clear differences in the way in which children's rights are conceptualised:

> A casual perusal of the 'children's rights' literature reveals a clear conflict between *welfare* rights to care and protection...and rights to *self-determination*...
>
> (Wyness, 2000, p. 5)

This, in turn, can be seen to be reflected in a divergence of position even amongst those who are strong advocates for the rights of children. Some sources have consciously taken an extreme position. Holt (1974), for example, argues that children should have the power to make decisions about all aspects of their lives, including employment, sexual activity, education and money. Thus, the child should be able to opt for autonomous status. As he puts it:

> I want more for the child than the right, in spite of being a child, to have all the protections of the law granted to adults. I want in addition the right to ... live as an independent, financially and legally responsible citizen.
>
> (Holt, 1974, p.180)

He argues that it should lie with the child to determine her/his living arrangements, which could be:

> (1) ... as dependents under the care and control of their parents (natural or adoptive) ...
> (2) ... as dependents but under the care and control of people other than their parents, *of their own choosing* ...
> (3) ... as fully independent, financially and legally responsible citizens.
>
> (Holt, 1974, p. 157)

Holt implicitly rejects arguments about childhood as a life stage characterised by developing competence and persistent moral and physical vulnerability. In this respect, he runs counter to a range of deeply embedded assumptions and attitudes. As James *et al.* (1998) put it, the belief that childhood is a 'natural' state, in which the processes of development and maturation are central, informs much of psychological and educational thinking. Corsaro (1997) identifies these ideas as offering an important contribution to our understanding of childhood, enabling us to understand the connections between physical development, intellectual progress and social learning. However, he also criticises them for focusing unduly on the child as the object of these processes, rather than as a participant with interests and perceptions of her/his own. Children should not be seen merely as the targets of 'socialisation' (Corsaro, 1997, p. 18), whose role is to internalise social norms and behavioural expectations; they should also be seen as social actors in their own right (Smith, 2000a). In ascribing full adult human rights to children from birth, Holt (1974) also confronts developmental assumptions which have almost attained the status of commonsense. Children and young people should, in his view, be treated as 'competent' participants in social life who should have the independent capacity to make choices and decide what happens to them.

Other proponents of children's rights have found it difficult to accept the extreme position which would ascribe full citizenship rights to children, accepting that autonomy, competence and personal integrity are attributes which are acquired over time. It is, in their view, more realistic to see the ability to exercise rights as emergent (Freeman, 1983). Distinctions can be made between different types of rights, and also the manner in which these should be realised. Some of these distinctions derive from inevitable limitations in children's experience or understanding. Children may, for example, need protection from their actions because of their limited knowledge of the risks involved. We should, therefore, be willing to act to prevent 'irrational' acts by children which might inhibit or compromise future outcomes. Children's interests should be seen in the context of their future as well as their present selves. Thus, within a broad framework of expanding rights and autonomy:

> We would choose principles that would enable children to mature to independent adulthood. Our definition of irrationality would be such as to preclude action and conduct which would frustrate such a goal...
>
> (Freeman, 1983, p. 57).

Thus, compulsory education can be justified, as can measures to protect the child against death or serious physical or mental harm taken without her/his consent. But beyond these bounds, children and young people should be encouraged to exercise their rights to make informed choices, for example, in the area of sexual behaviour and contraception (Freeman, 1983, p. 59). Age and understanding are important determinants here, in that rights are seen to be progressively acquired as children mature towards the (idealised) status of mature adulthood.

There is clearly a degree of complexity to the issue of children's rights. The pure form (Holt, 1974) presents challenges, particularly in relation to competence and protection, where it is assumed that children may expose themselves to the risk of harm through lack of knowledge or ability to make informed choices. Nevertheless, there is broad agreement amongst those who hold this perspective that children should be seen as autonomous beings with rights to participate in and influence major decisions about important aspects of their lives, such as education, care and lifestyle (James *et al.*, 1998). Recent developments in the sociology of childhood have been helpful here, notably in their recognition that children are active in creating the social world, and that they have distinctive interests, which cannot all be accounted for by reference to their future adult status:

All too often individuals and societies try to justify their actions in terms of their effects on children's futures as adults. This...can often blind us to how we treat and care for our children in the present.

(Corsaro, 1997, p. 277)

It is accepted by advocates for children that their rights have not been adequately recognised or respected in the past. However, things may be improving:

the idea that children possess rights which adults should respect and help to promote now informs aspects of government policy and legislation, the policy of voluntary sector and charitable organisations as a well as the practice of welfare professionals.

(Franklin, 2002a, p. 3)

Driving change: the policy context

It is undoubtedly true that greater recognition has been accorded to the rights of children and young people in recent years, both within and beyond the field of children's services. This trend appears to have been driven both by global developments, and by specific events within the child care sector.

As Fox Harding (1997, p. 140) observes, the emphasis on children's rights as a distinctive policy stream is a relatively recent phenomenon, coming to the fore in her view only in the 1980s and 1990s. However, the roots of the children's rights movement lie somewhat further back (Franklin, 2002a), and may ultimately be linked with the emergence of childhood (and adolescence) as a distinctive life stage (Aries, 1962). According to Freeman (1983), children's rights became an international policy issue, in the early part of the twentieth century. The first Declaration of the Rights of the Child was agreed by the League of Nations in 1924, following a campaign led by Save the Children which itself was launched in 1919. Freeman believes that this step was inspired by the 'devastation' of the First World War, and it emphasised basic material needs. By 1959, the United Nations had adopted a second Declaration of the Rights of Children including ten broad principles, such as the right to 'special protection' (Principle 2), the right to education (Principle 7) and the right to be protected from discrimination in all its forms (Principle 10). This, though, was felt to be mere rhetoric, having 'no real influence on the lives of children' (Freeman, 1983, p. 20). In retrospect, however, this rather critical stance seems to have underestimated the progressive nature of these international developments.

Moves towards the recognition of children as distinctive legal subjects were identified, including groundbreaking judgements such as *Re Gault* in 1967 in the United States. At the same time, steps were taken in the international arena to give greater substance to earlier aspirations. The year 1979 was sponsored by the UN as the International Year of the Child, leading, among other things to the establishment of the Children's Legal Centre. This gave further impetus to the development of a systematic instrument for the realisation of children's rights, culminating in the adoption in 1989 of the UN Convention on the Rights of the Child. Unlike earlier efforts, this prescribes in some detail the entitlements of children, and also begins to sketch out the mechanisms by which they can be realised (United Nations, 1989). Its 54 articles provide a substantial amount of detail, offering quite specific requirements against which states' provisions for children can be measured. Freeman (2002) acknowledges that there is some evidence of 'compromise' here, and that improvements could be made, but he still maintains that it is a good litmus test of individual nations' performance in meeting their obligations to children. By ratifying the convention,[2] states agree to abide by the rights it establishes for children, and each signatory is expected to report periodically on its progress and achievements in this respect.

Whilst the UN Convention is seen by most authorities in this field as a major step forward for children (see, for example, Franklin, 2002c), there are several major limitations, which limit the extent to which it exerts real influence on national and sub-national practice. The first of these, as already noted, is that the convention is, ultimately, characterised by a spirit of compromise. Thus, for example, Article 3 which requires that children's best interests be a 'primary consideration' in decisions made about them, is less stringent than the Children Act 1989, which requires that the child's welfare shall be 'paramount' in decisions falling under its remit (Section 1). More tellingly, the ratification process enables states to enter 'reservations' where they do not wish to be bound by specific articles of the convention. The UK government, for example, has declined to be bound by its requirements in relation to immigration and nationality (Candappa, 2002), with sometimes devastating consequences for individual children and their families.

Finally, the UN Convention is not binding on individual states unless they incorporate it into national legislation, in the same way as the European Convention on Human Rights forms the basis for the Human Rights Act 1998 (Franklin, 2002a). The only requirement which states must meet is to provide periodic reports to the UN Committee on the Rights of the Child (UNCRC). The pressure to comply which states experience is thus essentially moral rather than legal.

This limitation is illustrated in the case of the UK by the persistent nature of its failure to comply in certain key areas. The UN Committee has, on two occasions, for example, expressed concern about the UK government's reservation on immigration and citizenship (UNCRC, 1995; 2002), and also highlights recurrent failures in the areas of corporal punishment and detention of children and young people. The committee has been particularly concerned about this:

> The Committee is deeply concerned at the increasing number of children who are being detained in custody at earlier ages for lesser offences and for longer sentences as a result of the recently increased court powers...
>
> (UNCRC, 2002, p. 16)

More generally, the committee has expressed its concern at the persistence of social exclusion and child poverty. Whilst some improvements in the UK government's performance are noted, it is clear that the impact of the UN Convention in securing children's rights is limited. Freeman (2002, p. 114) concludes that government 'complacency about children's rights in England is totally misplaced'. By putting children's rights on the agenda, the UN Convention can only be seen as making a start. Beyond this:

> the lives of children will not change for the better until the obligations it lays down are taken seriously by legislatures, governments and all others concerned with the daily lives of children.
>
> (Freeman, 2002, p. 115)

Rights and children's services: a catalogue of failures?

Set against the relative, but limited, progress identified in the international arena, there have been some other fairly powerful drivers in enhancing the recognition of children's rights in the domestic context. In particular, as we have seen, the growing recognition of the importance of service user participation has affected the way in which children who use services are seen. This development has been further reinforced by a continuing catalogue of service failure, particularly in the care system, which have had damaging and sometimes tragic consequences for children and young people (for example, Levy and Kahan, 1991; Williams and McCreadie, 1992; Kirkwood, 1993; Williams, 1996; Utting, 1997; Waterhouse, 2000). The messages from these reports has seemed to suggest a pattern of mistreatment of children in the care system, at the very point at which their security should be most effectively guaranteed.

The 'Pindown' inquiry (Levy and Kahan, 1991, p. 167) found that children's homes in Staffordshire subjected their residents to a 'narrow, punitive and harshly restrictive experience'. Children and young people were kept in isolation and subjected to a systematically degrading regime, designed solely to gain 'control' over them. The denial of their rights was an integral and deliberate part of the practice philosophy. The report concluded that a fundamental change in management and practice was required, including the establishment of complaints procedures with an 'independent element' (Levy and Kahan, 1991, p. 175).

Similarly, abusive practice was identified in Ty Mawr Community Home in Gwent (Williams and McCreadie, 1992). A systematic example of institutional abuse was evidenced in Leicestershire, where a further inquiry (Kirkwood, 1993) found that the county's children's homes had become characterised by a series of repressive and humiliating practices, as well as specific instances of physical and sexual abuse. Children's (and others') complaints were not responded to appropriately or dealt with effectively, and their concerns were not heard.

Following this succession of scandals, Sir William Utting was commissioned to carry out a comprehensive inquiry into the 'safeguards for children living away from home' (Utting, 1997). Again, the inquiry observed a systematic pattern of mistreatment of children, which it attributes to the inadequacies of the 'system' itself:

> At the root of these failures is the unwillingness or inability of the organisation to implement its primary task of keeping children safe.
>
> (Utting, 1997, p. 119)

The evidence available led the inquiry to conclude that:

> the shift in the balance of power between children and adults has not been as great as the legislation intended, or as some believe.
>
> (Utting, 1997, p. 117)

The report of the Waterhouse Inquiry into the abuse of children in care in North Wales also contributed to this emerging policy agenda. It made a number of very specific recommendations which also highlighted children's rights, including the proposal for a Children's Commissioner for Wales;[3] a Children's Complaints Officer in every area; and 'appropriate indicators of compliance' for statutory agencies (Waterhouse, 2000, p. 221).

The combined impact of these investigations, culminating in the Children's Safeguards Review, was clear. The government took the message seriously and published its own response (Secretary of State for Health, 1998). The foreword represented a clear statement of intent:

> The Utting report... painted a woeful tale of failure. Many children who had been 'taken into care' to protect and help them had not been protected and helped. Instead some had suffered abuse...
>
> (Secretary of State for Health, 1998, p. 2)

The government undertook to put in place a programme of reforms to enhance the quality of care provided to 'children of the state', to be known as 'Quality Protects'. In this strategy, children's views and children's rights would be to the fore, with funding of £450,000 to promote 'the voice of the child' (Secretary of State for Health, 1998, p. 2). Children should be involved 'in decisions on their care'; they should be involved 'in developing policy and practice'; they should have access to 'children's rights services'; they should have access to 'independent visitors'; and they should be involved in 'local planning and in local developments' (Secretary of State for Health, 1998, p. 14). The children's rights agenda appeared to be moving to the centre of policy and planning for children's services.

Moving up the agenda: children's rights in law and guidance

In parallel with the increased attention to children's rights in policy and public debate, there is also evident a more explicit articulation of these principles in detailed legislation and in official guidance. This is supported by the increased recognition of the rights of the users of public services, which is articulated in instruments such as the Human Rights Act 1998 and the Race Relations Act 1976 (amended again in 2000).

In the specific context of children and children's services, however, it is important to make two distinctions before embarking on a discussion of the legislative context. First, rights are ascribed to children on a differential basis. Some, such as the right to education, apply universally. Others, notably, the provisions of the Children Act 1989, only fall to certain categories of children, those who are defined as meeting the threshold criteria for receipt of services. This distinction is helpfully illustrated for us by the Department of Health *et al.* (2000, p. 3) with, in 1999, a total child population of 11 million in England, including sub-groups of 'vulnerable children' (4 million, mainly in poverty) and 'children in need' (3–400,000), within which category lie smaller sub-groups of 'children looked after' (53,000) and children 'on child protection register' (32,000). It is only the latter three categories to which the Children Act applies. This, in turn, presents some operational challenges where the rights ascribed to children may differ at the interface between universal provision and specialised services – notably, for example, in the context of special educational needs.

The second area in which it is important to distinguish between aspects of children's rights, is the difference between what might be termed substantive and procedural rights. The entitlement to receive a service, for example, is not of the same order as the right to influence the management of that service, or to participate in decision-making processes. Roche (2002) helpfully distinguishes between what might be termed the 'welfare rights' of children and their 'liberty' rights; this is a distinction which again illustrates some of the complexities of taking an extreme pro-children's rights position (as discussed earlier in this chapter).

Section 17 of the Children Act might be seen as representing the first of these:

> the provision of such services was seen as the key to the safeguarding and promotion of children's 'welfare rights'.
>
> (Roche, 2002, p. 65)

On the other hand, 'liberty rights' are about the recognition of:

> the child's autonomy interest, e.g. the right to make their own decisions on matters that concern them.
>
> (Roche, 2002, p. 75)

There is thus a sense in which recent developments in the sphere of children's rights must be seen as multi-faceted, and potentially more complex than simply the advancement of a range of legalistic entitlements. Roche concludes that improving the child-centredness of services and institutions is the key factor:

> The rhetoric of rights is as much about shifting our imagination as it is about specific demands for legal change.
>
> (Roche, 2002, p. 73)

Despite this plea for attitudinal as well as legislative change, there has been evidence relatively recently of a more explicit emphasis on the rights of children within the terms of the law itself. The Children Act

1989, for example, puts a number of entitlements and expectations into place which enhance the position of children.

Parental responsibility

In one of the very few areas where it attributes rights to children universally, the Act establishes the principle of parental responsibility. This term is defined only in a circular fashion as 'all the rights, duties, powers, responsibilities which by law a parent has in relation to the child and his property' (CA 1989, Section 3(1)); whereas the equivalent legislation for Scotland (Children Act (Scotland) 1995) is more explicit in giving substance to this. For example, holders of parental responsibility, in Scotland, must:

> safeguard and promote the child's health, development and welfare....
> (CA (Scotland) 1995, Section 1(1))

Parents are therefore responsible for providing for children's 'welfare rights' (Roche, 2002). Whilst in Scotland this appears to establish a number of *positive* criteria by which a child's right to good parenting can be defined, in England and Wales this is effectively determined only in the *negative* sense that the quality of parental care does not fall below the threshold criteria for statutory intervention (CA 1989, Section 31(2)(b)).

Independent representation

The Children Act 1989 (Section 41) extended the provision originally established under the Children Act 1975, for a Guardian ad Litem to be appointed to represent the child's interests, to cover most proceedings involving the care of the child, including adoption hearings. The arrangements for delivering this service were substantially changed under the Criminal Justice and Court Services Act 2000, which created the Children and Family Court Advisory and Support Service (CAF-CASS). Whilst this new administrative arrangement has caused some controversy (Ball and MacDonald, 2002), it is also acknowledged that, for children, the principle of independent representation is more important than wrangles over the means of its delivery:

> Children do not care how we organise ourselves; they do not care what we call ourselves; children do not mind how much we get paid. Children simply want a good, reliable service....
> (Timmis, 2001, p. 280, quoted in Ball and MacDonald, 2002, p. 49)

The Guardian ad Litem (now Children's Guardian) has been shown to have an important role in ensuring that the distinctive voice and interests of the child are heard in complex proceedings, where other potentially powerful or influential voices are also present (such as parents, local authorities or expert witnesses). In some cases, this may be crucial in changing the way the issue is addressed and in determining the outcome. For example, it may be the first opportunity to gain a systematic disclosure of the nature and extent of sexual abuse (Dale-Emberton, 2001).

Consent to assessment/treatment

The Children Act 1989 is reported as seeking to put on a statutory footing the Gillick ruling of the House of Lords, which gave children limited rights to agree to or to refuse medical examination and treatment, where they are of sufficient understanding. Thus, for example, where either a Child Assessment Order (Section 43) or an EPO (Section 44) is sought in respect of a child, the child may if s/he:

> is of sufficient understanding to make an informed decision … refuse to submit to a medical or psychiatric examination or other assessment.
> (CA 1989, Section 43(8); Section 44(7))

Whilst this has implications for the child's right to be involved in other key decisions about her/his life, this principle has been subject to some judicial erosion subsequently. In one case, for example, the High Court used its powers to override the decision of a 15-year-old girl who had refused to undergo a psychiatric assessment, specified under an interim care order (CA, Section 38(6)):

> She did not consent and High Court exercised its inherent jurisdiction to order that the assessment proceed and therefore by-passed the 'right' given to mature minors under the Act.
> (Roche, 2002, p. 68)

For Roche, this leaves unanswered a crucial question, which is the extent to which it is:

> not just the courts but professionals who are uneasy and struggle with notions of children's rights once they extend beyond the right to welfare.
> (Roche, 2002, p. 69)

Consideration of wishes and feelings

Falling short of the right to determine decisions, but clearly establishing the 'right to be heard', the Children Act is explicit about the importance of considering the child's viewpoint in key decisions about her/his upbringing. Crucially, Section 1 of the Act requires courts to 'have regard' to:

> the ascertainable wishes and feelings of the child concerned (considered in the light of his age and understanding)
>
> (Children Act 1989, Section 1(3)(a))

when making any decision about the child's upbringing. In addition, local authorities providing services to children 'looked after' by them, must first 'ascertain', as far as possible, the child's wishes and feelings, and then, in making any decision with respect to the child:

> give due consideration – having regard to his age and understanding, to such wishes and feelings of the child as they have been able to ascertain....
>
> (Children Act 1989, Section 22 (5)(a))

The importance of this principle is therefore established, both at the point of judicial decision-making and during the process of service delivery. It should be noted that it is circumscribed in a number of respects, such as the child's age and understanding, the practicality of ascertaining her/his views, and the obligation only to take account of, rather than be bound by, her/his 'wishes and feelings'. Nevertheless, it has had a significant impact on attitudes and practice amongst practitioners (Brodie, 2001; Kirby, 2002).

However, Roche (2002) believes that progress in this area has been 'unsatisfactory' in some respects, arguing that professional attitudes and practices may still inhibit a clear airing of children's point of view, especially, he notes, where children's interests come within the purview of the private law aspects of the Children Act (Part II). Sometimes it seems that a reluctance to interfere in parental decisions combines with a concern to protect children from the burden of choice, leading to a presumption that it is better not to involve children in such matters (Smart et al., 1999). It has been demonstrated that children affected by parental separation want to have a role in discussing the new arrangements, even though they do not want to have to choose between parents (Smart et al., 2000).

Complaints

The emergence of complaints and representation procedures under the Children Act (Section 26) represents a further move towards giving fuller acknowledgement of the rights of children. The Act requires local authorities to establish procedures for the proper consideration of children's (and others') complaints on the discharge of their responsibilities. It has been suggested that this reflects a growing orientation towards a 'consumerist' view of public services (Ball and MacDonald, 2002).

The aim has been, in common with adult services, to provide a graduated structure of increasingly formal processes for hearing and resolving complaints about the quality of service provided. There is thus a clearly delineated 'official' route for the consideration and resolution of concerns about the treatment of children receiving statutory services. However, a number of studies (for example, Wallis and Frost, 1998) have given rise to fears that there are still problems of information and access – for example, where children are in foster care, suggesting that formal recognition of rights also needs to be supported by a genuine commitment to ensure that they are realised:

> Perhaps what is at stake here is the idea of actually listening to children and treating them with the same equality of concern and respect you would adults.
>
> (Roche, 2002, p. 71)

Child litigants

The Children Act 1989 also represents a significant advance in respect of treating children as 'litigants', that is, being able to initiate action to address concerns in their own right, both in public and private law. Children may apply under Section 10(8) of the act for a Section 8 order, which determines key issues about which parent (or other carer) they will live with, the nature of contact, and any specific issues or prohibitions relating to their living arrangements. The child is also able to make applications to the court on issues such as contact arrangements under a care order (Section 34(2)), or the variation or discharge of Child Assessment or EPOs.

It is of note, however, that this legislative attempt to extend the rights of children fell foul of the laissez-faire, familist perspective almost immediately on the Children Act's implementation. It is reported that:

> Following a few highly publicised early cases..., a Practice direction was issued restricting the hearing of children's applications for leave to the High Court...
>
> Early cases established that leave would only be granted if the issues were grave and not capable of resolution by the family... (Re C (A Minor) (Leave

> *to Seek a Section 8 Order)* [1994]; *Re SC (A Minor) (Leave to Seek a Residence Order)* [1994]).
>
> (Ball and MacDonald, 2002, p. 64)

Such conclusions established that there was, and remains, a degree of 'judicial unease' (Roche, 2002, p. 66) about the status of children as independent parties to court cases concerning their own welfare. In all probability, this has its roots in a continuing reluctance to intervene in the private domain of the family (Beck, 1997).

Children's rights beyond the Children Act

Subsequent developments following the implementation of the Children Act have concentrated largely on improving policy guidance in areas where children have been identified as particularly vulnerable. Thus, for example, the promotion of a children's perspective has become increasingly central in the development of the *Quality Protects* initiative. This derived from the concerns of the Utting Report that the Children Act itself might not achieve its intended objectives (Utting, 1997, p. 11), fears that were further amplified by the findings of the Social Services Inspectorate (1998).

The theme of giving children and young people a strong voice emerged consistently in these reforms. The White Paper, *Modernising Social Services*, promised to:

> promote the involvement of children in decisions on their care, local planning and national policy making [and] ... provide a national voice for children in care and those formerly in care ...
>
> (Department of Health, 1998a, p. 48)

The subsequent objectives document for *Quality Protects* set out as one of its key objectives:

> To actively involve users and carers in planning services ...; and to ensure effective mechanisms are in place to handle complaints.
>
> (Department of Health, 1999, p. 4)

To give substance to this aim, one of the mechanisms identified for its achievement was to ensure that children looked after would have 'trusted people' to act as their representatives to service providers and others. In keeping with the spirit of the interventionist Labour government post-1997, there appeared to be a real commitment to operationalising the aspirations of the Children Act 1989. The government used its muscle in terms of guidance, funding and performance monitoring to insist on the development of 'independent advocacy and children's right services' (Department of Health, 2002b). It also established a mandatory framework of national standards for such services (Department of Health, 2002b), linking this to Article 12 of the UNCRC and the Human Rights Act 1998. The standards document also referenced other documents aimed at promoting children's rights and participation, suggesting a broader strategy extending beyond the confines of the care system (Children and Young People's Unit, 2001a).

Representing children: the Children's Legal Centre

Against this backdrop of what must be acknowledged as a significant growth in political and policy commitment to the rhetoric of children's rights, it is also of interest to consider some of the major practice developments which might be associated with this. As in previous chapters, we will first consider an organisation which has been closely associated with this perspective for some time, the Children's Legal Centre (CLC).

The CLC was established in 1979 with government funding in recognition of the International Year of the Child becoming fully operational in 1981. Subsequently, it has gone through several changes, although its core objectives remain unaltered. The CLC:

> Promotes and campaigns for children's rights ... The centre believes that children ... have a right to be heard, to have their views considered and their interests independently represented at all levels of decision-making.
> (Children's Legal Centre, 2004)

Within this broad remit, the CLC has attempted to provide both an individual advice and advocacy service, and a broader campaigning role, reflecting its key principles. In practice, the Centre, in all its manifestations, has struggled with the tension between providing accessible individualised assistance, and finding time to develop its policy agenda. It argues, however, that these two aspects of its activities are often complementary, with the advice service providing the evidence so that:

> recurring issues can be taken up in our policy and campaigning work ...
> (Children's Legal Centre, 1999)

By and large, the areas of concern for children and their representatives contacting CLC are extremely diverse, although the largest categories relate to education (23 per cent) and private proceedings (22 per cent), with 6 per cent relating to public proceedings. Whilst this figure may appear relatively low, it is still significantly disproportionate to the relative number of children affected by care proceedings or entering the public care system (0.5 per cent are 'looked after' at any time; Department of Health, 2002c).

The prominence of education issues has prompted the centre to establish a dedicated service to deal with such matters. However, it has proved difficult to treat such cases in isolation from other concerns. Very often these have overlapped with matters concerning social exclusion and child protection. A common strand in these matters is the inadequacy and unfairness of quasi-judicial processes of investigation and disposal carried out within institutions. The centre cites the example of 'Samantha', excluded from school for allegedly setting fire to another student's hair. The CLC only became involved some five months later, when it transpired that there was no clear evidence to support the allegation – Samantha was reinstated, but at the cost of a substantial period of education.

The centre has also undertaken work directed at influencing practice for children 'looked after'; in some cases, this has meant taking a stand against other perspectives (such as the 'laissez-faire' position; see Chapter 2). In one instance:

> CLC's Development Worker did cite a specific case, concerning a fifteen year old who had left home. This young person wanted 'safe accommodation'. Her local authority, however, wanted to reconcile her with her family ... [S]he expressed a 'fear of abuse', should this be the outcome. It was the Centre's first priority, acting on her wishes, to 'make her safe'. On the other hand the social services department concerned perceived her to be 'wilful', and wanted the Centre to persuade her to go home. However, the Centre stood its ground, and found a place for her in a refuge for young people, in order to give her 'breathing space'. The critical point about this case for the Development Worker was that the CLC 'believed her, and acted to pursue her goals of safety and independent support'.
>
> (Smith, 1995, p. 238)

The CLC also initiated a number of specialist projects. For example, a scheme was established to provide an advice service for children relating to contact proceedings in the context of parental separation and divorce. Interestingly, this service was bedevilled by a recurrent problem for CLC, in that most of those seeking its services are adults, reportedly speaking on behalf of children (see also, Smith, 1995). Nevertheless, this initiative was important in seeking to reinforce the

Children Act principle that the child's interests should remain para-mount in contact decisions, rather than a matter for parents alone. A follow-up survey undertaken by CLC (French and Hamilton, 2000) showed that in only 16 out of 111 cases heard by courts was it felt that children's wishes were made known in full, and that in 73 cases they were not reported to the court at all. Whilst the survey suffered from the limitation of inferring children's wishes from other respond-ents, it appeared that, in many cases, contact orders (under Section 8 of the Children Act 1989) were being made where children did not want contact.

In this and other respects, the CLC has seen it as an integral part of its role to pursue the recognition of children's rights in judicial and quasi-judicial settings. In the course of its existence, the centre has claimed a significant role in advancing this cause. It has been observed that, in the context of the Children Act itself:

> the Centre was influential in developing proposals for children's involve-ment in complaints procedures (Section 26), and in opening up child care institutions to greater scrutiny (Sections 85–87)...
>
> (Smith, 1995, p. 219)

Despite its achievements and influence, there have been inevitable limitations to the work of the CLC. Firstly, like other small organisations (PAIN and FRG, for example) it has struggled to maintain an effective balance between its casework and its campaigning activities. But, in addition, CLC has made a number of strategic choices which have impacted on its achievements. It has, for example, opted for a 'modified' children's rights position (Freeman, 1983) which has meant that it has tended to avoid taking extreme positions and pursuing absolutist demands for children's rights. CLC has always accepted that children's 'understanding' may be limited in some circumstances, for example (Smith, 1995). A degree of pragmatism has been in evidence:

> The problem for advocates of children's rights of where, in practice, to draw the line between 'pure' advocacy, and recognising the political [and practical] limits to the articulation and promotion of children's rights is always likely to be a central tension in CLC's work.
>
> (Smith, 1995, p. 246)

In practice, this has had consequences too, with a clear readiness to work with and through children's representatives (parents, teachers, social work practitioners), rather than directly with children themselves.

Very few cases have come directly from children or young people themselves over the years (Smith, 1995). Whilst this was a matter of concern at one point, the plan to set up an advice service 'aimed exclusively at children and young people' (Children's Legal Centre, 1994, p. 2) was never realised. More recently, it seems, the distinctive role of the CLC has become less clear, with other organisations, and even government policy giving greater emphasis to the importance of recognising children's rights. This is perhaps a predictable and encouraging consequence of the gradual 'mainstreaming' of children's rights within public policy and welfare practice (Children and Young People's Unit, 2001b).

A new era? Children's rights and advocacy

The rights discourse appeared to be taking hold in the child care world with the establishment of a number of statutory measures to give substance to the reforms proposed during the 1990s. In particular, the government took action to create both a national framework and a local vehicle for representing the interests of children receiving services. The Care Standards Act 2000 provided for a Children's Commissioner for Wales (Section 72), with a brief to act as an advocate for children receiving services, both in individual cases and in general. The role of the Commissioner was further extended in line with the policy of the Welsh Assembly, to encompass the welfare and interests of all children by the Children's Commissioner for Wales Act 2001.

For England,[4] somewhat strangely, the position of Children's Rights Director was established only by statutory instrument under Schedule 1 of the Care Standards Act, which incorporated the role within the newly created National Care Standards Commission. The Children's Rights Director has a narrower brief (National Care Standards Commission, 2003), but is also required to consider both individual and general issues affecting children 'living away from home'. In both Wales and England, there is a clear attempt to make the service accessible, and child-friendly, in order to facilitate the expression of concerns and complaints.

These national bodies are complemented by a growing number of local children's rights and advocacy services, dramatically accelerated by the influence of the *Quality Protects* initiative. The number of such services increased from just over 40 in 1999 (Willow and Gledhill, 2001) to around 150 in 2002. Further emphasis was given to this area of work by the Department of Health (2002a) and by government (Department of Health, 2002b). Thus, the publication of National Standards set clear guidelines for the conduct of practice in this area. Whilst the standards document might appear at first glance to be somewhat anodyne, some important pointers are offered.

Thus, for example, the principles are established that:

> **Standard 1:**
> Advocacy is led by the views and wishes of children and young people ...
> **Standard 4:**
> Advocacy is well-publicised, accessible and easy to use ...
> **Standard 6:**
> Advocacy works exclusively for children and young people ...
> (Department of Health, 2002a, p. v)

The importance of this kind of document in establishing the legitimacy of a critical voice within (and sometimes against) statutory services should not be underestimated. It is stressed that children and young people should take the lead, that they should be able to exercise their choice of advocate, and that they should be able to determine when and how they make representations. The advocate is thus empowered to act as the child's representative:

> Children and young people are given help only if they want it. It is very important that children and young people have control over the advocacy relationship ...
>
> Only in exceptional circumstances would this standard be broken ...
> (Department of Health, 2002a, p. 3)

The advocate is expected to provide the child with sufficient information in an appropriate form to enable her/him to make informed decisions about expressing views and seeking change. The aim is to equip the child to express a view clearly and effectively, so the advocate must act as a 'champion' (Department of Health, 2002a, p. 5), and this must be the case irrespective of differences based on 'gender, race, religion, culture, age, ethnicity, language, disability or sexuality' (Department of Health, 2002a, p. 6).

Advocacy services and practices must, therefore be open, widely available and proactive in seeking to meet children who might find it hard to gain access, for whatever reason (see, for example, Wallis and Frost, 1998). This also means taking the message out to 'all relevant agencies and adults who are in a position to advise children and young people' (Department of Health, 2002a, p. 7). The service has to be independent and able to gain recognition as a legitimate voice. Conflicts of interest must be avoided in practice, and the advocate must be accorded the authority to act as an independent professional. Advocates should be:

> trained to act, and to be seen to act, independently and this is reflected in their behaviour when attending meetings with other professionals.
> (Department of Health, 2002a, p. 10)

The vision here is one of a body of confident, assertive, well-informed individuals and agencies ready to take up issues on behalf of children, irrespective of their circumstances, and equally, irrespective of the professional and personal risks, except in extreme cases.

This formalisation of the role and status of advocacy and children's rights services is important to the extent that it does achieve a powerful and independent voice for children in vulnerable circumstances. The establishment of Children's Commissioners in Wales, Northern Ireland and Scotland, and the commitment to do so in England (Chief Secretary to the Treasury, 2003) represent important manifestations of this process.

However, concerns have been expressed about the capacity of services to deliver all that is expected of them, especially given the likelihood of limited resources, and role conflict for those working within a statutory framework (Willow and Gledhill, 2001).

6

OF DISCOURSES AND DILEMMAS

Accounting for differences

Having established the nature of the distinctive perspectives discussed previously, it is important to move on to understand some of the issues which arise from their interaction. Inevitably, as we have seen, the 'pure' value positions identified come into conflict in certain key respects. It is necessary, for practical purposes, to try to develop a clearer understanding of the origin, nature and implications of these clashes. Most of us either work within, or feel a distinct affinity for one or other of the perspectives. Social work students, for example, appear to align themselves with the 'children's rights' and 'family support' positions. The consequence of these choices, of course, is that the underlying logic of a particular orientation may seem more persuasive, and will, in turn, have a specific influence on professional judgements and practice. The degree of certainty which underlies our choices may, to some extent, be based on presupposition, rather than evidence or reasoned argument. We are, therefore, likely to gain a degree of insight from taking a step back to reflect on the way in which such 'commonsense' understandings become established, in the form of paradigms and discourses.

The search for certainty

It was Kuhn (1970) whose investigation of the philosophy of science led to a recognition of the way in which particular 'paradigms' appear to operate to determine what counts as knowledge in different historical eras. These, in effect, constitute an interlocking and mutually validating set of beliefs which, in combination, ensure that there is only one coherent and acceptable way of addressing or understanding any particular phenomenon. Core assumptions set the terms for the way in which knowledge is organised in general. Kuhn identifies a number of epochs in the history of science, which he argues, have been dominated by coherent systems of conventional beliefs. These, in turn, effectively constitute the field of study, setting clear limits to what is acceptable, both in terms of ideas and what counts as evidence. As well as determining what can and should be investigated, conventional wisdom also dictates what can and cannot be thought. Some hypotheses become literally 'inconceivable'. In addition, anything that is found in the course of investigation is perceived and interpreted in a way which is consistent with and reinforces the dominant paradigm. This kind of normative process, it has been argued, can have an observable consequence in the field of child care and child protection. There is a predisposition to interpret behaviour in a particular way, despite the possibility of other explanations (British False Memory Society, 2002).

Taken to its extreme, this kind of functionalist analysis has fairly clear limitations. Nevertheless, even the most rigid system of belief is open to challenge, and therefore must leave room for alternative or dissenting views. It is virtually impossible to sustain a completely closed system of evidence and scientific beliefs over an extended period of time.

Modernism, post-modernism and social work

The concept of 'paradigms' is a helpful starting point for understanding recent developments in thinking about social relations and welfare systems. We can, for example, take the spirit of 'modernism' as one source of political and professional consensus about the appropriate means of organising and delivering children's services. The development of the welfare state can be portrayed as a reflection of this emerging body of thought and understanding:

> Enthusiasm for the idea of the paradigm was beefed up by the hope that life without a paradigm is but a temporary and curable condition, the manifestation of a momentary crisis, and at any rate an abnormal state...
> (Bauman, 1992, p. 68)

An agreed set of organising ideas and principles is therefore believed to be both desirable and necessary. This assumption, according to Bauman, is realised in the apparent 'certainties' of theory and practice in the 'modern' state. Social and behavioural sciences were developed as a means of establishing and maintaining this sense of coherence, structuring our understanding of what we encounter, whether as analysts or practitioners. This accounts, in Bauman's view, for a pre-occupation with behaviourist explanations of social phenomena, and with scientific methods based on 'quantifying' and 'statisticalizing' analytical techniques. The modern era, identified with the post-war welfare consensus represents the epitome of this development. This was a time characterised by a belief in a political middle ground reflecting a 'social contract' between different class interests, continued managed economic growth, and assumptions about the perfectibility of technological and scientific methods to improve the quality of life.

However:

> This resonance has been undermined, weakened, perhaps broken altogether with the gradual retreat of the political state (its actual and aspiring ruling forces alike) from the programmes of grand social organising...
>
> (Bauman, 1992, p. 81)

Even under New Labour, the statist tone of much government rhetoric (for example, Home Office, 1998) in the public sphere is arguably counter-balanced by a growing reliance on independent and private providers of services, and funding initiatives which appear to bypass the local state altogether.

The gradual withdrawal of the state from its central role in social welfare reflects a declining faith in the value of shared visions, monolithic state structures and universal services. This is further compounded by a belated recognition of the implications of increasing fluidity of social relations, leading to an acknowledgement of the importance of taking account of social and cultural diversity in what Dominelli (2002) describes as an evermore 'globalised' world.

James and her colleagues (1998) relate this argument to the specific context of childhood, arguing that we must recognise the relationship between universal and particular aspects of children's experiences. 'Modernity' has left a legacy in the form of global and common experiences, but these must be understood in their relationship to the specific nature of individual children's lives:

> What is crucial about this dichotomy...is that it places the universalism of 'childhood' in vivid relief with its particularity.
>
> (James et al., 1998, p. 205)

Parton (1996) develops these arguments in the specific context of children's services. He, too, distinguishes between the 'modern' and the 'postmodern', applying these terms to the field of child protection.

Like Bauman, he believes that there is a conjuncture between the emergence of the 'modern' welfare state and particular forms of social work intervention. The therapeutic orientation of professionals in the field played an increasingly central role in the development of sophisticated mechanisms of social regulation and service delivery. Foucault (1979) illustrates the way in which an 'army' of state-sponsored experts become associated with routinised forms of assessment, intervention and rehabilitation (Smith, 2003). Despite the apparently different professional and scientific traditions, these disciplines came to share a common orientation to principles of diagnosis and treatment, according to standardised operational codes:

> The central focus of modern systems of regulation was the classification of the population based on the scientific claims of different experts in the 'psy' complex.
>
> (Parton, 1996, p. 7)

The particular characteristics of 'modernity' can be discerned in its rejection of earlier beliefs in the 'natural' order of things, whereby outcomes are pre-determined or God given. Instead, there is substituted a belief in the human ability to explain, shape and control events and outcomes in both the natural and social worlds. This vision of order and predictability suggests the possibility of continual advancement towards greater levels of health and happiness. The quality of life itself could be subject to proven methods of evaluation and enhancement. A burgeoning self-confidence flowed through the modernist era:

> The vision of politicians joined with the practices of professionals and scientists to improve the world. The vision was of a hierarchical harmony reflected in the uncontested and incontestable pronouncements of reason.
>
> (Parton, 1996, p. 7)

The epitome of this emerging practice consensus could be found in the publication of the Seebohm Report (1968), and the establishment of social services departments under the Local Authority Social Services Act 1970.

In terms of the 'value positions' identified in this book (Chapter 1), the emergence of a welfare consensus based on notions of professional expertise and systematic intervention can be equated to a paternalistic, or 'child protectionist', orientation:

It was assumed that the interests of the social worker, and hence the state, were similar to, if not the same as, the people they were trying to help. It was to be an essentially benign but paternalistic relationship.

(Parton, 1996, p. 9)

The notion of legitimate professional authority also bestowed on statutory services legitimacy for the power to intervene against people's wishes (parents' or children's), in the broader interests of safety and well-being.

For a number of reasons, however, 'just at the point' where the validity of this perspective appeared to have been established fully, the 'welfarist' project began to break down, during the 1970s. This eventuality has been attributed to a series of political and economic crises, affecting the UK and other western societies, which undermined well-established belief systems, as well as the confidence of those in positions of political and professional authority. The collapse of the 'hegemony' (Gramsci, 1971) of interventionist social welfare services led to a more fundamental questioning of the rationale and effectiveness of social work intervention in general. The re-emergence on the public and political agenda of social problems such as juvenile crime, the emergence of new trends towards increased levels of lone parenthood, and the increased recognition of child abuse in its diverse forms, all combined to indicate a failure of statutory services and professional disciplines (Hall *et al.*, 1978). The mood changed, supported by new evidence, such as the body of critical research suggesting that professional practice was often inadequate or dangerous (Brewer and Lait, 1980; DHSS, 1985b; Otway, 1996). A series of child death inquiries in the 1980s underpinned the belief that social work was ineffective (Blom-Cooper, 1985; 1987; Parton, 1991).

Uncertainty and defensiveness were compounded by the increasing mood of political hostility, associated with a right-wing government, which sought to question both the principles of state intervention and the levels of expenditure committed to the public welfare system (Gamble, 1988).

Parton (1996) argues that the consequence of these challenges has been a 'reconstruction' of social work, based on 'market principles' and an actuarial approach to the assessment and management of risk. This, in turn, re-establishes a particular form of child protection activity at the heart of the social work project. However, in the new era, intervention is not based on notions of diagnosis and treatment, but risk assessment and control (representing a convergence of interests between 'laissez-faire' and 'state paternalist' perspectives, perhaps). The new shape of child welfare services has:

led to the discourse concerning child protection being reframed more and more by legal and administrative requirements and away from the concerns of predominantly female practitioners.

(Otway, 1996, p. 170)

A preoccupation with risk management has distorted the child protection process and the children and parents (particularly lone mothers) involved receive 'little or no practical or professional assistance' (Otway, 1996, p. 170). On the other hand, as the limitations of a scientific approach to risk management have become increasingly evident (Giddens, 1991; Beck, 1992), the nature of interventions in children's services has become more diversified, in Parton's (1996) view. In common with other theorists of late modernity and post-modernity (for example, Leonard, 1997), he argues that it is increasingly difficult to identify any particular perspective as dominant:

> social work is experienced as being subject to increasing diversity, uncertainty, fragmentation, ambiguity and change...
>
> (Parton, 1996, p. 12)

In the present context, this offers a better fit with the argument that there are a number of perspectives represented both in discourse and practice in children's services. As both Parton and others (for example, Williams, 1996) observe, there are different interpretations to be placed on this emerging evidence of the provisional and temporary nature of beliefs and practices in the field of social welfare. As Wyness puts it:

> in...analyses of prevention and identification, childhood seems to be much more contested. I am suggesting that the pressure policy makers, public commentators and professionals are under to protect the child have produced alternative, possibly unintentional models of childhood...
>
> (Wyness, 2000, p. 86)

However, the common strand to these observations seems to be that there is a need to be aware of the competing claims to validity of different perspectives of childhood, child welfare and child care practice.

Clarke (1996) agrees, suggesting that it is over-simplistic to think in terms of straightforward 'before' and 'after' scenarios, with a unified code of social welfare knowledge and practice straightforwardly giving way to fragmentation and chaos. Rather, it is important to think in terms of continuing shifts and modifications in the balance of authenticity between different social work traditions. This certainly equates with the position of Fox Harding (1997), to the extent that she describes a pattern of transitory dominance for each of the perspectives identified. There is according to Clarke a consistent pattern of attempts to construct unity and promote coherent practice norms out of 'fragments' (Clarke, 1996, p. 50).

The dilemmas of practice

In the following sections, I will focus on some of the recurrent conflicts affecting the provision of children's services, drawing on the value positions discussed previously. In due course, it will become clear that the key challenge is to clarify our understanding in order to achieve effective means of resolving these dilemmas in practice, according to the particular merits of any given set of circumstances. The decision-making process requires us to make choices, and it is of central importance that we are clear about the basis on which these choices are made.

Laissez-faire and child protection: keeping it in the family?

One of the most fundamental conflicts which arise in working with children concerns the extent to which it is right for public agencies to involve themselves in the private life of the family. As we have seen, this is at least partly attributable to the persistence and strength of the belief that the family, as an institution, should be sacrosanct. Fox Harding (1996), for example, describes a 'continuitarian' position which holds the belief that the 'traditional' family remains strongly established as a social form; interestingly, this is a belief which is held by commentators with diametrically opposed views. Whilst for some, relationships within the family are characterised by male power and control, which disadvantages women and children, for others the family remains a safe and secure haven for the upbringing of children. These polarised perspectives reflect, at the extremes, some of the arguments about when and how it is appropriate for statutory agencies to intervene in the family. In many ways, this is epitomised by the controversy surrounding events in Cleveland in 1987, which brought divergent perspectives into direct confrontation (Parton, 1991).

The 'crisis' in Cleveland (Butler-Sloss, 1988) revolved around the practices of medical and social work professionals in relation to child sexual abuse. During 1987, there was a significant increase in the number of cases identified, with children being removed from their families under Place of Safety Orders.[5] The upsurge of cases resulted in the appearance of a routinised approach to the removal of children under these orders, and subsequent problems concerning the quality of care provided for them. Amongst the consequences of this were a breakdown of professional consensus about appropriate intervention, and a challenge to the legitimacy of the state's actions in relation to the family. Extreme positions were taken up by some of those associated with the issue, including, notably, the local MP. He lent his weight to a campaign organised by a parents support group (Butler-Sloss, 1988, p. 19), and proceeded to challenge both the validity of the medics' diagnostic techniques and the professional competence of the social work professionals responsible for the removal and care of the children. He accused the local authority of 'conspiring and colluding' with the doctors involved (Butler-Sloss, 1988, p. 166).

The picture he painted was of a state-inspired reign of terror, in which professional independence and disagreement was subsumed to a routinised practice of screening and intervention, which took no account of the effect on children and families. The MP, Stuart Bell, believed there had been:

> a fundamental attack on family life, disrupting the lives of people, including children...in dealing with these matters social workers adopted an attitude of insensitivity and a lack of compassion towards the parents...
>
> (Butler-Sloss, 1988, p. 165)

According to this line of argument, any form of state intervention in the family must be treated with suspicion, because of its inherent propensity to do damage to those affected. There must, therefore, be an inbuilt presumption against taking any such action.

The counter-argument (Campbell, 1988; Parton, 1990; McLeod and Saraga, 1991) was that it was precisely this ideology of family autonomy which had disguised the extent of child sexual abuse, and had allowed male power to be misused in the domestic setting. The evidence from surveys that 10 per cent of children may be sexually abused by 'family members and close relatives' (Parton, 1990, p. 51) suggests that the sudden increase in the number of cases in Cleveland may have resulted from *improved* professional awareness and practice. For Campbell, it is simply a matter of 'belief', and once the possibility of widespread sexual abuse of children is accepted, it becomes possible to act against it. For McLeod and Saraga (1991) the suggestion that intervention itself may be damaging is not an acceptable defence. There must be a readiness to suspend disbelief, and to act positively in children's interests. One social worker from Cleveland is quoted as saying:

> We had to distrust everything we knew. We could disbelieve the suspicion, and my god we wanted to. But we didn't, because if we ignored the evidence

that sexual abuse is an under-discovered activity, then it would have been like being presented with two different diagnoses and accepting the no-abuse option because it was easier...

(quoted in Campbell, 1988, p. 141)

It is precisely at this point, however, that others seek to find a middle way. Parton (1991) argues that the role of social work in intervening in the family is justified, but that it should not be subjugated to standardised practices or fixed preconceptions:

> What was crucial was that social workers interpret, construct and mediate the 'subjective' realities of the children and families with whom they work... objective criteria... needed to be interpreted so that their true significance could be weighed and judged.

(Parton, 1991, p. 115)

Likewise, the report of the Cleveland inquiry itself, in famously arguing that the 'child is a person and not an object of concern' (Butler-Sloss, 1988, p. 245), tried to set out a middle path:

> It is a delicate and difficult line to tread between taking action too soon and not taking it soon enough.

(Butler-Sloss, 1988, p. 244)

For practitioners in children's services, then, the challenge remains one of moving beyond nakedly ideological perspectives on the role of the

---

Case example:

Eddie and Julie are brother and sister. Both attend their local primary school, where teachers have noticed that they have been coming in late and sometimes a bit dishevelled.

The children have also told their teacher that they have missed breakfast some days, because 'daddy has hit mummy, and she is hiding from him'. The school has made a referral to the local authority social services department according to its child protection procedures.

However, initial inquiries with the police show that the children's mother has been unwilling to pursue formal complaints of assault (domestic violence) against their father in the past.

What action is appropriate to protect the children from significant harm?

---

state in relation to the family, to making informed judgements, in the light of the social realities underlying those beliefs, and the professional knowledge available to them.

Laissez-faire vs family support

The focus of this debate concerns the extent to which it is legitimate for the state and its representatives to intervene to support families and children, or whether action should only be taken in extreme circumstances. There is a significant 'moral' dimension to the arguments in this context, revolving around the question of dependency and personal responsibility. Too great a willingness to intervene, it is argued, creates a dependent, unproductive and weak social grouping, which is a source of moral decline, anti-social behaviour and fragmented communities (Page, 1999). It is, therefore, inadvisable to invest the resources of the state in 'propping up' inadequate parents and failing families since this will just compound the problem. This kind of argument is perhaps most famously associated with Charles Murray, who has developed and pursued the argument that excessive state intervention is indulgent, and gives rise to a range of social and personal problems (Murray, 1996a). For Murray, writing mainly in an American context, the emergence of the 'underclass' is best represented by three phenomena: crime, joblessness and 'illegitimacy'.[6] In particular, the lack of two parents to provide consistent and secure upbringing for their children, is likely to lead to further and more substantial social failures.

Murray (1996a, p. 26) distinguishes between 'raising a child without ever having been married' from the state of widowhood or divorce because 'illegitimacy is less ambiguous than other forms of single parenthood'.

According to Murray, 'illegitimacy' has 'sky-rocketed' in Britain (Murray, 1996a, p. 27); he cites the fact that births outside marriage had reached 31.2 per cent by 1992 (Murray, 1996b, p. 101). The absence of a formal legal relationship is, in his view, indicative of a certain attitude towards parenthood and childrearing, which is becoming more pervasive.

Inferring a causal connection from this evidence, he argues that '[i]llegitimacy produces an underclass', primarily because of the absence of fathers. The underclass itself is characterised by a number of consequential social problems, including high crime rates (especially violent crime), poor educational attainment, poor health and unemployment (Murray, 1996b, p. 100). The lack of positive role models, especially male ones, is said to have negative consequences:

> Children grow up making sense of the world around them in terms of their own experience . . .

> A child with a mother and no father, living in a neighbourhood of mothers with no fathers, judges by what he [sic] sees.
>
> (Murray, 1996a, p. 31)

The consequences are, he believes, inevitable. Higher crime rates, unemployment and general social disorganisation will ensue, which, in turn, will generate further social problems, ensuring that the spiral of decline will continue, intensifying as it goes. In terms of policy and practice, Murray is critical of responses which tend to support the state of lone motherhood. The 'dependency culture' is likely simply to underwrite emerging patterns of behaviour:

> the problem in providing money to single women is that the income enables many young women to do something they would naturally like to do.
>
> (Murray, 1996a, p. 46)

Other provisions, such as the availability of accommodation, are also criticised for making it too easy to maintain a lone-parent family. In this, Murray is supported by other theorists of the underclass (Morgan, 1995; Field, 1996). Perverse incentives are created for young women to have babies, it is suggested. By extension, other forms of family support, such as early years child care or Sure Start, could also be criticised for having the same effect, and for being 'oversold' (Morgan, 1995, p. 140).

Murray's proposed solution is to remove any incentive to encourage lone parenthood, and restore the two-parent family as the norm. Having children 'out of wedlock' should be more 'painful'. Economic and other means of coercion should re-establish the place of men in the family: 'Babies need fathers. Society needs fathers' (Murray, 1996b, p. 127). We should be explicit, in his view, about putting policies in place which do not encourage the maintenance of existing one-parent families because that will simply create more, and undermine social cohesion to a greater extent. Policies which provide support for 'living children', which sustains such living arrangements, merely compound the problem, creating 'more pain than they alleviate' (Murray, 1996b, p. 92). On the contrary, the state should 'end welfare' (Murray, 1994) and 'adoption at birth' should be encouraged for the children of single women:

> Any comparison of what is known about child abuse and neglect, emotional development or educational success suggests that the child of a never-married teenager has a better chance in an adoptive home.
>
> (Murray, 1994)

These arguments are not just rhetorical, and it is possible to trace their influence on policy and practice, notably in the field of adoption. The concerns of the New Labour government about social exclusion appeared to coalesce around a belief in the need to address the problem of teenage pregnancy, for example: 'Teenage pregnancy is bad for parents and children' (Social Exclusion Unit, 1999, p. 90). The same report makes reference to the merits of adoption, and proposes the establishment of an advisory service to assist pregnant teenagers to 'make a positive choice', which might include adoption (Social Exclusion Unit, 1999, p. 101). Alongside this considered policy development, government ministers have also been reported as promoting the value of adoption (*The Guardian*, 26.02.99). The underclass thesis seemed to have taken hold – babies should not be allowed to 'suffer' because of parental inadequacy, according to the then Home Secretary:

> Everybody knows that some teenage mothers may not have the necessary skills to look after their children during their childhood.
>
> (Straw, 1999)

Tunstill (2003, p. 101) has expressed a clear concern that this might lead to the prioritisation of adoption over family support services. The prime minister's support for increased use of adoption (see Chapter 2) must be viewed in this context. Adoption policy is framed in terms of 'putting children's needs at the centre of the process', ending delay, and actively helping children 'out of care' and into 'adoption' (Blair, 2000, p. 3). In particular, drift and delay should be avoided, either because of excessive emphasis on same race placements (Cabinet Office, 2000, p. 18), or because of a sentimental attachment to the virtues of birth parents:

> once a child has been admitted into LA care the focus can too often tend to be exclusively on rehabilitation with the birth family... [A] permanent home for the child may be delayed if contingency plans, including... adoption... have not been considered
>
> (Cabinet Office, 2000, p. 25)

Following this lead, substantial increases in the number of children adopted suggested that there was, in fact, a rebalancing exercise under way. From 1998 to 2002, for example, the number of 'looked after' children who were subsequently adopted rose from 2200 to 3400 (55 per cent) (Department for Education and Skills, 2003b).

On the other hand, proponents of the 'family support/birth family defender' perspective were understandably concerned at the implication of these trends:

> Put bluntly, are the most 'needy' families – emotionally and socially as well as materially – now at risk of falling through the gap between *universal family support* on the one hand, and if it fails to work, the draconian step of *having their children permanently removed* on the other?
>
> (Tunstill, 2003, p. 101)

Tunstill's fears offer a clear insight into the impact of changing discourses on policy and practice at the point of service delivery. The reassertion of laissez-faire and familist ideologies is apparent, even in detailed procedural requirements. The absence of any specific requirement by the adoption standards (Department of Health, 2001b) of 'evidence of a concerted effort' to promote the upbringing of the child by her/his birth family is 'not promising', in her view. A fully child-centred approach must attempt to locate the child in the family environment, and promote flexible services aimed at maximising the nurturing potential of this environment. Standards and bureaucratic timetables cannot be allowed to override this complex and sometimes painstaking process. Adoption targets and guidelines must not cut across a developmental approach, by providing a 'premature answer' to difficult and demanding child and family circumstances. A properly child-centred approach should enable adoption and family support to coexist as legitimate options within the portfolio of professional responses to meeting the needs of children at risk (Tunstill, 2003).

Case example:

Davina is 22 years old, and she is due to have her second child in two months' time. She has been assessed as having moderate learning difficulties, and her parenting capacity is said to be significantly impaired.

Her first baby was taken into care and subsequently adopted, shortly after his birth, when she was 17.

This time, her parents have said that they will support her, having refused to do so previously, and there is a Sure Start programme available in the area where she lives.

What is your immediate preference: Should the new baby be adopted, or should services be put in place to enable Davina to care for it?

Laissez-faire vs children's rights: 'seen and not heard'?

The recent emergence of children's rights and the user perspective as influential elements in discussion of child welfare has introduced significant challenges, especially to the laissez-faire perspective. The caricature of the traditional patriarchal model of the family suggests that children have been expected historically to adopt a passive role, to accept parental discipline unquestioningly, and to follow the life course mapped out for them. According to this model, they would have no right to challenge decisions taken by adults within the family, or to make important decisions independently.

Associated with this perspective is the assumption that, *de facto*, state intervention in the life of the family is to be discouraged, in that it acts rather in the way that Murray (1994) suggests, destabilising relationships and undermining legitimate parental authority. Thus, as Fox Harding (1997) observes, even supposedly benevolent legislation to control the working hours of children in the nineteenth century could be seen as an unwarranted intrusion. Similarly, perhaps, it might be argued that the state should not be in the business of prescribing the precise form and duration of children's homework in the modern era (Smith, 2000b).

These constraints on the role of the state in relation to the family can be seen to persist in a number of areas. Firstly, as we have seen, the relevant legislation tends to be less prescriptive about the rights and safeguards of children in the family than in state care. As we have already seen, children's rights services tend to be restricted in their remit to children 'looked after'; children have very limited access to complaints procedures and other administrative forms of redress in relation to the family; and children have relatively limited influence on decisions made between separating parents about their upbringing, at least in the court setting. For example, it is reported that in disputed contact cases between parents:

> children were rarely seen, and when they were, 'seeing' children did not necessarily entail listening.
>
> (Cull, 2001, p. 84)

The assumption persists, even where the 'conventional' family unit breaks down, that it should be the parents and not the child who make such fundamental decisions about her/his upbringing. The private law elements of the Children Act do appear to reinforce this, assuming that it is better for parents to negotiate arrangements between themselves, and only providing very limited opportunities for the child's interests to be represented directly (Harding, 2003).

The most striking (!) illustration of this dichotomy between children's rights within and outside the family is that of physical punishment, which remains legal *only* within the family, having been progressively outlawed in all extra-familial forms of provision, from education settings, through the care system and finally incorporating childminding (Department for Education and Skills, 2003a). Unlike other countries, however, and contrary to the recommendations of the UNCRC, the UK government has not banned physical punishment by parents. Connections have been made between the tolerance of corporal punishment and child abuse, with the NSPCC's evidence to the Victoria Climbie inquiry noting that her brutal mistreatment had begun with 'a few "slaps" to instil discipline' (*The Observer*, 4 May 2003). This problem is held to be compounded by the 'rule of optimism' (Dingwall *et al.*, 1983), by which professionals ascribe to parents the most benign possible interpretation of their actions.

The point is made forcibly by the organisation *Children are unbeatable* (2001), which contrasts the UK's position with that of Sweden, which banned all physical punishment of children in 1979. The very low level of child deaths from physical abuse in Sweden is partly attributed to this prohibition.

Further support for this line of argument is provided by the overview report of child abuse inquiries, published by the Department of Health (Noyes, 1991). In a number of cases where children subsequently died from physical abuse, there was a history of 'corporal punishment of children in a "disciplinary" context' (Noyes, 1991, p. 64). Kimberley Carlile's stepfather had contacted the social services department and informed them that he had 'shaken' and 'smacked' her (Noyes, 1991, p. 66). The acceptance of 'smacking', and the reluctance of the state to intervene to prevent it appears to represent a significant clash between the ideology of family autonomy, and the principles of children's rights. Whilst public opinion (amongst adults) appears consistently supportive of the 'right' of parents to 'smack a naughty child' (*The Observer*, 4 May 2003), children and young people consistently draw attention to the humiliating and oppressive nature of physical punishment:

> Some people go overboard. They're gonna hit them hard and it's gonna get harder and harder.
>
> (A young person quoted in Willow and Dugdale, 1999, p. 40)

It is not just in this context that the tensions between the rights of children and the authority of the family are evident. However, the issue of discipline does help to illustrate another area where there are significant implications for service delivery and for practitioners, that of 'cultural relativism'. In criticising some of the assumptions which informed decisions in the Victoria Climbie case (and previous cases, such as Jasmine Beckford; Parton, 1991), *Children are unbeatable* stated that:

> some parents and professionals may (and do) consider that it is 'reasonable' for, say, a West African or Caribbean or Romany parent to apply harsher forms of physical punishment than would be considered reasonable by indigenous British families, because this is part of these other societies' 'child-rearing traditions'. We are confident that the [Climbie] Inquiry will make clear that such cultural relativity is discriminatory.
>
> (*Children are unbeatable*, 2002)

Likewise, the tensions between cultural sensitivity, family autonomy and the rights of the child emerge in other contexts, posing similarly awkward questions for those who are seeking to negotiate and resolve intergenerational conflicts (Craig and Coles, 2002).

Case example:

Nita is a young woman who has arrived at the women's refuge, having left home to try to avoid an arranged marriage.

She says that she does not wish to reject her culture or her religion, nor does she want to be isolated from her friends, her sisters and her family, but she says she cannot agree with something that doesn't feel right.

On contacting her family, it appears that there is no room for negotiation, as the family insists that it is not acceptable for her to break with history and tradition. She must return home and accept the family's decision.

As a worker in the refuge, how could you negotiate the conflict between the young person's rights, and the family's independence and cultural expectations?

Child protectionism vs family support: the 'refocusing' debate

The fourth value conflict to be discussed here is the one which is perhaps most central to professional practice in child and family social work. It is experienced and perceived as a perennial debate, which has its roots in competing positions established at least fifty years ago (Smith, 1995). In brief, it concerns the question of when to act to protect children at the expense of and as an alternative to supporting their care and upbringing within families. Of course, lying behind this crucial decision point are also a range of ideas, perceptions, theory and evidence, which are likely to affect professional perspectives.

It is widely assumed that the period after the Second World War was characterised by a power struggle between elements which favoured a more coercive role for state intervention and those which, whilst also interventionist, believed that the approach should be based on principles of family support, partnership and prevention. Thus, for example, the Children Act 1948 and the Children and Young Persons Acts of 1963 and 1969, appear to reflect a greater commitment to children being supported in their own homes, even when they were in great need. This might include direct material help for children and their families. For example:

> the Children Act 1948 reflected an entirely new ethos... there was a notion of positive discrimination to compensate the deprived child...
>
> (Fox Harding, 1997, p. 101)

Subsequently, the 1963 Act incorporated specific provisions to require local authorities to use 'advice, assistance and guidance' to reduce the need to receive children into care (Smith, 1995). As a result, there was a substantial increase in the use of material assistance to help families and children in need. Whilst the 1969 Act re-emphasised this aspiration, the upheaval that followed the Maria Colwell case prompted a re-evaluation, and the Children Act 1975 represented a reassertion of the state's role in child protection. The primacy of the biological tie between children and parents was called into question:

> Notable was the provision requiring parental notice prior to reclaiming a child staying in care for a period of more than six months. In addition the grounds on which a local authority could assume parental rights were widened...
>
> (Smith, 1995, p. 66)

These changes in law were paralleled by a number of practice developments, such as a more extensive use of statutory provisions such as Place of Safety Orders and wardship, and the greater reliance on the assumption of parental rights by local authorities. These trends were also reflected in the emergence of 'permanency' as a core principle in child care, reflecting the child protectionist belief that psychological ties are more important than biological ones (Fox Harding, 1997).

However, the change of government in 1979 was followed by a further ideological shift (Gamble, 1988). The mood became one of hostility to state intervention, and support for the independence of the family. The Child Care Act 1980 and the HASSASSA Act 1983[7] both included limited measures to promote the integrity of the family and restrict the authority of statutory agencies. At the same time, the numbers of children in state care began to decline sharply – practice taking its cue from the spirit of the times, rather than from dramatic legislative or policy change.

Despite the events in Cleveland, and the anti-statist views of the government of the day, the Children Act 1989 did not pursue an explicitly libertarian line. The act cannot be seen simply as the end product of another pendulum swing, away from state intervention, and towards supporting families:

> Concerns about both the child care agents of the state doing too much, too coercively, and about them doing too little, too ineffectually, resulted in a wish for legislation and policy to attempt to proceed in two directions at once – both towards better protection of the child and better protection of the parent...
>
> (Fox Harding, 1997, p. 186)

It is, indeed, this intentional ambiguity in the legislation which subsequent policy and guidance has grappled with. The 'refocusing' debate has emerged from a desire to harmonise interventions to protect children with those that address their needs; that is, to reconcile Sections 17 and 47 of the Children Act 1989.

By 1994, however, the Audit Commission was arguing that this balance had not been achieved, and that a greater degree of emphasis should be placed on preventive work, utilising resources such as family centres. This line of argument was further bolstered by the Department of Health overview report *Child Protection: Messages from Research* (Department of Health, 1995a), which argued that too much effort was being invested in 'front end' investigations into allegations of child abuse, and too little was being done to support those families where children had 'needs' but were not 'at risk'. The report noted that 160,000 children were the subject of child protection referrals each year, of whom 24,500 (15 per cent) were added to the child protection register, where concerns were substantiated. However, 96 per cent (154,000) of all children referred remained with their families, and only about 7000 (4.5 per cent) received services following the investigation. Other findings suggested that there was an undue emphasis on formal decision-making, and too little on planning interventions, whilst parents seemed to be routinely alienated by the investigative process.

Subsequent guidance (Department of Health *et al.*, 1999; 2000) has therefore sought to emphasise the importance of an integrated, holistic, forward-looking approach, which emphasises the indivisibility of needs and the risk of significant harm to children. The *Framework for the Assessment of Children in Need and their Families* makes the position clear:

> safeguarding children should not be seen as a separate activity from promoting their welfare. They are two sides of the same coin.
> (Department of Health *et al.*, 2000, p. 5)

This orientation should ensure that inquiries where there is reason to believe children are at risk of significant harm should be informed by the same principles as those addressing children's needs.

Case example:

Maya has a baby son, Evan, who is prone to chest infections. She has had problems of drug and alcohol addiction, and she has been abused by previous partners.

At present she is living alone with her son, and her mother lives nearby, offering occasional assistance when needed.

When she is clean, Maya manages her parental responsibilities well, but when she has relapses, real concerns arise about the possibility of neglect, and risks to the baby's health.

Is it possible to achieve a 'balance' between protecting the child and supporting the family in this case?

Child protection vs children's rights: 'it's for your own good'

The increasing prominence of children's rights has generated a recognition that it is not sufficient for practice simply to provide services which are determined to be 'in the child's interests', without at least checking this assumption out. The notion of children's 'competence' to contribute to, and in some cases, to make key decisions about their lives has become more widely accepted in recent years (see Chapter 5), with a corresponding weakening of the hegemony held by those in positions of professional power over them. This generates significant tensions about the way in which children's capability is judged, and the extent to which they are authorised to make independent choices. These issues are compounded in specific contexts, where, for example, children are assessed as having learning difficulties, or where they may be deemed to have mental health problems.

Nevertheless, the starting point is one where professional authority and the assumption of expert infallibility have increasingly come into question. Concrete examples of this growing trend are provided by accounts of children's residential care, where the quality of service provided, ostensibly in children's interests, has been found inadequate from their own perspective.

In particular, the institutional nature of care seems to create inherent tensions between the aim of providing for children's needs, and engaging them effectively in exercising choice and control over important aspects of their lives. Stein and Carey (1986), for instance, found that there was a general sense of 'loss' experienced by children and young people in care, which was not always recognised. For most of the young people they interviewed, there:

> was the feeling that being separated from their families had been a "bad thing" ... It was this particular aspect of separation from their families that made them insist that no one else ... could understand what it was really like to be in care ...
>
> (Stein and Carey, 1986, p. 72)

This sense of loss may be compounded by a deeper sense of unfairness. The very nature of the institutional regime, with standardised rules and requirements, is likely to seem arbitrary. Children and young people resent restrictions on bedtimes and going out, and are reported to have felt that being in care was like a form of punishment.

Other concerns voiced by young people relate to the arbitrary exercise of authority by staff (Triseliotis *et al.*, 1995). Thus, while the proportion of those who felt unfairly treated was found to be relatively low in one study, there were complaints of excessive use of power, physical assault and arbitrary decision-making:

> By far the most disliked aspect of care was having to conform to rules ... Other examples of unfair treatment included informally making plans for a young woman's future in her absence and being subject to too many restrictions.
>
> (Triseliotis *et al.*, 1995, pp. 180–181)

Such conflicts between the demands of the regime and the rights and interests of young people are particularly acute in the context of secure accommodation (Harris and Timms, 1993; O'Neill, 2001). Whilst some young people are admitted to secure accommodation on grounds of criminal behaviour, others may be there on 'welfare' grounds, but this does not seem to affect the quality of the experience. The nature of the institution seems to override the individual interests of those accommodated:

> In the experiences of the young people, the need for security and control took precedence over everything else, including their rights to privacy, confidentiality and participation...
>
> (O'Neill, 2001, p. 232)

Reviews of children's experiences in care have shown us their perspective, and offer some ideas about establishing rights in an institutional setting. *People Like Us* (Utting, 1997) notes first the impact of entering 'the care system', and the impact of losing control over key decisions. Children and young people experience 'bewilderment, displacement and loss' (Utting, 1997, p. 76). They have no control over 'choice of placement, location, school, social worker or who one lives with'. They are reported to feel that they are not listened to, and have no input into planning and decision-making – all areas where institutional practices appear to override children's own preferences or views. The report summarises the feelings of children and young people in residential care in terms of a desire to be treated with respect and recognised as distinct individuals, whose particular circumstances and aspirations need to be attended to:

> The inadvertently oppressive nature of professional systems was exposed by the Camden child who said, very simply, 'I don't like people making decisions about me and they think they know what's best for me just by reading my file'.
>
> (Utting, 1997, p. 77)

Children and young people clearly aspire to be involved in determining outcomes. They expect to be provided with information and options, and they would like to take part in deciding what happens to them. This does not necessarily extend to being expected to shoulder responsibility beyond what can reasonably be expected:

> Although important, children's perspectives should not necessarily outweigh other considerations.
>
> (Berridge, 2002, p. 90)

Children and young people themselves expect to be challenged, and to have boundaries set (Utting, 1997), so it is not simply a matter of giving them a free hand. Similarly, in the context of parental separation, children are found to want a say, but not to be the final arbiters; understandably, they do not want to be put in the position of choosing between their parents (Smart *et al.*, 1999).

The difficulty of negotiating a path between children's interests and their wishes is also highlighted in other aspects of the child welfare system. For example, whilst the *Gillick* judgement apparently gave children the right to *consent* to medical treatment, subsequent court rulings have suggested that children may not have the right to *refuse* treatment in some circumstances (Standley, 2001). For instance, in the case of *South Glamorgan County Council* v. *W and B* [1993] 1 FLR 574, the court made an interim care order with a requirement that a 15-year-old girl receive a psychiatric assessment:

> When she refused to consent to the examination and assessment, the court under its inherent jurisdiction overrode her wishes and gave the local authority permission to take the necessary steps for her to be treated and assessed.
>
> (Standley, 2001, p. 199)

Thus, the assumption cannot be sustained that children of 'sufficient age and understanding' have absolute control over crucial decisions such as this. A path must be negotiated between their rights and their best interests.

Case example:

Leia is 14 years old, and she has been subject to a care order for three years. Her behaviour at school and elsewhere is often disruptive, and is highly sexualised.

She has been accommodated in a number of foster homes, and in residential care. She has absconded on a number of occasions, and she has been admitted to secure accommodation under Section 25(1)(a) of the Children Act 1989, on the grounds that she is at risk of 'significant harm'.

She does not want to be in care, and when she absconds she returns to live with her father, a known sex offender.

It is believed by all agencies involved that theirs is an incestuous relationship.

What is the balance between Leia's 'rights' and her' 'interests' in this situation?

Family support vs children's rights: 'the rule of optimism'?

The possibility of conflict between meeting the needs of families and enhancing the rights of children may not always be clear, but there are some general and specific issues which arise from straightforward assumptions in this context.

For some, it seems relatively self-evident that services which benefit families in general will also contribute to children's well-being. Thus, Tunstill (2000) emphasises the broader possibilities arising from a generous interpretation of the local authority role under Section 17 of the Children Act 1989. She stresses that the emphasis of the Act and its accompanying guidance (Department of Health, 1991a) is on supporting children in their own homes, and on social services departments meeting need as well as responding to indications of risk. The positive response of parents to the provision of family support services is taken as evidence that they are contributing to children's well-being. For example, one study is reported as finding a high level of parent satisfaction with family centre provision, whilst parents also believed that the service had been beneficial to their children (Aldgate and Statham, 2001, p. 223). It is claimed elsewhere that family support, in the form of a changed 'environment' or a compensatory programme can enhance children's well-being (Buchanan, 2002). The number of risk factors can be reduced and the number of 'protective factors' increased by carefully planned and well-delivered programmes.

However, criticisms can be directed at the extent to which the family support perspective conflates children's interests with those of their parents. These are made at three distinct levels: the political agenda; the quality of provision; and the misreading of children's needs or wishes.

Morgan (1992) argues that the move towards more extensive provision of services such as children's day care is driven not by an interest in children's welfare, but by a concern to promote parents' (particularly mothers') involvement as participants in the paid workforce. Children lose out in two ways, it is argued. They miss out on the direct experience of being parented; and, the quality of day care provided may also fail to meet their needs. For her, the apparent success of 'model projects', such as the Perry Preschool programme in the United States, does not justify 'unwarranted generalisation' (Morgan, 1995). Small-scale gains from well-run preschool programmes do not justify a massive and uncontrolled expansion of services, or the assumption that benefits will arise from 'virtually any non-parental care'. As far as she is concerned, 'parental involvement' is a far more crucial factor in children's upbringing.

Certainly, concerns about the quality of provision have been echoed elsewhere (Aldgate and Statham, 2001). Out-of-school services, for example, seem to show some of the signs of being expected to meet a multiplicity of expectations. According to Petrie *et al.* (2000), they have grown up out of a diverse history:

> They have not been developed in any holistic or purposeful way within the context of a broadly educational policy ... [P]roviders and staff were aware that what was on offer failed to meet the needs of young people.
>
> (Petrie *et al.*, 2000, p. 70)

In the out-of-school provision studied by these researchers, children themselves appeared to have little role in determining either the activities undertaken or the way in which these services were provided, and there was a considerable degree of dissatisfaction expressed about being 'bored', controlled, and in the case of girls, exploited as unpaid helpers. Children are often marginalised or problematised, and their perspective is subordinated to 'adult interests' (Petrie *et al.*, 2000, p. 194).

Not only do 'family support' services sometimes prioritise adult concerns at the expense of the quality of service, but they can also be criticised for failing to address specific needs of children (Social Services Inspectorate, 1998). An inspection of services provided for 'children in need' found a high level of parental satisfaction, but at the same time, there was evidence of significant needs 'not being properly recognised or assessed' (Social Services Inspectorate, 1998, p. 1). Thus, 80 per cent of families expressed satisfaction with the support provided by the eight local authorities inspected, but:

> It concerned us that ... in 40% of the cases we examined in detail, we considered there to be possible indicators of abuse or neglect ... which were not being adequately recognised or evaluated.
>
> (SSI, 1998, p. 3)

The inspectors' interpretation of these observations was that the services themselves were often unclear about who the service user was:

> Our findings strongly indicate a need to guard against losing sight of the position of children [in light of] a concern to meet the needs of parents or carers ...
>
> (SSI, 1998, p. 17)

This coincides with the stipulation in policy guidance to ensure that the child remains at the heart of all stages of assessment and intervention. The child must not be 'lost during assessment', for example, in the face of other issues and needs facing the family (Department of Health *et al.*, 2000, p. 10).

In addition, the fact that families are making use of support services should also be considered in light of the 'rule of optimism' (Dingwall *et al.*, 1983), which suggests that professionals have sometimes taken an overly positive view of parents' readiness to cooperate and take up services (see also Noyes, 1991).

Not only should we be wary about making simplistic assumptions in respect of family support services in general, but there are also several quite specific areas where children's perceptions of their needs may conflict with the approach taken to the family as a whole. Again, the guidance on assessment draws attention to the needs of young carers, where there may be:

> differences of view between children and parents about appropriate levels of care. Such differences may be out in the open or concealed.
>
> (Department of Health *et al.*, 2000, p. 49)

For example, young carers may be torn between completing school-work and providing personal care for other family members, leading to disagreements, stress and feelings of guilt.

In another context, it may be difficult to distinguish between the needs of parents and other family members, and children with disabilities. The example of respite care is cited (Marchant and Jones, 2000), where the lack of availability of 'natural breaks' may lead to contrived solutions. This can be problematic, and children's interests can become secondary:

> Defining the purpose of any service as respite can create a confusing situation. The child's experience of the service can become incidental since its defined purpose is to give the child's parents a break.
>
> (Marchant and Jones, 2000, p. 87)

For young people with learning difficulties, money can be a contentious issue. In discussing this question with a focus group of young people, the present author found a very strong body of opinion to the effect that money provided to the family in respect of their special needs should be theirs to spend (Allard *et al.*, 1994). Middleton (1999), too, refers to the impact of 'parental pressure' on children with a disability, which again underlines the importance of distinguishing between parental and family needs, and those of young people receiving services.

> *Case example*:
>
> George is disabled and also has learning difficulties. His needs require a significant level of attention, especially at night. He attends a special unit at a mainstream school, but for the rest of the time, it is his parents who have to meet his care needs.
>
> He has an older sister and a younger brother, and his parents sometimes arrange for him to go into short-term foster care so that the rest of the family can spend time together.
>
> He resents having to go into short-term care, and he lets the rest of the family know this when they return.
>
> His parents, however, feel that it is only fair on his brother and sister to give them time to do things they want to do. They also feel they need a break from time to time.
>
> *How could you ensure that everybody is able to have a say in deciding how family members' differing needs are met? What approach would you take to reconciling their different interests?*

Tackling dilemmas: some final thoughts

In posing these issues, which are recurrent themes in children's services, as a series of dichotomies, there is a risk of oversimplifying complex choices and challenges. The aim here is not to suggest that the options are straightforward, or that they can always be resolved one way or the other. Rather, it is to highlight the persistence of professional challenges, and the fact that these are usually posed in the light of competing belief systems. These inbuilt assumptions can help to illuminate the choices available, but they are unlikely to provide clear-cut answers. Instead, they must be seen primarily as providing the basis for understanding competing expectations, and achieving coherence and clarity in decision-making.

VALUES AND ANTI-DISCRIMINATORY PRACTICE

Dilemmas and diversity

By this point, it will be clear that working in children's services involves both understanding and resolving a series of complex and challenging dilemmas. We have identified a number of major discourses in child welfare, all of which appear to have a degree of validity, and all of which are held to strongly by a variety of stakeholders concerned with the well-being of children. Significantly, however, there are a number of key issues which generate conflict between these perspectives, and where the resolution of differences is not routine. It is, of course, important to do more than simply restate these challenges, and to go on to consider some of the ways in which they can be analysed and resolved. The notion of 'balance', for example, may appear unhelpful because it suggests a comfortable middle ground when, in fact, the requirement may be for a clear choice in favour of a particular position.

In developing an approach which is practice relevant, it will be worthwhile to consider the questions which arise in the specific context of anti-discriminatory practice, before moving on to consider the application of 'value positions' in the general context of professional decision-making and intervention. As Thompson (2001, p. 29) points out, the role of ideology and fixed beliefs is of crucial significance in generating a 'logic of discrimination'. Understanding the impact of prior assumptions, and recognising the need to challenge and rethink these, are essential tasks for practitioners.

The aim here will be to show how the perspectives identified earlier can contribute to these objectives by offering us a 'road map' which will support the application of a reflective and critical approach (Fook, 2002), providing a degree of flexibility, whilst also retaining a sense of 'groundedness'. Decisions and actions should thus be seen to draw on a lexicon of values and principles, which, crucially, are applied to particular situations and personal circumstances thoughtfully and creatively, rather than as a routinised checklist.

Anti-discriminatory and anti-oppressive practice:[8] overarching principles

There is, of course, no doubt that anti-discriminatory practice is a fundamental requirement in the delivery of services to children (Thompson, 2001). However, the simplicity with which this can be stated may be misleading to the extent that it underestimates the challenges involved in delivering something which is seen, in the abstract, as an unqualified good. The fundamental need to practice in a way which identifies and challenges all forms of discrimination is not disputed. This has been clearly and consistently stressed by many authors (for example, Dominelli, 1988; Dominelli and McLeod, 1989; Dalrymple and Burke, 1995; Middleton, 1999; Thompson, 2001). The field of social care has witnessed a 'thread of historical continuity' (Dominelli, 1988), reflecting a concern to promote social justice. The commitment to challenging unfair treatment and promoting equality has been characterised by a progressive recognition of the interests of particular groups, moving through class divisions (Corrigan and Leonard, 1978), the treatment of women (Dominelli and McLeod, 1989), anti-racism (Dominelli, 1988; Ahmad, 1990), the disability movement (Oliver, 1990), and to a lesser extent, sexuality and the social exclusion of marginal groups such as refugees and asylum seekers.

These professional concerns of those 'in the field' have been paralleled by a growing number of policy measures to promote equal treatment (Banks, 2001b). Legislation has progressively sought both to outlaw discriminatory action and also to impose expectations on organisations and services that they will take a proactive approach to preventing discrimination (for example, the Race Relations (Amendment) Act 2000). It is perhaps inevitable that the emergence of general public and political concern about discrimination should act most directly to influence ideas and practice in those areas of social welfare where services are focused on those people who are most likely to experience unfair or oppressive treatment – people who are marginalised because of their perceived characteristics, such as disabilities, race or country of origin. Garland (2001) refers to the sense of 'otherness' which is attributed to certain groups, which then predisposes them to discriminatory treatment, and contributes to their vulnerability. The connection between anti-oppressive practice and securing social improvements therefore becomes firmly embedded in the beliefs and practices of many working in the human services:

> Anti-oppressive practice, insofar as it is preoccupied with the implementation of social justice, is intimately bound up with notions of improving the quality of life or well-being of individuals, groups and communities...
>
> (Dominelli, 1998, p. 5)

Perhaps also because of this close connection, the insertion of anti-discriminatory principles into the fabric of training, particularly in social work has become a standard expectation:

> During the late 1980s social work education became increasingly aware of the impact of oppression and discrimination on clients and communities.
>
> (Thompson, 2001, p. 1)

Anti-discrimination and professional training

Following this development, moves were made to establish the principles of anti-discriminatory practice as core elements in the training and preparation of the workforce in the social care professions. As well as making an explicit commitment to anti-racist practice, the regulations for the Diploma in Social Work (the influential 'Paper 30') stated that:

> CCETSW [the Central Council for Education and Training in Social Work] will also seek to ensure that students are prepared to combat other forms of discrimination based on age, gender, sexual orientation, class, disability, culture or creed.
>
> (CCETSW, 1989, p. 10)

The paper further emphasised that it was not just enough to be able to recognise 'structural oppression' but that 'qualifying social workers' must demonstrate the ability to act to challenge discrimination (CCETSW, 1989, p. 15).

This commitment has been retained by CCETSW and its successor organisations (the General Social Care Council and TOPSS), although in a modified and less radical form (Harris, 2003). Similar aspirations are incorporated into the requirements for the new social work degree (from 2003 onwards). Students should learn to 'challenge constructively individual, institutional and structural discrimination' (QAA, 2002, p. 12), so that on gaining the social work degree, they will have 'the knowledge and skills they need to prevent unjustifiable discrimination' (GSCC, 2002a, p. 8).

As the context for delivering services to children has changed, so has the commitment to anti-discriminatory practice extended to other areas of practice (see, for example, Sure Start, 1999). So, the guidance issued for Sure Start early years services emphasises the importance of an inclusive approach, which recognises and 'celebrates' diversity. The principles of inclusion, participation and relevant services are emphasised, and the importance of challenging stereotypes is stressed (Sure Start, 1999, p. 12). In addition, the problems of discriminatory behaviour must be addressed:

> Strategies need to be in place to support victims of harassment and to deal with racist behaviour. This can be very difficult when the service users themselves, or indeed young children display racism, but it must be tackled.
>
> (Sure Start, 1999, p. 16)

In this example and elsewhere, it is consistently made clear that anti-discriminatory practice requires an active commitment, and should be seen as a 'non-negotiable' core component of professional activity in delivering services for children.

Anti-discriminatory practice and belief systems

Thompson's (2001) approach to anti-discriminatory practice also attempts to ensure that practitioners adopt an integrated approach. For him, the level of inter-personal relations and individual practice must not be disengaged from the cultural and societal influences within which it is 'embedded'. His PCS (personal, cultural, social) analysis enables practitioners to locate their own and service users' experience of discrimination within their structural and communal origins. It is not possible, in his view, for individuals to act in a way which is sheltered or isolated from the influence of the dominant forces which shape our understandings and beliefs. The idea, for example, of 'colour-blind' practice becomes unsustainable:

> Even if we are full of good intentions in relation to anti-discriminatory practice, unless we are actively seeking to eliminate racist thoughts and actions from our day-to-day dealings, they will 'filter through' from the culture and structure into which we were socialised.
>
> (Thompson, 2001, p. 25)

Practitioners in children's services must recognise the sources and patterns of power in their relationships with service users, in order to be clear about the factors which determine the preconditions for any intervention (see also the analytical model set out in Chapter 4).

Practice must be committed to empowerment as a goal, rather than as a technique, and it must be open to criticism and change in the light of our own experience. Anti-discriminatory practice, in Thompson's view, lies at the heart of any intervention, which must therefore reflect a set of emancipatory values. However, practice at the individual level must achieve two linked but potentially contradictory aims. As the PCS model makes clear, the nature of discrimination at the different levels is interactive. Work with a particular service user on what may appear to be personal issues cannot be 'isolated' (Banks, 2001b) from wider systems and attitudes which may crucially affect individual experience. It will be the practitioner's task to build links between immediate personal concerns and needs, and wider factors in the community and social structure which impact on service users' life chances. Whilst the practitioner may be part of a network of power and authority which exercises control over the individual service user, and this must be recognised, it is also important to assist recipients to gain power for themselves and to challenge oppression and inequality – this is, for Thompson, an integral part of the professional task:

> each individual has a part to play in the major change from traditional approaches to social work to a form of practice based on principles of emancipatory practice...
>
> (Thompson, 2001, p. 162)

The aim here is to establish an acceptance that a commitment to anti-discrimination must permeate every aspect of the activities of those who deliver services to children in the welfare field. However, as we shall see, establishing this as a core principle leaves open a number of questions about realising this aspiration in practice.

Challenges to the anti-discriminatory agenda

Whilst it may seem that the core aim of working in a way which is anti-oppressive is uncontentious, there have been a number of questions raised and challenges identified. First, as Dominelli (1998) acknowledges, it has been argued in some quarters that to adopt an explicit anti-oppressive stance is inappropriate, unnecessary, or even counter-productive. The argument is made that the level and nature of inequality is exaggerated; that anti-discriminatory principles are imposed on service providers in a 'draconian' and inflexible manner; and that it is not part of the helping professions' role to adopt a political stance against oppression.

Davies (1981), for example, has argued that social work should be modest in its aims, focusing on helping individuals, rather than taking an explicit stance in favour of structural and political change. In contrast to Thompson, this perspective makes a clear distinction between individual problems and individualised solutions on the one hand, and political action and social change on the other. For Davies:

> all societies have imperfections... the business of social work is necessarily concerned with ameliorating the pains of these imperfections, and, furthermore,... the individualist approach of traditional social work is both necessary and sufficient to justify the existence of the profession.
>
> (Davies, 1981, p. 10)

Though social workers may have a role in policy change or improving social conditions, this should not be seen as their primary purpose; but they should seek to maintain both the social fabric and the quality of life of those who are disadvantaged within society. Transformational aims are not fundamental to service delivery, according to this view. Likewise, Banks (2001b, p. 81) talks of 'bracketing off societal and agency constraints' so that 'we can try to treat the user as a person to be respected'. The rules and restrictions which define the worker–service user relationship may be taken as given:

> For example, a social worker making an assessment of the needs of a person with a disability is doing so within a framework prescribed by her agency... Yet within this framework, the service user can be spoken to and treated with respect and honesty.
>
> (Banks, 2001b, p. 81)

Others, as Dominelli (1998) and Thompson (2001) acknowledge, have argued that an anti-oppressive approach to practice is, itself, oppressive, removing 'common sense' from the practitioner's repertoire and replacing it with a standardised, prescriptive and ultimately self-defeating set of procedures (Brewer and Lait, 1980, for example). However, the idea that good practice is just a matter of applying common sense is robustly challenged by Thompson (2001), who argues that this itself is a repository of ideological assumptions, and cannot be taken to be value free:

'Common sense' amounts, in fact, to a mixture of dominant ideologies – sexist, racist and so on. It is a collection of taken-for-granted assumptions which are likely to be discriminatory and oppressive in their impact.

(Thompson, 2001, p. 166)

We must, therefore, have a clear and comprehensive understanding of theory and structures in order to inform practice. The assumption that we can just practice with individuals, in isolation, poses significant risks for the quality and outcomes of our work. For example, in working with the consequences of domestic violence or child prostitution, to avoid recognising and challenging the structural origins of victims' experience amounts to blaming them, or at least holding them partly responsible, for their own mistreatment. The work of Barnardo's and The Children's Society, in challenging paternalist assumptions about promiscuity and irresponsibility (Utting, 1997), and transforming our conceptions of the nature of child prostitution, is an example of the positive consequences for practice of making the connection between individual circumstances and the structural origins of sexual exploitation. Interestingly, this has also meant 'reframing' the issue from one defined in terms of 'child protection' to one which emphasises the rights of children and young people not to be exploited in this way.

More difficult questions for anti-discriminatory practice are posed by the risks of adopting a routinised approach. As Fook (2002) puts it, it is not enough merely to strive for equality of treatment. The process of empowerment must be adapted to differences in 'personality, social or cultural background, or present circumstances' (Fook, 2002, p. 50).

Obvious examples might include the need to vary our approach to the communication needs of children, depending on their age and understanding, or whether they use forms of communication other than speech. Fook also points out that 'striving for sameness' might, in itself, be disempowering to different interests. Ahmad (1990), for instance, draws attention to the real complexities of seeking to apply a policy of 'same-race placements'. In one case she discusses, this appeared to mean separating one child of 'mixed parentage' from the child's white siblings, at the point where the children were accommodated by the local authority. The existence of the same race placement policy resulted in a prolonged search for a 'mixed parentage' family for the one child, whilst the siblings were placed with white foster carers. While arguments were raised for placing all the children with black[9] carers, these were treated as 'problematic' (Ahmad, 1990, p. 24).

Gupta (2003), too, demonstrates some of the problems of a 'stereotypical' and 'superficial' approach, which routinises anti-discriminatory practice. She acknowledges the legitimate anti-racist origins of the movement for same race placements, and the continuing importance of racial and cultural identity in the matching process, in the face of some politicians' preference for a 'colour blind' approach:

> In a society like Britain, where racism is endemic...a black child will receive negative messages about being black and needs a positive internal model of identity to counteract these negative messages.
>
> (Gupta, 2003, p. 210)

However, adherence to a policy which is inflexible and insensitive to the child's 'wishes and feelings' and sense of identity can lead to poor or harmful outcomes. Gupta cites evidence that local authorities are not able to provide continuity of support for 'ensuring that a child's needs in terms of ethnicity, culture, religion and language were met on a daily basis' (Gupta, 2003, p. 211). She also cites a case example of a placement of an Asian child in an 'Asian' family, which was disrupted because the assessment process failed to take account of religious and linguistic differences. Kirton (2000), too, identifies the problems that arise when 'two camps' seem to 'talk past each other' in the argument over 'same race' placements, without recognising the validity of alternative viewpoints.

Whilst part of the reason for such shortcomings might be the desire to avoid delay, the risks are self-evident. As Gupta argues, there is a need for agencies to adopt a more thoroughgoing strategy of recruitment and support of carers from a range of backgrounds, as well as the promotion of kinship care (Ince, 2001). In addition, however, it may be necessary to adapt 'same race' policies to focus on issues of 'positive identity and self-concept':

> where it is not possible to place a child in a same race placement within a reasonable time or because of other factors...specific interventions need to be considered. These include recruiting and supporting families who are able to demonstrate an understanding of the developmental needs of black children and an active understanding of racism and commitment to challenging racism and discrimination; and promote the child's access to cultural, religious and linguistic frameworks...
>
> (Gupta, 2003, p. 212)

In terms of the 'value positions' which we have identified, this involves making a shift from an emphasis on the integrity and autonomy of the family and culture, to one which is more concerned with putting in place active and flexible support mechanisms, which help to build the family's capacity to meet the child's needs in terms of identity, self-image and 'socio-genealogical connectedness' (Owusu-Bempah and Howitt, 2000).

The problems of routinisation in anti-oppressive/anti-discriminatory practice are closely linked with a further problematic area, which is that of conflicting principles and the potential for contradictory impacts. As Fook (2002, p. 50) puts it, monolithic conceptions of power and oppression are relatively unhelpful in enabling us to deal with 'uncertainty, contradictions and difference'. Individuals or groups who are oppressed in a particular respect may also espouse attitudes or behave in ways which discriminate against others. Thus, for example, children and young people, and their parents may become the object of authoritarian attitudes in neighbourhoods which are characterised by a range of social and economic disadvantages.

The contradictory nature of interventions intended to be anti-discriminatory can be demonstrated in a variety of settings. For instance, Middleton (1999) draws attention to some of the difficulties arising from attempts to prevent the bullying of disabled children. Victimisation is often cited as a reason for choosing to send disabled children to special schools rather than maintaining them in mainstream education. The focus on bullying appears to be part of a broader 'protective' agenda, which assumes that special education is better suited to meeting the needs of children with disabilities (Middleton, 1999, p. 43). On the other hand, the very fact of segregation imposes a range of other constraints on children and young people, which might themselves be experienced as disempowering:

> Sharon [recognised] that the problems lay not with her disability but having to live away from home. She missed her family and had difficulties fitting back in when she left school ...
>
> (Middleton, 1999, p. 10)

Far from being anti-oppressive, special education can become a 'form of social control'. Moving children rather than challenging the discriminatory attitudes that underlie bullying can be seen as another example of victim-blaming, which locates the 'problem' with the individual, and fails to challenge oppressive behaviour and structures. Being away from home may result in children feeling less valued, and thus more vulnerable to exploitation and abuse (Middleton, 1999, p. 117).

The contradictory aspects of anti-discriminatory practice can also be identified in other areas. Barn (1993) has argued that much intervention with children from minority ethnic backgrounds suffers from a kind of 'double bind'; services are found to be both over- and under-interventionist. Her findings suggested that there were different patterns to the care careers of black and white children, which in turn partly reflected 'qualitative differences in the social work help employed' (Barn, 1993, p. 102). In particular, there was less evidence of social workers intervening to 'engage black families...in preventative work'; that is, to provide family support services. At the same time, intervention with black children appeared to be characterised by a greater sense of urgency and readiness to resort to compulsory measures to keep them in care. This apparent inconsistency appeared to be rooted in conflicting assumptions about black families and children: on the one hand, that they should not be subject to state interference (a 'laissez-faire' position; see, Laming, 2003, p. 345), whilst, on the other hand, where intervention is needed in children's interests, this should be decisive and authoritative ('child protectionist'), in order to safeguard children who may be at risk. Examples of cases where particular cultural assumptions have informed a non-interventionist strategy which has contributed to tragic outcomes (Blom-Cooper, 1985; Laming, 2003) can be adduced to support such levels of intrusion:

> Cultural heritage is important to many people, but it cannot take precedence over standards of childcare embodied in law...

> There can be no excuse or justification for failing to take adequate steps to protect a vulnerable child...
>
> (Laming, 2003, p. 346)

Equally, however the fact that there appear to be good and effective kinship support networks available in many cases does not always lead to the offer of suitable family support services when these could be beneficial:

> Social services need to continue working in partnership at the stage when the child is in care, and facilitate better links between black families and children.
>
> (Barn, 1993, p. 123)

Indeed, the provision of family assessment and support is an important mechanism for both recognising and addressing the structural inequalities which ensure that black and ethnic minority families are 'more likely to live in deprived areas, have less access to employment and good housing and are likely to face discrimination' (Ince, 2001, p. 142).

Dealing with tensions and challenges

Having acknowledged that there are tensions and challenges in applying an anti-discriminatory approach to practice, it will now be useful to consider some of these problematic issues in more detail in relation to the specific positions which have provided our analytical framework thus far. In this way, we will be able to assess the extent to which specific aspects of discrimination and oppression must be recognised in developing responses to identified areas of concern.

The family: safe haven or site of oppression?

As already noted, the concept of the family as a 'natural' institution, which is generally the safest and most conducive site for children's upbringing and development has continued to exercise consider-able power, in both professional circles and in more widely held patterns of belief. It is therefore held to be, *de facto*, oppressive and potentially counterproductive for the state to intervene in the arena of the family. In other words, there exists a notional threshold which must be breached before intervention can be accepted as legitimate. The clearest example of this, in statute form, would be the threshold criteria for determining risk of 'significant harm' provided by Section 31(2) of the Children Act 1989, which must be met to justify the imposition of care or supervision orders in respect of a child.

This, of course, is also supported by the 'no order' principle (Section 1(5)), which creates a presumption against making a statutory order unless its beneficial effects can be demonstrated. Thus, the legislative context provides some support for the assumption that any action which impacts upon the family will be experienced as oppressive, and must therefore be justifiable. Evidence to support a 'hands off' approach to families is also offered by research which suggests that parents often experience professional intervention as intrusive and oppressive. It has been repeatedly observed that parents feel alienated and disempowered by formal procedures and impersonal official settings. Parents attending case conferences to discuss concerns about their children, and who were unsupported, are reported to have found:

> the experience 'daunting', feeling 'overwhelmed with long words' and 'unable to speak'. Those who did speak complained 'they don't listen', 'your point of view never gets heard or understood'.
>
> (Hunt *et al.*, 1999, p. 150)

This finding reiterates earlier evidence of the impact of professional power on families, in the context of statutory intervention (Fisher *et al.*, 1986; Farmer and Owen, 1995), which seems to suggest that formal systems and processes tend to be experienced as denying the opportunity for participation rather than encouraging it. That this is a persistent strand emerging from evaluations of child welfare practice (particularly when focusing on child protection) is fairly clear. Parents involved in care proceedings remain very negative about the experience (Aldgate and Statham, 2001).

The combined impact of research findings, the conclusions of public inquiries (Butler-Sloss, 1988) and media images (Franklin, 2002b) is potentially powerful. It should perhaps be no surprise that intervention in the lives of families is affected by these perceptions. The view of social workers and other child welfare professionals as, by nature, potentially oppressive is widely established, and, indeed, may well be shared by practitioners themselves. Ironically, as Banks (2001b) points out, this view is notably held by those from a 'radical' tradition, who would see human services as, at least partly, a vehicle for state control. However, the notion of 'radical non-intervention' (Schur, 1973) fails to take sufficient account of the oppressive potential of 'natural' structures, such as the family. This is demonstrated in a very direct way by the impact of domestic violence on children (Mullender *et al.*, 2002). Not only is it clear that children are profoundly affected, directly and indirectly by (predominantly male) violence within the family setting, but it is also evident that, if anything, there is a degree of under- rather than over-involvement of statutory services in responding to the harm caused. Violence at home is a routine experience for many children and young people (Monaghan and Broad, 2003), and it appears to be associated with many other damaging outcomes, but statutory agencies seem to be peripheral to this. Children appear to seek help primarily from other family members, and sometimes from voluntary services, such as refuges (Mullender *et al.*, 2002), but they make little use of other agencies. Children affected by domestic violence feel that their needs are 'invisible' to agencies:

> As they were not asked about domestic violence, far from these encounters having been used as opportunities for exploring the underlying causes of their problems, children had felt judged and anxious.
>
> (Mullender *et al.*, 2002, p. 106)

This study also reports examples of 'professionals' knowing about children's 'home situation', but doing nothing about it. This apparent reluctance of agency representatives to accept responsibility for children's needs is also reported as extending to cases where there is clear evidence of physical harm to their mothers (Stanko *et al.*, 1998).

Despite this, there are examples of workers who are prepared to take the risk of appearing to act 'oppressively' in respect of the use of their own powers, in order to counter another form of oppression. One such case is cited by Mullender *et al.* (2002, p. 106):

> I thought the social workers would help me and my mum, and if he harmed me they would know what happened. I think they finally made my mum see how risky it was for all of us to be living with him. They threatened that we would be taken into care if she stayed on after he had hit me so badly (16-year old South Asian girl).

For practitioners, then, the question is not one of eschewing the use of their own statutory powers, but of understanding the ideological context of the family as well as their own value perspectives, and making practice decisions in the light of these.

Child protection, cultural relativism and 'colour blindness'

There is no doubt that the interaction between anti-discriminatory practice and principles associated with a child protectionist perspective remain highly problematic. The challenge is one of taking account of cultural differences in perceptions of childhood, whilst at the same time providing a comprehensive service to safeguard children's welfare. It might be argued, for example, that the agreement of an internationally recognised instrument such as the UNCRC (United Nations, 1989) might provide the basis for a common and consensual approach to protecting children. Article 19 stipulates that:

> States Parties shall take all appropriate legislative, administrative, social and educational measures to protect the child from all forms of physical or mental violence, injury or abuse, neglect or negligent treatment, maltreatment or exploitation, including sexual abuse, while in the care of parent(s), legal guardian(s) or any other person who has the care of the child.
>
> (UN, 1989)

Stated in this way, this seems to suggest an objective and effectively trans-cultural basis for applying measures to protect children from harm or abuse. However, translating these principles into practice appears rather more complex. Firstly, it must be acknowledged that the Convention itself incorporates a recognition of the importance of diversity, under Article 30:

> In those States in which ethnic, religious or linguistic minorities or persons of indigenous origin exist, a child belonging to such a minority or who is indigenous shall not be denied the right, in community with other members of his or her group, to enjoy his or her own culture, to profess and practise his or her own religion, or to use his or her own language.
>
> (UN, 1989)

It is precisely at this point, however, that conflicting principles come into play. It has been clear that negotiating the dividing line between cultural sensitivity and protecting children has been, and continues to be, problematic. Parton (1991), for example, draws attention to the problems arising from applying 'the rule of optimism' (Dingwall *et al.*, 1983) in this specific context. This allowed social workers in the Jasmine Beckford case, for example, to apply the most positive interpretation possible to the way she was treated. It was reportedly felt by those involved as professionals that they could not apply 'white middle-class' attitudes about child care to 'black working-class parents' (see also, Channer and Parton, 1990).

By the time of the death of Victoria Climbie (Laming, 2003), it appeared that little had changed, however. A preoccupation with race and culture may, in itself, divert attention from 'fundamental' needs of children, according to the inquiry report:

> it may be that assumptions made about Victoria and her situation diverted caring people from noting and acting upon signs of neglect or ill-treatment.
>
> (Laming, 2003, p. 345)

A number of examples of such assumptions are cited: beliefs about the strict nature of children's upbringing in 'Afro-Caribbean families'; preconceptions about the impact of migration from elsewhere; and judgements about the origins of 'marks' on children's bodies. All of these suppositions may have contributed to a diminution of concern about the nature of treatment to which Victoria Climbie was subject. As the inquiry report makes clear, the consequences of generalisations can be very misleading in individual cases:

> The concept of Afro-Caribbean behaviour referred to in Victoria's case illustrates the problem. The range of cultures and behavioural patterns it

includes is so wide that it would be…potentially damaging to an effective
assessment of the needs of the child.

(Laming, 2003, p. 345)

However, the inquiry's rather anodyne conclusion that children should
be 'kept safe', irrespective of colour or culture is of limited practical
value. Indeed, there are also risks in taking a 'colour blind' approach
(Channer and Parton, 1990). For example, approaches based on identifying 'high-risk' populations may show a tendency to over-identify
black families as being a source of potential harm to their children
because of the use of indicators of poverty, disadvantage and social
exclusion. Responding appropriately to risk and need affecting black
children therefore needs a more sophisticated model which 'factors in'
individual, cultural and structural elements (Thompson, 2001).

Dutt and Phillips (2000, p. 45) have articulated a model of assessment
which provides a basis for integrating our knowledge of the impact of
structural discrimination, including our own professional and organisational preconceptions, in the specific context of the individual child,
her own self-image, and her personal and social development. This, in
turn, enables us to bring an understanding of general concepts, such as
'attachment' or 'culture' to the specific circumstances of the child. The
significance of attachment for the child may therefore lead the professional
to seek evidence of positive and healthy relationships, but knowledge
of the particular culture may sensitise the worker to seek these in the
context of a culturally specific family configuration.

Culture, too, is a concept that must be applied flexibly. Otherwise, 'all
children' from a particular background might be judged to be at risk:

> Culture can explain the context in which abuse takes place, it can explain
> the values, beliefs or attitudes of a parent at the time when an abusive
> incident took place, but it cannot provide an explanation for the parent's
> action in response to those values, beliefs or attitudes.
>
> (Dutt and Phillips, 2000, p. 56)

The goal should be to achieve a degree of sensitivity and adaptability in
practice, rather than apply standardised concepts, such as 'cultural
relativism':

> The goal of ethnically sensitive practice is inaccessible and impossible
> without the worker allowing their practice and their values to be chal-
> lenged and without time and effort being put into unlocking deep-rooted
> stereotypes.
>
> (Channer and Parton, 1990, p. 119)

Family support and children's needs: who is the service user?

The notion of anti-oppressive practice may appear relatively more straightforward in the context of supporting families, where providing services to counter the effects of disadvantage may be assumed to be of automatic benefit to children. Holman (1988) is strongly identified with the argument that it is almost always in children's interests to meet their needs through providing improved resources and services for their families. The fact that children can generally be seen to 'develop best' within the natural or biological family is sufficient to endorse an approach to welfare intervention which seeks to counter the effects of social exclusion and maintain children with their families, rather than removing them. 'Prevention' is therefore the ideal. Holman links the principle of preventive measures for specific children 'in need' with broader principles of 'social justice' (Holman, 1988, p. 204), although it could equally easily be argued that it is not always possible to identify *which* specific children are at risk of being removed from their families, so a generalised programme of social investment in families may be required in any case. As Hardiker *et al.* (1991) point out, the particular approach to prevention that will be taken largely depends on the model of intervention which 'holds sway'. Where, for example, principles of social inclusion and equality of opportunity are espoused, it might well be the case that practice will be informed by a holistic commitment to improving children's life chances. The specific example cited by Hardiker *et al.* (1991) is the Pen Green Centre in Corby, Northamptonshire, which combines projects to provide parenting support and meet children's developmental needs with community programmes to enhance the quality of life for families in the wider community.

The Pen Green Centre was one of the initiatives which provided the blueprint for the Sure Start programme, which by 2004 would comprise a network of 524 projects 'helping up to 400,000 children living in disadvantaged areas, including a third of under 4s living in poverty' (Sure Start, 2003a). Sure Start aims to promote opportunities for families, through offering child care, helping children and parents and helping children with special needs, improving support for parents and enhancing their ability to find paid work. In practical terms, this means providing services which are available to and involve 'all local families', promoting the programme actively, and being 'culturally appropriate and sensitive to particular needs'.

The Sure Start model is consistent with the aims of Schedule 2 of the Children Act 1989, and represents an attempt to give substance to the principle of 'empowerment' (Shardlow, 1998; Adams, 2003). Intervention is to be based on principles of inclusion, enabling and voluntarism. Service users are to be encouraged, not just to determine which services they receive, but also to participate in the design and management of provision. As Adams (2003, p. 129) observes, the role of the professional worker in this context becomes one of facilitator and broker, with the aim of building up individual and community resources.

However, a number of issues remain problematic for service providers. Firstly, concerns have been raised about the 'targeted' approach, which identifies communities and groups within communities (teenage mothers, for example: Allen and Dowling, 1998; Social Exclusion Unit, 1999) as problematic in some way. Whilst these groups may receive the benefits of additional investment and services, there remains a risk that they will be stigmatised in some way. As Percy-Smith (2000) observes, targeting will result in 'needy people being missed', whilst at the same time, 'negative perceptions' of identified communities or groups can be exacerbated. Ahmad (1990) notes that this is compounded for black and minority ethnic people who are more likely than the population in general to live in 'disadvantaged' areas. The inherent risk is that in trying to find criteria to justify intervention to provide support and assistance, we require families and children to accept a label which they may experience as demeaning. It is noticeable, for example, that many of those on low incomes do not see themselves as 'poor', nor do they wish to be categorised in this way (Smith, 1990b; Roker, 1998). Tunstill (2000) fears that the anti-oppressive 'rhetoric of social inclusion/ exclusion' can easily spill over into assumptions about the 'underclass', which, in turn, legitimises social engineering and more intrusive and controlling forms of 'service'. This, indeed, may be one of the consequences for those who do not make use of the voluntary options on offer through universal measures such as Sure Start. Some of the Sure Start targets relate to the reduction of harm to children (Melhuish, 2003) which may appear to justify a greater degree of effort to engage 'hard to reach' families, with the risk of becoming 'interfering'.

On the other hand, such targets should act as a reminder that the well-being of children is the underlying objective; there is a risk of assuming that parents can always be seen as a proxy for children's interests. Services which rely on parents 'opting in' may not always be best suited to safeguarding children. The provision of assistance to parents or the family should not deflect attention from the child (Cleaver *et al.*, 1998). The Victoria Climbie Inquiry found evidence that, despite indicators of possible risk to her, one agency, at least, did not distinguish between these and the needs of the family (Laming, 2003, p. 63).

When problems arise, parents may find it increasingly difficult to participate in normal activities and mainstream services (Cleaver *et al.*, 1998, p. 38). The child may slip from view:

> the impact of parental problems on children was not always recognised... [C]hildren's needs may not be responded to appropriately.
> (Cleaver *et al.*, 1998, p. 3)

The need for an integrated approach between adult-focused and child-centred services is stressed here (Cleaver *et al.*, 1998, p. 99).

The tension between competing expectations and responsibilities can also be linked with inadequate resources (Adams, 2003). An acute shortage of provision, results in a recurrent struggle for those seeking to provide universal family support services whilst simultaneously addressing urgent needs and crises. 'Gate-keeping mechanisms' (Tunstill, 2000) may have a distorting effect on the both the form and content of services offered, with children being categorised according to the funding available rather than systematic or professionally applied judgements (see Laming, 2003, p. 74, on the impact of under-funding on decision-making and practice).

Children's rights and 'repressive tolerance'[10]

In the context of children's services, it should perhaps be unsurprising that there is an emerging concern with the need to avoid discriminating against children on the basis of age or 'competence'. This, as we have seen, is associated with a much wider movement aimed at securing user participation and control of services, on the one hand, and a recognition of the rights of children, on the other.

In practice, this has led to an emphasis on securing children's participation in deciding what services they want, how they want them to be provided, and in ensuring their continued involvement. This 'participatory' (O'Kane, 2000) principle has been extended to areas of work such as child protection, which by their nature present real challenges and dilemmas (Cloke and Davies, 1995).

Notably, however, a genuinely anti-oppressive approach to children's services might be expected to start from a 'reframing' of definitions of need, and a prioritising of what is provided according to their own perspectives, rather than those of traditional service providers (Moss and Petrie, 2002). It is argued, for instance, that even the notion of 'children's services' contains some potent connotations, which establish a particular view of the nature of provision. What is delivered may be seen as a technical exercise, where workers are expected to 'follow clearly laid down procedures to produce prescribed outcomes' (Moss and Petrie, 2002, p. 66). Such forms of intervention are associated with a 'narrative' of childhood, which assumes that the child is vulnerable, immature, dependent and 'unfinished'. This, inevitably, creates a passive view of children (Smith, 2000a), which does not attribute them with the capacity to take an active part in shaping services, and controlling decisions made about them. By contrast, in order to be genuinely anti-oppressive, children must be recognised as participants in the design and construction of provision:

> Within our alternative discourse, children are understood as citizens, members of a social group, agents of their own lives (although not free agents...).
>
> (Moss and Petrie, 2002, p. 101)

This means reconceptualising the way in which provision is made for children. As opposed to a consumerist model based on 'services', they argue that it is more important to think of 'children's spaces'. These are places 'out-of-home' where children meet and act together, and experience a wide range of events and activities; crucially, they are places in which children can set and live by their own 'agendas'. This requires, they acknowledge, a complete overhaul of the way in which policies and structures designed for children are conceived. Children should not be 'processed and normalised to a limited set of predetermined ends', and this, in turn, requires a change in the nature of procedures and practice. Staff working with children would need to learn the skills and attributes of 'reflective practice' (see Chapter 8). They must be prepared to collaborate with, and learn from, children in the design and delivery of services, in a process of 'constant critical analysis' (Moss and Petrie, 2002, p. 111), based on relations of mutual respect and equality. Some examples of this developing model of working with children are provided, from Italy and Scotland. Children are thus given the opportunity to respond to potentially oppressive initiatives, such as the banning of ball games (Moss and Petrie, 2002, p. 168), and to contribute to the development of their own facilities, such as improvements to school toilets (p. 169). Not only is it possible to develop a participatory approach, but it may also be the case that involving children in this way can reduce the incidence of mistreatment. Involving children in rule-making and control may help to reduce unacceptable behaviour such as bullying (Petrie *et al.*, 2000), for example. However, it is observed, there may be drawbacks to the pursuit of children's participation as an anti-oppressive goal. Petrie *et al.* (2000) note that involving children in setting rules and maintaining discipline in their own 'spaces' can be uncomfortable for them. First, the very rules of behaviour which children draw up may then be 'turned against them by staff'; and, secondly, the fact of being involved in organisational structures which give them positions of power can be problematic. For those involved as committee members at one after-school club, this resulted in a degree of 'role conflict'. For one young person:

> the worst thing about it was telling staff when other children broke the rules: 'Well it's a bit like grassing up . . .'.
>
> (Petrie *et al.*, 2000, p. 130)

In other respects, too, the concession of power to control outcomes and make decisions may not always appear to be in children's best interests. For example, whilst some children feel empowered by being involved in decision-making meetings in the context of child protection concerns, others appear to find the responsibility of making choices too demanding (Katz, 1995). Thus, one young person is quoted as saying:

> I felt that I influenced the meetings and that my choices were always respected . . . they were making the decisions but I was telling them what to do
>
> (in Katz, 1995, p. 162)

However, for another young person offered the same opportunity to participate in the decision-making forum:

> I'm stuck in the middle, torn between my own foster parents and my own mother.
>
> (in Katz, 1995, p. 163)

Likewise, in the context of separation and divorce, it is apparent that sometimes children and young people can be put in the impossible position of making choices between parents (Bradford and Smith, 1998; also, see Chapter 6). Equally, where domestic violence is involved, children and young people may feel highly ambivalent, and very uncomfortable about being expected to voice an opinion about maintaining or ending contact with a violent father. It is reported that one 15-year-old boy:

> was very unhappy about the way he felt pressurised by a series of court welfare officers' interviews to say he wanted contact when the opposite was the case.
>
> (Mullender *et al.*, 2002, p. 201)

We may perhaps find it helpful to reflect on Marcuse's (Wolff *et al.*, 1969) concept of 'repressive tolerance'. The devolution of control to children and young people may, of itself, contain some hidden traps. First, as we have seen, it may create real tensions and difficulties for them in resolving feelings of ambivalence and guilt – they may feel that they are being asked to take responsibility for choices which should lie with others (family members or agencies, for example). They may also fall victim to assumptions that because power is nominally delegated to them, that they are, in practice, able to exercise it. For example, it has been found that despite the existence of complaints procedures, young people in certain settings, such as foster care, have been unable to access them (Wallis and Frost, 1998). It is important, therefore, to avoid making simplistic assumptions about the desirability of devolving authority to children and young people. It is not automatically desirable or anti-oppressive, and in some cases may compound feelings of help-lessness and isolation.

Dealing with ambiguity

The illustrations considered in this chapter have helped to demonstrate some of the potential challenges in delivering anti-discriminatory or anti-oppressive practice. The notion that this can be prescribed and delivered in straightforward fashion must be tempered by a recognition of competing demands and the contradictory impact of overlapping forms of oppression. Drawing on the value positions we have previously identified, it can be seen that there is a need to identify different dynamics at play, and to avoid superficial judgements. Practice must be sensitive, grounded and based on a systematic approach to inquiry and understanding.

A FRAMEWORK FOR ACTION

Awkward questions and hard choices

The preceding chapters have, effectively, helped to crystallise some important challenges for those working with children. We have seen, first, that the role of values as a motivating force for the provision of children's services is central. Values are both powerful drivers of individual preferences and practice orientations, and they are both implicitly and explicitly incorporated in many of the prescriptive statements which are intended to underpin service delivery. This is notably the case for those in the field of statutory social work, but it is also becoming more prevalent in other areas of service delivery, such as Sure Start and Connexions.

In addition to the service-specific role of values, there are also wider sets of principles deriving from law and policy, through human rights and anti-discriminatory legislation, for example. These instruments provide a mandate for organisational policy, planning and service development – and they are, in many cases, associated with explicit monitoring procedures (see, for example, the Race Relations (Amendment) Act 2000). In addition to these formal expressions of values, we have also observed the impact on policy and procedures of influences and ideological traditions embedded in the broader social terrain.

There is an extensive and influential framework of ideas and beliefs which sets the terms for interventions to promote the well-being of children. Values are, therefore, instruments of social welfare delivery. However, it has also been recognised that these may, when operationalised, come into conflict with one another. This is at least partly due to the unavoidable fact that, in practice, choices will need to be made between contradictory outcomes and competing interests, in situations of imperfect knowledge. The notion of 'empowerment', for example, is both laudable, in the abstract, and problematic in its delivery (Burke and Dalrymple, 2002). The example provided, of the task of empowering a mother with learning difficulties, helps to illustrate this issue. Whilst the ideas of partnership and family support are described as 'central' to service provision for children and families, it is also noted that concerns about protecting children 'create tensions', forcing practitioners into a strategy of continuous risk assessment and risk management, which can be characterised as 'defensive and reactive'. At the same time, service users' trust in practitioners can also be undermined (Cleaver and Freeman, 1995). Equally problematic is that an approach based initially on engaging with and providing resources for the mother may lead to the emergence of concerns about the safety of the children (Macdonald, 2002). The complexities of the situation are compounded by other variables, including social norms and expectations, and the perspectives of other members of the network of service providers. For instance, 'inter-agency sharing of information' may focus on risks and safety issues for the children rather than on the parent's needs and wishes. There appears to be an inherent risk of 'splitting' between value positions, as represented by different professional and personal interests. The consequence may be a lapse into an 'over-zealous' approach. Over-reliance on scrutiny may magnify child protection concerns at the expense of other issues:

> The problem for a practitioner attempting to work from a child-centred perspective is balancing the range of needs identified within the family.
> (Burke and Dalrymple, 2002, p. 59)

By implication, therefore, any one value perspective should not be allowed to dominate at the point of initial engagement and assessment. The idea of 'balance' introduced here is of particular interest because it *seems* to offer a mechanism for resolving practice dilemmas and achieving a workable solution. However, some concerns have been raised about the value of the term 'balance' in this context, since it seems to imply the possibility of an achievable and reasonable middle ground, when this may not be the most appropriate outcome (Harris and Timms, 1993). For instance, the attempt to find a compromise in determining levels of 'contact' between a violent father and his children may be a dangerous route to follow:

> In child-care policy . . . we are not dealing with different commodities 'balanced' thus but with human judgements about how a range of factors should contribute to a decision which is, literally, in imbalance, affording precedence to one set of values over another.
> (Harris and Timms, 1993, p. 36)

We shall return subsequently to the difficult question of 'balance', 'synthesis' or 'compromise', but for the present the important observation to be made is that practitioners must employ a reflective and critical approach, in order to identify conflicting demands or expectations, and to establish a basis for decision-making which avoids making pre-judgements.

Values and critical practice

It has been argued that a 'critical' approach is essential in the task of giving life to core service values, and making it possible to resolve potential conflicts (Dominelli, 2002). This observation is partly a response to the well-documented search over many years for a common set of fixed principles as the basis for action. The work of Biestek (1961), for example, is acknowledged as a pioneering example of this kind of thinking:

> The most commonly recognised values in social work emanate from Biestek (1961) and consist of the following:
>
> • individualisation
> • purposeful expression of feelings
> • controlled emotional involvement
> • non-judgemental attitude
> • self-determination
> • confidentiality.
>
> (Dominelli, 2002, p. 17)

Much subsequent thinking on the question of values in human services has originated from this starting point. It has generated critical responses as to its content (it is said to be ethnocentric, for instance; Dominelli, 2002). It is also the case that fundamental challenges arise from the demands of putting into practice abstract ideals. The principle of 'self-determination', for instance, is difficult to challenge, but is also 'very difficult to understand in any absolute form' (Horne, 1999, p. 13). As Dominelli observes:

> If we are asked whether respecting the person is a key social work value, the question is cast in a decontextualised form and it is hard to imagine a social worker who would not endorse it. However, posing the question in terms of practising values in context, the answer would be more nuanced and complex.
>
> (Dominelli, 2002, p. 17)

The illustration she provides is that of a sex offender (who could be a child), where those responsible for working with that individual might seek to differentiate between the individual (who should be treated with respect and whose rights to self-determination must be acknowledged), and his/her offending behaviour, which must be controlled. Whilst Dominelli argues that this is a 'mythical' distinction, it nonetheless enables the practitioner to maintain a professional approach to intervention, and to work with the service user, irrespective of her/his personal views. Whilst it may be difficult to see why this distinction is characterised as illusory, it does illustrate an important quality of practitioners in children's services. They:

> have to become skilful mental acrobats who can juggle contradictory positions with ease when it comes to putting their values into practice.
>
> (Dominelli, 2002, p. 18)

For her, this is not simply a matter of acquiring circus skills, however. The approach to be taken needs to be grounded in the principles of 'critical practice'. According to Lishman (1998), the ability to think critically and reflect on our work (and on our own views and preconceptions) is an essential quality of the skilled practitioner. Adams (2002) argues that the application of this principle is no easy matter, since many of the systems and structures within which child care professionals operate are not conducive to original thinking, or the design of creative solutions which might, themselves, have an empowering effect. Nevertheless, such a strategy is both possible and desirable, in his view (but, see Jones (2001) for a more pessimistic account of the potential for positive practice). 'Practising critically' is an iterative process which 'links theory and action'. Practice should not be based on routine proceduralism or reactive responses to crisis situations, where the preservation of core values may be problematic:

> critical practitioners are engaged in and committed to the struggle to develop their practice through a questioning rather than a defensive approach.
>
> (Adams, 2002, p. 83)

Fook (2002) describes this as a process whereby the 'reflective practitioner' takes a questioning approach to knowledge obtained through observation and reflection. This enables the practitioner to identify different possible constructions of what is 'known', which, in turn, provides a basis for developing responses which are 'inclusive, artistic and intuitive', and are responsive to the specific circumstances of each intervention. For Adams (2002), there are a number of elements, or stages, in developing a critical approach:

- engaging with clients;
- engaging with ourselves;
- engaging with knowledge; and
- engaging with paradoxes and dilemmas.

Thus, for example, as suggested earlier, the context, including both structures and belief systems, is of crucial importance in providing us with an insight into the forces which shape our prior orientation to intervention. As we have seen, value positions, and some of the influences which underpin them, can have a significant influence on the assumptions which underlie children's services. The long running tension, for instance, between the aims of providing child care either as a developmental resource for children, or as a means of enabling parents to take up or keep employment is reflected in the forms and diversity of services offered in this service area.

Not only must we adopt a questioning approach to the operational environment, but we must also, according to Adams (2002), be 'reflexive'; that is, we must also take account of our own 'starting points', and, in particular, our untutored feelings and emotional responses to particular situations. Our beliefs clearly have the potential to influence our practice, and we must therefore be willing to critically assess and modify them.

In addition, our understandings should be informed by an open and enquiring approach to 'knowledge', both what counts as knowledge (epistemology) and how it should be interpreted (hermeneutics). The evidence and information resources available to practitioners are continually expanding, and offer ever-changing insights. Whilst Frost (2002) offers a note of caution about treating all 'knowledge' at face value, or privileging certain types of research evidence, notable advances have been made by the adoption of ideas from new and emerging sources. Adams (2002) cites the example of feminism and its insights as a major influence on changing perceptions of the nature of family relationships (see, for example, Barrett and McIntosh, 1982). The ambiguous and transient quality of family forms has become much more apparent as a result.

The importance of 'engaging with practice' is also highlighted. Interventions which aspire to the 'critical' ideal themselves need to be informed by certain principles, such as empathy, a sense of purpose and a commitment to change. Distinctions need to be made between strategies which are ungrounded, partial or unsystematic and those which develop a coherent approach, based on a comprehensive under-standing of the service user's expectations and needs. We might, for instance, view the development of an assessment framework for children in need (Department of Health *et al.*, 2000) as an attempt to operationalise an inclusive strategy of this kind. Critical practice is necessarily holistic:

> Critical practice is not just an adjective bolted onto practice to give it the appearance of professionalism and respectability but purposeful, creative, assertive, committed to change, the promotion of people's rights and the elimination of injustice.
>
> (Adams, 2002, p. 91)

Whilst this represents a powerful call to arms, it does not help to any great extent with the need for critical practice also to meet the challenge of resolving 'paradoxes and dilemmas'. We need to recognise that in some situations, straightforward solutions are impractical, and in other circumstances, we may be forced to 'take sides', opting to achieve one goal at the expense of others. Certain strategies may be adopted for dealing with uncertainty, however. First, it is important to take account of all available perspectives and evidence on the issue in question, rather than, say, accepting only the beliefs or perceptions of the most powerful participants. This may, in turn, lead to insights which enable the practitioner to 'reframe' the situation, as in the example of a disabled young person who was given a 'voice' as a result of the perceptive intervention of a student social worker (Sapey, 2002). In this instance, the rights of the child/young person were acknowledged and acted upon, as against the prevailing service strategy based on a 'family support' perspective, which had confined the young person to a day centre which he did not wish to attend.

It is also important, in taking a critical approach, to accept that there may not be available 'easy' or 'best' solutions. It may rather be a matter of 'holding on' to unresolved tensions, instead of moving towards premature closure, and falling prey to pressures from outside to resolve difficult situations, make firm decisions and close case files. Jones (2001), for example, has identified these pressures as a real threat to creative, developmental practice.

'Grounding' critical practice

Whilst the merits of a critical approach are clear, it is important to be aware of possible criticisms. These will lead us, in turn, to consider the need to 'ground' our work, in the light of specific, concrete value positions, such as those explored in previous chapters.

Fook (2002) is very helpful in this respect, both opening up the real possibilities offered by critical practice, and, appropriately, offering some reflective criticisms as well. She explicitly links the idea of critical practice with the emergence of postmodernist thinking, suggesting that there are many 'points of similarity', including the recognition that knowledge is not just 'given', but also comes from self-reflection. Postmodernism is particularly helpful in recognising the multiplicity of perspectives likely to be encountered in the practice setting, and in recognising and validating diversity. This helps to break down perceived hierarchies of knowledge and leads to a more creative and varied approach to practice:

> The critique (deconstruction) of mainstream practices potentially upends taken for granted hierarchies and power differences, and allows for the possibility of new forms of empowerment.
>
> (Fook, 2002, p. 14)

However, the very fact that this approach denies a privileged position to any particular perspective or way of knowing also generates some of the problems encountered by postmodernism. As Fook acknowledges, the fact that it appears to consciously eschew the adoption of a moral stance causes some problems for those in practice who are likely to be committed to a strong sense of social justice and equal treatment. The loss of any clear set of principles leaves a kind of moral vacuum, which may, in turn, inhibit, rather than encourage positive action. The post-modernist analysis 'does not provide guidance about appropriate or desirable knowledge and ways to act' (Fook, 2002, p. 15). This argument can be extended to critical practice, in the sense that it encourages welfare professionals to adopt a spirit of challenge towards accepted forms of intervention, but may not offer much of a guide to alternative strategies. In questioning standardised and routine procedures, there also needs to be a sense of purpose, and a willingness to put constructive alternatives in place. Fook's solution is to seek an accommodation between postmodern and structural forms of analysis, so that a critical approach is *situated*, and is able to engage with concrete systems and distributions of power. For critical practice to be effective and relevant, it must, therefore, be sited within an understanding of the social order in which it is constructed and maintained. Creative and progressive practice depend on this integrated approach to understanding the needs and interests of service users:

it is through a process of dialogue and interaction, self-reflection and analysis, in conjunction with knowledge obtained empirically, that an understanding of how power relations are specifically expressed and used in a particular situation will be achieved.

(Fook, 2002, p. 18)

It seems clear from this that effective practice depends on an ability to link critical analysis with a perspective on the meaning of structures, ideas and processes which create the social context for service users' experiences and aspirations. Whilst the merits of critical thinking are clear, this must also be 'grounded'.

The disciplines of 'grounded theory' (Glaser and Strauss, 1967) provide one means by which we can begin to bridge the gap between critical analysis, and generating ideas for practice. Whilst the principles of grounded theory were originally generated to inform the develop-ment of qualitative research, they also offer some valuable pointers for the task of developing a systematic approach to intervention. The grounded approach to theory generation is explicitly opposed to the empiricist approach of applying preconceived ideas and assumptions, but rather lets our understanding emerge from what is observed. This, it is argued, is not only a more considered approach, but it also fits more accurately what is actually going on when we engage with an analytical problem:

Theory as process, we believe, renders quite well the reality of social inter-action and its structural context.

(Glaser and Strauss, 1967, p. 32)

Importantly for a critical perspective, this approach is based on allow-ing theory to emerge from the social context, rather than finding our analysis unnecessarily constrained by prior assumptions. Supporting this general strategy, Glaser and Strauss offer a number of techniques and methods to support the process of information gathering, assessment and analysis. This, they argue, is important in order to avoid the accusation that their findings and conclusions might be based on arbitrary choices and speculation. They suggest, for example, 'theoretical sampling', whereby the process of observation and data collection generates ideas and possibilities which, in turn, inspire the next stage of the investigation, which can include more systematic information gathering. This is important in the context of practice in children's services precisely because it avoids premature closure:

data collected according to a pre-planned routine are more likely to force the analyst into irrelevant directions and harmful pitfalls.

(Glaser and Strauss, 1967, p. 49)

Also of value in this context is the suggestion of a comparative approach to investigation, whereby the evidence collected can be utilised to generate a series of 'theoretical categories', which provide the basis for comparison and detailed understanding. This, in effect, is the role posited for 'value positions' in the present context. Emerging evidence and information can be categorised in a way which illuminates alternative explanations, and leads to the generation of practice options.

The starting point

For practitioners, however, the starting point must be an understanding of their own perspective and its possible impact on their own judge-ments and actions. Lishman (1998) points out that there is always likely to be a personal factor which shapes professional motivation; but, she cautions, this should not be the 'driving force' in determining practice.

Carrying out this exercise (Table 8.1) is valuable for a number of reasons. First, it does enable us to see ourselves as practitioners who carry certain beliefs and assumptions into the work setting. Our own preferences, both in general and in specific situations of conflict (see Chapter 6) are important elements to be 'factored in' to our evaluative and decision-making processes, since they are likely sources of bias and may inhibit us from considering all available possibilities in any given situation.

As we have already observed, for example, a preference for family support measures over statutory child protection procedures, combined with the 'rule of optimism' may lead to an unjustifiably positive view of problematic and dangerous circumstances:

> We fear that their attitude in regarding the parents of children in care as the clients, rather than the children in their own right, may be widespread...We...have detected this attitude which is the negation of any authoritarian role in the enforcement of Care Orders...Jasmine [Beckford]'s fate illustrates all too clearly the disastrous consequences...
>
> (Blom-Cooper, 1985, p. 294)

This is not to suggest that an attitude which favours supporting families over statutory measures of intervention is always 'misguided', but that it is important to recognise this preference in oneself and

Table 8.1 'Where do I stand?'

Families should be left to look after themselves	1	2	3	4	Our first priority should be to ensure the safety of children
Families should be left to look after themselves	1	2	3	4	The state should provide support to families to improve children's well-being
Families should be left to look after themselves	1	2	3	4	Children should have the final say in how they are brought up
Our first priority should be to ensure the safety of children	1	2	3	4	The state should provide support to families to improve children's well-being
Our first priority should be to ensure the safety of children	1	2	3	4	Children should have the final say in how they are brought up
The state should provide support to families to improve children's well-being	1	2	3	4	Children should have the final say in how they are brought up

Note: For each pair of statements, you should locate your own preference on one side or the other. It is important to make a clear and considered choice, as this is likely to reflect your 'starting point'.

others when potential conflicts arise or difficult judgements have to be made.

The recognition that we all have 'starting points' illustrates another important consideration, and this is the 'situated' nature of values. They are based in experience and ideology, and they are negotiated rather than fixed. Thus, for example, differences in orientation between social groupings and professional interests are also significant (Leathard, 2003), particularly in a context where inter-professional working is becoming increasingly the norm (Department of Health *et al.*, 1999). It is argued, for example, that professional differences partly reflect the fact that career choices derive from personal values (Rawson, 1994), which are then compounded by differential training regimes and occupational socialisation.

Social work students, for instance, have been found to show a distinct preference for value positions which emphasise children's rights and family support.[11] However, alternative perspectives are likely to predominate in other professional circles and in the wider public sphere. We have already observed that specific organisations are associated with and campaign in support of specific viewpoints, and it is also clear that the media and public opinion may well be located at particular points in the spectrum (see, for example, Franklin, 2002b). These, however, are not merely interesting observations, but they may also have direct relevance for practice. Both in general and in specific individual cases, it is important to make some sort of assessment of service users' preferences, given that these are likely to be formed on the basis of a quite different range of inputs than those of professionals in children's services. Values are negotiated rather than simply applied, and the status of 'expert' is of little value if it is negated by the commonsense (and equally valid) perceptions of other participants whose views are shaped by rather different discourses.

The implications for practice here can be illustrated by the events in Cleveland in 1987–88, where, whatever the merits of the situation, the absence of support for protective interventions, and the dominance of the 'laissez-faire' perspective amongst other professional groups, some sections of the media and community groups, critically hampered the possibilities of intervening effectively in the interests of children:

> It is unacceptable that the disagreements and failure of communication of adults should be allowed to obscure the needs of children both long and short term in so sensitive, difficult and important a field.
>
> (Butler-Sloss, 1988, p. 244)

The implication of this is not that professional practice should be dictated or circumscribed by the anticipated response of other participants, but that the presence, and the possible validity, of other perspectives as well as our own must be accommodated in the investigative, assessment and decision-making process. Values should be negotiated, explored and achieved in the practice setting, although this will not always obviate the need to make hard choices.

Balance, synthesis, compromise or choice?

The need to take account of divergent 'starting points' also illustrates another challenge for the delivery of appropriate services, which is to resolve differences of perspective. Value conflicts are inevitable in practice, and they often revolve around strongly held views and powerful positions:

> While each perspective has a degree of internal coherence, and while each
> may be identified as more influential than others in actual policy and
> practice at different times, the 'real world' of such policy and practice...
> always represents an uneasy and incoherent synthesis of views.
>
> (Fox Harding, 1997, p. 171)

The search for 'balance' has been a sustained effort, and it is notable
that the Children Act 1989, for example, offers legitimacy to a range of
perspectives. For example, it appears to 'proceed in two directions
at once' (Fox Harding, 1997, p. 186), offering improved protection for
children and, at the same time, a greater emphasis on the rights of
parents in family support. It is possible to see this either as a 'denial of
conflict', or as a genuine attempt to achieve 'balance':

> What will be achieved, it may be argued, is not simply a redistribution of
> muddle but a genuinely more effective solution correcting tendencies to
> both over- and under-react...
>
> (Fox Harding, 1997, p. 186)

The aspiration towards reaching an accommodation between alternative
positions is reflected elsewhere. This has been a prominent feature of
the 'refocusing' debate which has sought to bring about an alignment
between 'safeguarding' and 'promoting the welfare' of children, that is,
reconciling Sections 17 and 47 of the Children Act 1989 (Department of
Health, 1995a). Significant guidance documents such as *Working Together
to Safeguard Children* emphasise the importance of integrating perspectives:

> Effective measures to safeguard children cannot be seen in isolation from
> the wider range of support and services available to meet the needs of
> children and families.
>
> (Department of Health, 1999, p. 2)

Although tensions are acknowledged between families and professionals,
it is argued that a balance can be achieved between promoting family
autonomy and offering services to meet the needs of children
(Aldgate and Statham, 2001, p. 42). The aims of safeguarding children
and promoting their well-being should not be seen as contradictory
according to this perspective. However, it is also acknowledged
that this leaves some tensions unresolved. In this sense, it could be
argued that policy and guidance documents simply restate a perennial
problem:

what are the factors to be weighed in giving parents 'one more chance' or in grasping the nettle and deciding which children will be best served by growing up in another family ...?

(Aldgate and Statham, 2001, p. 42)

It has been shown that the attempt to achieve balance has sometimes led to indecision and inertia. As far back as the 1970s, when 'drift' was identified as a problem in the care system (Rowe and Lambert, 1973), this could be attributed to an over-optimistic aspiration to see children returned to their families, which may have inhibited the making of alternative plans (Rowe and Lambert, 1973; Parker, 1999). Equally, it has sometimes been difficult for social work professionals to judge when to intervene, and which set of values should take precedence. One case which 'could have dragged on' demonstrates the professional challenges involved:

You would visit and the baby was fine but everything else you saw made you concerned. This young and very immature couple seem to be waiting for us [social services] to say, 'enough is enough'.

(Social worker quoted in Hardiker and Barker, 1994, p. 47)

In another case in the same study, involving 'an ethnic minority single parent' with mental health problems, it took over a year for decisive action to be taken in the form of an Interim Care Order application. This appears to have been partly because the search for balance took precedence, even though 'various forms of intervention were attempted without success' (Hardiker and Barker, 1994, p. 47).

Competing priorities?

We can identify other contexts where the notion of 'balance' may be unhelpful. For example, the question of the appropriate level of contact between children and absent fathers may also generate assumptions that this is a matter of negotiating a reasonable compromise. Beliefs about the inherent value of the 'natural' family may lead to contact arrangements being made which do not offer protection to children. It is reported that contact can be used as a route to the perpetration of further 'abuse and aggression' (Mullender *et al.*, 2002, p. 202), which impacts on children as well as their mothers.

The problem for child welfare professionals may well be one of negotiating different perspectives, reflecting sometimes deeply embedded societal assumptions or organisational imperatives, in challenging situations, where the way forward may not be clear. This is particularly the case for those working in what I have termed 'hybrid' organisations (Smith, 1995) where there is a requirement to satisfy a diverse range of interests. Family centres in the voluntary sector, for example, have been found to reflect a real diversity of practice (Smith, 1996). Similarly a range of new initiatives, including Sure Start, Children's Centres, Children's Trusts and Connexions are also likely to encounter some of the same tensions, as they become integral to the service landscape. These new organisational forms are likely to engender differing and potentially competing priorities for action in children's services. It is in the arena of statutory agency practice, however, that the challenges are most acute. Local authorities will be expected to provide effective child protection services to support families, and, increasingly, to incorporate a strategy for promoting children's rights. Whilst conflicts are inevitable at the level of organisational strategy and spending, so also will they be manifested in direct practice. Laming (2003) has already rejected the argument for creating a structural division between protective and supportive services, arguing that this assumes a much greater capacity to distinguish between different 'types' of case than is achievable, and may thus be counterproductive. Nevertheless, for practitioners, the issue remains one of making informed decisions about how to intervene.

It is possible to illustrate this by revisiting the case example (Chapter 6) of the possible adoption of a child of parents with learning difficulties. Each value position offers the potential for insight and understanding, but there may also be a choice to be made between them (Table 8.2).

Thus, consideration can be given to a range of key questions under each of the value positions, and the nature and content of our observations can also enable us to make a judgement about the relative weighting to apply in the specific context – and determine our actions accordingly.

Considered decisions: using value positions creatively

At this point, it will be helpful to reflect briefly on the rationale for applying the kind of framework offered by 'value positions' to the task faced by practitioners in delivering services for children. In particular, it is important to stress the importance of bringing reference points to bear on our assessments and interventions in a context of rapid and significant structural, ideological and personal change.

It has been argued, justifiably, that the context is one which has come to be dominated by the rhetoric of 'modernisation' (Moss and Petrie, 2002). There is a sense in which a number of transformations in ideas and practice have been implemented which have combined

Table 8.2 Weighing up the options

	Laissez-faire: family integrity	Child protection	Family support	Children's rights
A couple, both of whom have learning difficulties are expecting a baby. The mother has already had one child, who was subsequently adopted.	Are we making discriminatory assumptions about this family not being 'normal'? *How are we applying our thresholds for intervention ('no order')?*	What sort of risks are evident? *Are these risks short, medium or long-term?* *How will specific needs be met, e.g. attachment?*	What resources are available to promote 'good parenting'? *Have the parents' rights/service needs been considered separately?* *What about 'kinship' care/ support?*	What are the child's rights in relation to identity? *What factors such as culture and religion should be considered?*

to reshape our understanding and experience of interventions with children. According to Moss and Petrie (2002), these changes appear to be driven by the search for a 'technical' solution to the need to manage the impact of market capitalism on children and families, whilst also ensuring the preparation of the next generation of responsible, wage-earning, child-rearing adults. For them, however, this project has a number of flaws, including the fragmentation and 'compartmental-isation' of services between agencies, age groups, identified 'needs' and different user perspectives. The problem, they believe, lies in the influence of a 'dominant discourse about children', characterised by three central tenets:

> that children are the *private* responsibility of parents; that children are *passive* dependents; and that parents are *consumers* of marketised services for children.
>
> (Moss and Petrie, 2002, p. 5)

However, this, in itself, may underestimate the complexity of the challenge facing those working with children. It is not simply a matter of working within one dominant pattern of ideas and organisational structures, but of being able to understand and integrate a range of competing and equally plausible viewpoints, as we have seen. Fox Harding (1997), importantly, shows that different belief systems do appear to gain greater influence in certain historical phases of child care policy. As she observes, a number of factors combine to create a more favourable climate for specific ideologies of child welfare at particular points in time. Thus, we must take account of 'social and economic change', government policy, the influence of interest groups (such as PAIN and the CLC), specific 'scandals' and the public response, as well as the impact of dominant 'paradigms' (Kuhn, 1970) amongst the professions involved in children's services. The impact of change and the diversity of potential influences are important in shaping the context for practice:

> Many change factors could be listed...The relationship of all these variables to child care problems and the need for state intervention is complex...but the general point is that child care problems and the response to them do not arise in a social vacuum.
>
> (Fox Harding, 1997, p. 178)

However, she makes it clear that whilst one perspective may dominate at any one time, others will be in evidence. Negotiating the inconsistencies and competing demands between them will remain a challenge for those delivering services. Thus, for example, in child care terms, the 1980s and 1990s are seen as a period of 'great complexity', epitomised by the Children Act 1989, which incorporates and, indeed, strengthens all four value positions to some degree.

The origins of this complexity do not lie just in the differential flow in the currents of opinion over time. They are also to be found in the way in which the changing nature of children's services impacts on professional thinking, and the contested nature of orthodoxy itself. As we have observed, major shifts in government policy and the profile of expenditure on children will have a corresponding impact on the orientation of those responsible for developing and delivering services.

Notably, the establishment of the Children and Young People's Unit provides formal, 'official' endorsement of the importance of hearing and acting on children's voices. The expectation is that this will infuse all aspects of service delivery for children and young people, and not just new initiatives or experimental projects:

The best services for children and young people are already actively engaging with them and their families, so that policies and services are designed around their individual needs. We want this to be the norm.

(Children and Young People's Unit, 2001b, p. 27)

At the same time, Sure Start has become the primary vehicle for delivering family assistance and developmental services for children 'in need', effectively becoming the mechanism for meeting the requirements of Part III and Schedule 2 of the Children Act 1989, at the expense of local authorities. Sure Start, in turn, is strongly imbued with a 'family support' ideology, emphasising the importance of working with parents to meet children's needs:

> Every family should get access to a range of services that will deliver better outcomes for both children and parents...
>
> But not the same service for everyone. Families have distinctly different needs... Services should recognise and respond to these varying needs.
>
> (Sure Start, 2003b)

By contrast, the policy stream flowing from the *Quality Protects* (Department of Health, 1999) initiative utilised the language of vulnerability and child protection, effectively re-emphasising this as the core approach for those in statutory social services departments. The supporting documentation seeks to redefine the way in which the term 'children in need' is understood, encompassing those who are 'highly vulnerable' and requiring protective services:

> Quality Protects is about improving the management and delivery of services for children for whom social services have taken on direct responsibilities: children who are looked after by local authorities, children in the child protection system and other children in need requiring active support from social services.
>
> (Department of Health, 1999, par. 12)

Thus, a 'protectionist' agenda is effectively built into the way in which services are characterised.

The emergence of strands in service development which operate in parallel, and which reflect clear ideological differences (especially if we also include the essentially *private* arena of children's day care; Moss and Petrie, 2002), creates some very real challenges for those who are engaged in the task of delivering coherent interventions to children, young people and their families whose own life trajectories sometimes traverse these service boundaries.

The separation of distinct aspects of practice into mutually exclusive service systems may seem superficially attractive, but it has been questioned as something of an arbitrary exercise. The report of the Victoria Climbie Inquiry (Laming, 2003) expresses this view strongly, in arguing against the establishment of a 'National Child Protection Agency':

> It is not possible to separate the protection of children from wider support to families. Indeed, often the best protection for a child is achieved by the timely intervention of family support services.
>
> (Laming, 2003, p. 6)

The separation of these functions into different agencies is, it is stated, 'neither practical nor desirable'.

Despite this observation, the fact is that there already exists a *de facto* separation of functions and practices between different types of children's services. Different perspectives, different organisational dynamics and different operational imperatives already impact on the priorities accorded to specific aspects of intervention to meet children's needs. The impact of organisational boundaries has been noted previously (Rawson, 1994), but we should also be aware of the professional implications of alternative perspectives which may operate within agencies or disciplines.

In taking account of difference, practice must achieve several tasks for which the values framework identified in this book provides a helpful basis:

- avoiding tramlines;
- accepting and exploring distinctive viewpoints;
- resting assumptions and decisions;
- remaining child-centred.

Avoiding tramlines

The previous discussion will have shown that, whatever our work setting, it is likely that we will approach the task with a series of preconceptions. These may be based in our own personal values, they may be dictated by the organisational culture (assumptions which come to prevail in an established team, for example), or they may be dictated by procedural requirements. Whichever of these applies, it will still be important in addressing individual circumstances and needs to consider alternative possibilities, and invite contributions from other perspectives.

Accepting and exploring distinctive viewpoints

The very changeability of what is accepted as conventional practice in children's services requires practitioners to retain a spirit of flexibility and exploration. The task of incorporating challenging perspectives into our approach must be accepted. Thus, for example, it is important to explore and try to give substance to the principle of 'partnership' in the course of child protection assessments. Equally, the need to listen to children as distinct interests, even in the context of supportive services such as Sure Start will ensure that differences of perspective between children and parents can be identified and acted upon.

Testing assumptions and decisions

As I have already argued, the task of achieving 'balance' or 'synthesis' between perspectives is not easy. However, the process of negotiation or comparison between competing positions does provide the opportunity to test our assumptions fairly rigorously. It is important to bring each of the value positions to bear in any situation where significant decisions are likely to be made. For example, the application of principles of laissez-faire and family support in relation to a child who is at risk of significant harm and needs to be accommodated may open up the possibility of 'kinship care' (Broad, 2001) as a placement option.

Remaining child-centred

Perhaps most importantly, an approach which is flexible in applying different perspectives is one which is most likely to achieve the objective of being child-centred. As noted in previous chapters, each of the positions identified has elements which are beneficial to children, and it is therefore important that each is taken into consideration in any practice setting. This is encapsulated for us by the evidence of the limited progress made thus far in taking account of children's own wishes and feelings in the context of domestic violence (the 'children's rights' perspective):

> we are still not listening to children sufficiently...
> A little child-centredness can go a long way...
>
> (Mullender *et al.*, 2002, p. 231)

To conclude this discussion of the practical application of a framework based on identified 'positions', it is perhaps important to reiterate a number of key observations. First, there are a number of distinct perspectives which flow through the development and delivery of children's services. These viewpoints are, in turn, likely to be associated with specific interests, both within and beyond the immediate focus of intervention. The partial nature of these interests is likely to lead to certain preconceptions about the appropriate nature of intervention in specific circumstances. Because of this, it is important for those in practice to identify and negotiate the implications of each perspective in reaching decisions and intervening to 'safeguard and promote' children's welfare. This is a necessary, but constructive and purposeful challenge:

> The reflective practitioner needs to be aware of... tensions and contradictions, in order to understand her role in relation to users and to realise that she is both a publicly paid professional with some 'expert' knowledge whose aim is to change and control behaviour, and a fellow human being whose aim is to relate to and empathise with the user.
>
> (Banks, 2001b, p. 83)

Hindsight may show that professional judgements can be open to question (for example, Laming, 2003). The response should not be to seek absolute certainty in every conceivable case, but more modestly (and realistically) to establish a coherent basis for taking justifiable decisions which have the potential to improve the lives of children. The framework offered here is one mechanism for enabling practitioners to achieve this aim. Rather than simply stating these as opposed and contradictory positions, the objective has been to encourage a willingness to engage with them, to acknowledge one's own preferences, and then to develop a considered and rounded strategy for action in the best interests of children.

Conclusion: THE ROAD AHEAD

The changing terrain

In seeking to provide a kind of route map for resolving complex challenges and conflicting expectations, one recurrent problem facing service providers is that of dealing with change. This is made particularly acute by the turbulent climate which has characterised children's services for a number of years. For those attracted by postmodernist arguments, this is perhaps only to be expected as a consequence of global dynamics which are beyond our control. On the other hand, this perhaps also serves to re-emphasise the importance of having the available means of bringing intelligibility and order to the service settings which are relevant to children and impact on their lives. It seems likely that competing agendas will continue to exert contradictory demands on professional judgements and powers to act.

In particular, the field of children's services is subject to considerable upheaval as a result of recent government initiatives, including the transfer of ministerial responsibilities from the Department of Health to the Department for Education and Skills in 2003. Associated with this has been the initiation of a programme of reforms which is intended to transform child welfare. Whilst this has been inspired to a considerable extent by the Victoria Climbie inquiry (Laming, 2003; Secretary of State for Health et al., 2003), this is not the only 'driver' of change. Different strands of thought can therefore be identified in the reforms package:

> The policies set out in the Green Paper [*Every Child Matters*] are designed both to protect children and maximise their potential. It sets out a framework for services that cover children and young people from birth to 19 living in England. It aims to reduce the numbers of children who

experience educational failure, engage in anti-social behaviour, suffer from ill-health, or become teenage parents.

(Chief Secretary to the Treasury, 2003, p. 5)

The intention is to create a network of children's services which 'addresses' risk within the context of universal services to the benefit of all children. Child protection and family support agendas will be integrated.

In terms of the alternative value positions, there are some interesting developments associated with the government's strategy. Despite the document's title (*Every Child Matters*), little attention is paid to the needs of children and families in general, unlike the government's previous venture into this territory, *Supporting Families* (Home Office, 1999). The focus of concern appears to have shifted in the aftermath of the Victoria Climbie inquiry, and the tone has become decidedly more interventionist. This is perhaps best typified by the planned 'information hub' and 'common assessment framework' (Chief Secretary to the Treasury, 2003, p. 51), which will act as the mechanism for sharing concerns and triggering early action where children may be at risk. Whilst this conjures up similar echoes of Foucault (1979) to current practices within youth justice (Smith, 2003), it also suggests a shift of the parameters for decision-making and intervention. State paternalism appears to be making a significant move centre stage. However, this does not invalidate other perspectives, and may generate real fears for those who believe in a spirit of genuine partnership with families (Tunstill, 2000).

Not only is there a continuing challenge in adapting practice to changing demands at the level of policy and strategy, but the changing organisational context also creates its own peculiar dynamics. The shape of children's services is undergoing fundamental change, with recent years seeing the emergence of Sure Start, Children's Trusts, Youth Offending Teams, Connexions and a series of short-term targeted programmes (such as 'On Track', Quality Protects and the Children's Fund). Other trends should not go unrecognised, too, such as the influence of 'marketisation' (Smith *et al.*, 2002) and the expansion in the use of privately provided services for children (in the early years and the residential sector, notably). These are not merely shifts in the structural and logistical arrangements for service provision; they also carry implications for the way we think about and utilise services.

Many involved in the direct provision of children's services feel themselves under pressure (Jones, 2001), and the risk is that responses become deprofessionalised and reactive. In this context 'what works'

(McNeish *et al.*, 2002) takes on a different and rather more pragmatic ethos than is ascribed to it in the research literature.

Despite this, it remains centrally important that decisions and interventions are based on the application of professional judgements and values of the kind which have been discussed here. The importance of considered judgement, based in a grounded understanding of the issues, cannot be overstated. The aim of this book has been to provide some ideas and strategies to assist in the application of skilled and informed assessments in working with children. The core principles and value positions which we have considered will remain central to children's interests, and they will therefore also remain relevant to the varied and changing exigencies of practice. In this sense, they will continue to provide a way through, round or beyond some of the more immediate distractions arising from media alarms, abrupt policy shifts or organisational upheavals. The underlying purpose of providing supportive, empowering and effective services for children remains constant and enduring.

NOTES

Keeping it in the family: 'laissez-faire' and minimal intervention

1. More recently, attempts have been made to resuscitate PAIN (PAIN, 2003).

Rights and empowerment in children's services

2. At the time of writing, only two states (Somalia and the USA) have declined to ratify the UN Convention.
3. In contrast to the position in England, this was acted upon and implemented almost immediately.
4. By 2004, legislation was in progress to give England its own Children's Commissioner.

Of discourses and dilemmas

5. The place of Safety Order provided for under the Children and Young Persons Act 1969 was superseded by the Emergency Protection Order in 1989, partly as a result of the Cleveland case.
6. Murray's use of this pejorative term may give some indication of 'where he is coming from'.
7. Health and Social Services and Social Security Adjudications Act 1983.

Values and anti-discriminatory practice

8. Following Thompson (2001), this chapter will use the terms 'anti-discriminatory' and 'anti-oppressive' practice interchangeably, although it is recognised that there may be room for debate on this point, and that there is not always an absolute equivalence between them.
9. Whilst the terms themselves are a matter of some debate (Kirton, 2000), the use of 'black', 'minority ethnic' and 'Asian' here generally follow the sources used.

10. The phrase 'repressive tolerance' was coined by Marcuse (Wolff *et al.*, 1969), to alert us to the possibility that freedom may, in some respects, be disempowering.

A framework for action

11. This was an exercise carried out by the present author with a group of child and family social work students shortly after the beginning of their course.

BIBLIOGRAPHY

Adams, R. (2002) 'Developing critical practice in social work' in Adams, R., Dominelli, L. and Payne, M. (eds) *Critical Practice in Social Work*, Basingstoke, Palgrave, pp. 83–95.

—— (2003) *Social Work and Empowerment* (3rd edn), Basingstoke, Palgrave.

Adcock, M. (2001) 'The core assessment: how to synthesise information and make judgements' in Horwath, J. (ed.) *The Child's World*, London, Jessica Kingsley, pp. 75–97.

Ahmad, B. (1990) *Black Perspectives in Social Work*, Birmingham, Venture Press.

Aldgate, J. and Statham, J. (2001) *The Children Act Now: Messages from Research*, London, The Stationery Office.

Allard, A., Brown, G. and Smith, R. (1994) *The Way It Is*, London, The Children's Society.

Allen, I. and Dowling, S. (1998) *Teenage Mothers*, London, Policy Studies Institute.

Allen, N. (1998) *Making Sense of the Children Act* (3rd edn), Chichester, Wiley.

Althusser, L. (1977) *Lenin and Philosophy and Other Essays*, London, Verso.

Amphlett, S. (1992) 'System abuse and gatekeeping' in Office for Public Management and National Institute for Social Work (eds) *The Strategic Management of Child Protection*, London, OPM/NISW.

Aries, P. (1962) *Centuries of Childhood*, London, Cape.

Audit Commission (1994) *Seen but not Heard*, London, HMSO.

Baher, E., Hyman, C., Jones, C., Jones, R., Kerr, A. and Mitchell, R. (1976) *At Risk: An Account of the Work of the Battered Child Research Department, NSPCC*, London, Routledge & Kegan Paul.

Ball, C. (1990) 'The Children Act 1989: origins, aims and current concerns' in Carter, P., Jeffs, T. and Smith, M. (eds) *Social Work and Social Welfare Yearbook 2*, Buckingham, Open University Press, pp. 1–13.

Ball, C. and McDonald, A. (2002) *Law for Social Workers*, Aldershot, Ashgate.

Banks, N. (2001a) 'Assessing children and families who belong to minority ethnic groups' in Horwath, J. (ed.) *The Child's World*, London, Jessica Kingsley, pp. 140–149.

Banks, S. (2001b) *Ethics and Values in Social Work*, Basingstoke, Palgrave.

Barn, R. (1993) *Black Children in the Public Care System*, London, Batsford.

Barrett, M. and McIntosh, M. (1982) *The Anti-Social Family*, London, Verso.

Bauman, Z. (1992) *Intimations of Postmodernity*, London, Routledge.

Beck, U. (1992) *Risk Society*, London, Sage.

—— (1997) 'Democratisation of the family', *Childhood*, 4, 2, pp. 151–168.

Bell, S. (1988) *When Salem Came to the Boro*, London, Pan.

Beresford, P. (2000) 'The user review of the personal social services', *Shaping Futures*, www.elsc.org.uk/users and carers/shaping/prez2.html.

—— (2003) 'A missed chance to listen to the child', *The Guardian*, 5 Feb.

Berridge, D. (2002) 'Residential care' in McNeish, D., Newman, T. and Roberts, H. (eds) *What Works for Children?* Buckingham, Open University Press, pp. 83–103.

Besharov, D. (1990) *Recognizing Child Abuse*, New York, Free Press.

Biestek, F. (1961) *The Casework Relationship*, London, Allen & Unwin.

Blair, T. (1998) *The Third Way*, London, Fabian Society.

—— (2000) 'Foreword' in Cabinet Office, *Prime Minister's Review: Adoption*, London, Cabinet Office, pp. 3–4.

Blair, T. and Schröder, G. (1999) *Europe: The Third Way – die Neue Mitte*, London, Labour Party and SPD.

Blom-Cooper, L. (1985) *A Child in Trust*, Harrow, London Borough of Brent.

—— (1987) *A Child in Mind*, London, London Borough of Greenwich.

Bowis, J. (1995) 'Foreword' in Department of Health (1995a) *Child Protection: Messages from Research*, London, HMSO.

Bowlby, J. (1953) *Child Care and the Growth of Love*, Harmondsworth, Pelican.

Bradford, J. and Smith, R. (1998) *Children and Divorce*, London, Church House Press.

Brewer, C. and Lait, J. (1980) *Can Social Work Survive?* London, Temple Smith.

Broad, B. (1998) *Young People Leaving Care: Life after the Children Act 1989*, London, Jessica Kingsley.

Broad, B. (ed.) (2001) *Kinship Care*, Lyme Regis, Russell House Publishing.

Brodie, I. (2001) 'Children looked after' in Cull, L.-A. and Roche, J. (eds) *The Law and Social Work*, Basingstoke, Palgrave, pp. 155–162.

British False Memory Society (2002) *Newsletter*, 10, 1, Oct.

Buchanan, A. (2002) 'Family support' in McNeish, D., Newman, T. and Roberts, H. (eds) *What Works for Children?* Buckingham, Open University Press, pp. 252–273.

Burke, B. and Dalrymple, J. (2002) 'Intervention and empowerment' in Adams, R., Dominelli, L. and Payne, M. (eds) *Critical Practice in Social Work*, Basingstoke, Macmillan.

Butler-Sloss, E. (1988) *Report of the Inquiry into Child Abuse in Cleveland 1987*, London, HMSO.

Cabinet Office (2000) *Prime Minister's Review: Adoption*, London, Cabinet Office.

Campbell, B. (1988) *Unofficial Secrets*, London, Virago.

Candappa, M. (2002) 'Human rights and refugee children in the UK' in Franklin, B. (ed.) *The New Handbook of Children's Rights*, London, Routledge, pp. 223–236.

Cannan, C. (1992) *Changing Families, Changing Welfare*, Hemel Hempstead, Harvester/Wheatsheaf.

Central Council for Education and Training in Social Work (CCETSW) (1989) *Requirements and Regulations for the Diploma in Social Work*, London, CCETSW.

Central Council for Education and Training in Social Work (CCETSW) (1995) *Assuring Quality in the Diploma in Social Work – 1: Rules and Requirements for the Diploma in Social Work*, London, CCETSW.

Channer, Y. and Parton, N. (1990) 'Racism, cultural relativism and child protection' in The Violence Against Children Study Group (eds) *Taking Child Abuse Seriously*, London, Routledge.

Chief Secretary to the Treasury (2003) *Every Child Matters*, London, The Stationery Office.

Children and Young People's Unit (2001a) *Building a Strategy for Children and Young People*, London, CYPU.

Children and Young People's Unit (2001b) *Tomorrow's Future*, London, CYPU.

Children are unbeatable (2001) 'Briefing for MSPs – Debate in the Scottish Parliament' on Thursday 13 Sept.

Children are unbeatable (2002) *Submission to the Victoria Climbie Inquiry by the 'Children are unbeatable!' Alliance*, www.childrenareunbeatable.org.uk/pages/news/climbie.html.

Children's Legal Centre (1994) *Annual Report 1993*, London, Children's Legal Centre.

Children's Legal Centre (1999) *The Children's Legal Centre Annual Report 1998–1999*, Colchester, Children's Legal Centre.

Children's Legal Centre (2004) 'About the centre', www2.essex.ac.uk/clc/hi/centre.default.htm.

Clark, C. (2000) *Social Work Ethics*, Basingstoke, Palgrave.

Clarke, J. (1996) 'After social work?' in Parton, N. (ed.) *Social Theory, Social Change and Social Work*, London, Routledge, pp. 36–60.

Clarke, J., Cochrane, A. and Smart, C. (1987) *Ideologies of Welfare*, London, Hutchinson Education.

Clarke, J., Gewirtz, S. and McLaughlin, E. (2000) *New Managerialism, New Welfare?* London, Sage.

Cleaver, H. and Freeman, P. (1995) *Parental Perspectives in Cases of Suspected Child Abuse*, London, HMSO.

Cleaver, H., Unell, I. and Aldgate, J. (1998) *Children's Needs – Parenting Capacity*, London, The Stationery Office.

Cloke, C. and Davies, M. (eds) (1995) *Participation and Empowerment in Child Protection*, Chichester, Wiley.

Committee on Local Authority and Allied Personal Social Services (Seebohm Committee) (1968) *Report of the Committee on Local Authority and Allied Personal Social Services*, London, HMSO.

Connexions (2002) 'Your Brand', www.connexions.gov.uk/partnerships/brand/words/cx_brand_philosophy.pdf.

Corby, B. (1996) 'Risk assessment in child protection work' in Kemshall, H. and Pritchard, J. (eds) *Good Practice in Risk Assessment and Risk Management*, Volume 1, London, Jessica Kingsley, pp. 13–30.

—— (2000) *Child Abuse: Towards a Knowledge Base* (2nd edn), Buckingham, Open University.

Corrigan, P. and Leonard, P. (1978) *Social Work Practice Under Capitalism*, Basingstoke, Macmillan.

Corsaro, W. (1997) *The Sociology of Childhood*, California, Pine Forge Press.

Craig, G. and Coles, B. (2002) 'The needs of excluded young people in multi-cultural communities', *Findings*, 212, York, Joseph Rowntree Foundation.

Croft, S. and Beresford, P. (2002) 'Service users' perspectives' in Davies, M. (ed.) *The Blackwell Companion to Social Work*, Oxford, Blackwell, pp. 385–393.

Cull, L.-A. (2001) 'Family breakdown' in Cull, L.-A. and Roche, J. (eds) *The Law and Social Work*, Basingstoke, Palgrave.

Dale, P., Davies, M., Morrison, T. and Waters, J. (1986) *Dangerous Families*, London, Routledge.

Dale-Emberton (2001) 'Working with children: a guardian *Ad Litem*'s experience' in Cull, L.-A. and Roche, J. (eds) *The Law and Social Work*, Basingstoke, Palgrave, pp. 198–202.

Dalrymple, J. and Burke, B. (1995) *Anti-Oppressive Practice*, Buckingham, Open University Press.

Davies, M. (1981) *The Essential Social Worker*, London, Heinemann.

Department for Education and Skills (2003a) *Day Care and Childminding (National Standards) (England) Regulations 2003*, London, The Stationery Office.

Department for Education and Skills (2003b) *The Children Act Report 2002*, London, The Stationery Office.

Department of Health (1989) *An Introduction to The Children Act 1989*, London, HMSO.

Department of Health (1991a) *Children Act Guidance and Regulations*, Volumes 1–9, London, HMSO.

Department of Health (1991b) *Patterns & Outcomes in Child Placement*, London, HMSO.

Department of Health (1991c) *Working Together under the Children Act 1989*, London, HMSO.

Department of Health (1995a) *Child Protection: Messages from Research*, London, HMSO.

Department of Health (1995b) *Children Act Report 1994*, London, HMSO.

Department of Health (1998a) *Modernising Social Services*, London, The Stationery Office.

Department of Health (1998b) 'The Quality Protects programme: transforming children's services', LAC 98(28), London, Department of Health.

Department of Health (1999) *The Government's Objectives for Children's Social Services*, London, Department of Health.

Department of Health (2000a) *Adoption: A New Approach*, London, Department of Health.

Department of Health (2000b) *Assessing Children in Need and their Families: Practice Guidance*, London, The Stationery Office.

Department of Health (2000c) *The Children Act Report 1995–99*, London, The Stationery Office.

Department of Health (2001a) *The Children Act Now: Messages from Research*, London, The Stationery Office.

Department of Health (2001b) *National Adoption Standards for England*, London, Department of Health.

Department of Health (2001c) *Statistical Bulletin: Children Looked after in England*, London, Department of Health.

Department of Health (2002a) *National Standards for the Provision of Children's Advocacy Services*, London, The Stationery Office.

Department of Health (2002b) *The Quality Protects Programme: Transforming Children's Services 2003–04*, London, Department of Health.

Department of Health (2002c) *Statistical Bulletin: Children Looked after in England: 2000/2001*, London, Department of Health.

Department of Health and Department for Education and Employment (2000) *Guidance on the Education of Children and Young People in Public Care*, London, DfEE/DoH.

Department of Health, Home Office and Department for Education and Employment (1999) *Working Together to Safeguard Children*, London, The Stationery Office.

Department of Health, Department for Education and Employment and Home Office (2000) *Framework for the Assessment of Children in Need and their Families*, London, The Stationery Office.

Department of Health and Welsh Office (1993) *Children Act 1992*, London, HMSO.

Department of Health and Social Security (1974a) *Non-Accidental Injury to Children*, London, HMSO.

Department of Health and Social Security (1974b) *The Family in Society: Preparation for Parenthood*, London, HMSO.

Department of Health and Social Security (1976) 'Non-accidental injury to children: area review committees', LASSL 76(2), London, DHSS.

Department of Health and Social Security (1985a) *Review of Child Care Law*, London, HMSO.

Department of Health and Social Security (1985b) *Social Work Decisions in Child Care*, London, HMSO.

Department of Health and Social Security, Home Office, Lord Chancellor's Department, Department of Education and Science, Welsh Office, Scottish Office (1987) *The Law on Child Care and Family Services*, London, HMSO.

Dingwall, R., Eekelaar, J. and Murray, T. (1983) *The Protection of Children: State Intervention and Family Life*, Oxford, Basil Blackwell.

Dominelli, L. (1988) *Anti-Racist Social Work*, Basingstoke, Macmillan.

—— (1998) 'Anti-oppressive practice in context' in Adams, R., Dominelli, L. and Payne, M. (eds) *Social Work: Themes, Issues and Critical Debates*, Basingstoke, Macmillan, pp. 3–22.

—— (2002) 'Values in social work: contested entities with enduring qualities' in Adams, R., Dominelli, L. and Payne, M. (eds) *Critical Practice in Social Work*, Basingstoke, Palgrave, pp. 15–27.

—— (2004) *Social Work*, Cambridge, Polity Press.

Dominelli, L. and McLeod, E. (1989) *Feminist Social Work*, Basingstoke, Macmillan.

Donzelot, J. (1979) *The Policing of Families*, Baltimore, Johns Hopkins.

Dutt, R. and Phillips, M. (2000) 'Assessing black children in need and their families' in Department of Health (ed.) *Assessing Children in Need and their Families*, London, The Stationery Office, pp. 37–72.

Eekelaar, J. (1991) 'Parental responsibility: state of nature or nature of the state?', *Journal of Social Welfare & Family Law*, 1, pp. 37–50.

Esping-Andersen, G. (1990) *The Three Worlds of Welfare Capitalism*, Oxford, Polity Press.

—— (1999) *Social Foundations of Postindustrial Economies*, Oxford, Oxford University Press.

Family Rights Group (FRG) (1986) *FRG's Response to the DHSS Consultation Paper: Child Abuse – Working Together*, London, FRG.

Family Rights Group (FRG) (1987) *Submission to the House of Commons Select Committee on Children in Care*, London, FRG.

Family Rights Group (FRG) (1991) *The Children Act 1989 – An FRG Briefing Pack*, London, FRG.

Family Rights Group (FRG) (2003) 'More about us', www.frg.org.uk/More/more.asp.

Family Rights Group (FRG) (2004) 'Policies', www.frg.org.uk/More/policies.asp.

Family Rights Group, Family Welfare Association and Parentline Plus (2003) *Every Child Matters: A Joint Response from Family Rights Group, Family Welfare Association and Parentline Plus*, London, FRG/FWA/Parentline Plus.

Farmer, E. and Owen, M. (1995) *Child Protection Practice: Private Risks and Public Remedies*, London, HMSO.

Field, F. (1996) 'Britain's underclass: countering the growth' in Lister, R. (ed.) *Charles Murray and the Underclass: The Developing Debate*, London, IEA Health and Welfare Unit, pp. 57–60.

Fisher, M., Marsh, P. and Phillips, D. with Sainsbury, E. (1986) *In and Out of Care*, London, Batsford.

Fitzgerald, T. (1987) 'The new right and the family' in Loney, M., Bocock, R., Clarke, J., Cochrane, A., Graham, P. and Wilson, M. (eds) *The State or the Market*, London, Sage, pp. 46–57.

Fook, J. (2002) *Social Work: Critical Theory and Practice*, London, Sage.

Foucault, M. (1979) *Discipline and Punish*, Harmondsworth, Peregrine.

Fox, L. (1982) 'Two value positions in recent child care law and practice', *British Journal of Social Work*, 12, pp. 265–290.

Fox Harding, L. (1991a) 'The Children Act 1989 in context: four perspectives in child care law and policy (1)', *Journal of Social Welfare and Family Law*, 3, pp. 179–193.

—— (1991b) 'The Children Act 1989 in context: four perspectives in child care law and policy (2)', *Journal of Social Welfare and Family Law*, 4, pp. 299–316.

—— (1996) *Family, State & Social Policy*, Basingstoke, Macmillan.

—— (1997) *Perspectives in Child Care Policy* (2nd edn), Harlow, Addison Wesley Longman.

Franklin, B. (2002a) 'Children's rights: an introduction' in Franklin, B. (ed.) *The New Handbook of Children's Rights*, London, Routledge, pp. 1–12.

—— (2002b) 'Children's rights and media wrongs: changing representations of children and the developing rights agenda' in Franklin, B. (ed.) *The New Handbook of Children's Rights*, London, Routledge, pp. 15–42.

Franklin, B. (ed.) (2002c) *The New Handbook of Children's Rights*, London, Routledge.

Freeman, M. (1983) *The Rights and Wrongs of Children*, London, Frances Pinter.

—— (1992) 'In the child's best interests?', *Current Legal Problems*, 45, 1, pp. 173–211.

—— (2002) 'Children's rights ten years after ratification' in Franklin, B. (ed.) *The New Handbook of Children's Rights*, London, Routledge, pp. 97–118.

French, M. and Hamilton, C. (2000) *Contact and Children: A Review of Contactline*, Colchester, Children's Legal Centre.

Forrest, V. (2003) 'How post-adoption support can make adoption a success' in Douglas, A. and Philpot, T. (eds) *Adoption: Changing Families, Changing Times*, Routledge, London, pp. 132–138.

Frost, N. (2002) 'Evaluating practice' in Adams, R., Dominelli, L. and Payne, M. (eds) *Critical Practice in Social Work*, Basingstoke, Palgrave, pp. 46–54.

Frost, N. and Stein, M. (1989) *The Politics of Child Welfare*, Hemel Hempstead, Harvester/Wheatsheaf.

—— (1990) 'The politics of the Children Act', *Childright*, 68, pp. 17–19.

Gamble, A. (1988) *The Free Economy and the Strong State*, Basingstoke, Macmillan.

Garland, D. (2001) *The Culture of Control*, Oxford, Oxford University Press.

Geach, H. (1983) 'Child abuse registers: a time for a change' in Geach, H. and Szwed, E. (eds) *Providing Civil Justice for Children*, London, Edward Arnold.

General Medical Council (GMC) (2004) 'The duties of a doctor', www.gmc-uk.org/standards/default.htm.

General Social Care Council (GSCC) (2002a) *Accreditation of Universities to Grant Degrees in Social Work*, London, GSCC.

General Social Care Council (GSCC) (2002b) *Codes of Practice for Social Care Workers and Employers*, London, GSCC.

George, V. and Wilding, P. (1976) *Ideology and Social Welfare*, London, Routledge & Kegan Paul.

—— (1985) *Ideology and Social Welfare* (2nd edn), London, Routledge & Kegan Paul.

—— (1994) *Welfare and Ideology*, Hemel Hempstead, Harvester/Wheatsheaf.

Ghate, D. and Ramella, M. (2002) *Positive Parenting*, London, Policy Research Bureau.

Gibbons, J., Conroy, S. and Bell, C. (1995) *Operating the Child Protection System*, London, HMSO.

Giddens, A. (1991) *Modernity and Self-Identity*, Cambridge, Polity Press.

Gilligan, R. (2001) 'Working with social networks: key resources in helping children at risk' in Hill, M. (ed.) *Effective Ways of Working with Children and Their Families*, London, Jessica Kingsley, pp. 70–91.

Glaser, B. and Strauss, A. (1967) *The Discovery of Grounded Theory*, Chicago, Aldine.

Goldstein, J., Freud, A. and Solnit, A. (1973) *Beyond the Best Interests of the Child*, Chicago, Free Press.

—— (1980) *Before the Best Interests of the Child*, London, Burnett Books.

Gramsci, A. (1971) *Selections from Prison Notebooks*, London, Lawrence and Wishart.

Gupta, A. (2003) 'Adoption, race and identity' in Douglas, A. and Philpot, T. (eds) *Adoption: Changing Families, Changing Times*, London, Routledge, pp. 208–214.

Hall, S., Critcher, C., Jefferson, T., Clarke, J. and Roberts, B. (1978) *Policing the Crisis*, London, Macmillan.

Hardiker, P. and Barker, M. (1994) *The 1989 Children Act: Social Work Processes, Social Policy Contexts and 'Significant Harm'*, Leicester, University of Leicester School of Social Work.

Hardiker, P., Exton, K. and Barker, M. (1991) *Policies and Practices in Preventive Child Care*, Aldershot, Avebury.

Harding, L. (2003) personal communication.

Harris, J. (2003) *The Social Work Business*, London, Routledge.

Harris, R. and Timms, N. (1993) *Secure Accommodation in Child Care*, London, Routledge.

Hendrick, H. (1994) *Child Welfare 1872–1989*, London, Routledge.

Higgins, J. (1981) *States of Welfare*, Oxford, Basil Blackwell/Martin Robertson.

Holman, B. (1988) *Putting Families First*, Basingstoke, Macmillan.

—— (1993) *A New Deal for Social Welfare*, Oxford, Lion Publishing.

Holt, J. (1974) *Escape from Childhood*, Harmondsworth, Pelican.

Home Office (1998) *Supporting Families*, London, Home Office.

Home Office (2000) *Crime and Disorder Act 1998 – Community-Based Orders*, London, Home Office.

Hopkins, J. (1996) 'Social work through the looking glass' in Parton, N. (ed.) *Social Theory, Social Change and Social Work*, London, Routledge, pp. 19–35.

Horne, M. (1999) *Values in Social Work* (2nd edn), Aldershot, Ashgate.

Horwath, J. (ed.) (2001) *The Child's World*, London, Jessica Kingsley.

House of Commons Social Services Committee (Short Committee) (1984) *Second Report on Children in Care*, London, HMSO.

Howitt, D. (1992) *Child Abuse Errors*, Hemel Hempstead, Harvester/Wheatsheaf.

Humphries, B. and Truman, C. (eds) (1994) *Re-thinking Social Research*, Aldershot, Avebury.

Hunt, J., Macleod, A. and Thomas, C. (1999) *The Last Resort: Child Protection, the Courts and the 1989 Children Act*, London, The Stationery Office.

Ince, L. (2001) 'Promoting kinship foster care: preserving family networks for black children of african origins' in Broad, B. (ed.) *Kinship Care*, Lyme Regis, Russell House Publishing.

Jackson, S. (1995) 'Introduction' in Ward, H. (ed.) *Looking After Children: Research into Practice*, London, HMSO, pp. 3–18.

James, A., Jenks, C. and Prout, A. (1998) *Theorising Childhood*, Polity Press, Cambridge.

Johnson, T., Dandeker, C. and Ashworth, C. (1984) *The Structure of Social Theory*, Basingstoke, Macmillan.

Jones, A. (2003) 'The fiction of permanence' in Douglas, A. and Philpot, T. (eds) *Adoption: Changing Families, Changing Times*, London, Routledge, pp. 172–178.

Jones, C. (2001) 'Voices from the front line: state social workers and New Labour', *British Journal of Social Work*, 31, pp. 547–562.

Jones, D., Pickett, J., Oates, M. and Barbor, P. (1987) *Understanding Child Abuse*, Basingstoke, Macmillan.

Jones Finer, C. (1999) 'Trends and developments in welfare states' in Clasen, J. (ed.) *Comparative Social Policy*, Oxford, Blackwell.

Kalberg, S. (1994) *Max Weber's Comparative-Historical Sociology*, Cambridge, Polity Press.

Katz, I. (1995) 'Approaches to empowerment and participation in child protection' in Cloke, C. and Davies, M. (eds) *Participation and Empowerment in Child Protection*, Chichester, Wiley, pp. 154–169.

Kenward, H. (2002) *Ainlee*, Newham, Newham Area Child Protection Committee.

King, M. and Trowell, J. (1992) *Children's Welfare and the Law*, London, Sage.

Kirby, P. (2002) 'Involving young people in research' in Franklin, B. (ed.) *The New Handbook of Children's Rights*, London, Routledge, pp. 268–284.

Kirkwood, A. (1993) *The Leicestershire Inquiry 1992*, Leicester, Leicestershire County Council.

Kirton, D. (2000) *'Race', Ethnicity and Adoption*, Buckingham, Open University Press.

Kuhn, T. (1970) *The Structure of Scientific Revolutions* (2nd edn), London, University of Chicago Press.

Laming, H. (2003) *The Victoria Climbie Inquiry*, London, The Stationery Office.

Leathard, A. (2003) 'Introduction' in Leathard, A. (ed.) *Interprofessional Collaboration*, Hove, Brunner-Routledge, pp. 3–11.

Lee, P. and Raban, C. (1985) 'Welfare and ideology' in Loney, M., Boswell, D. and Clarke, J. (eds) *Social Policy and Social Welfare*, Milton Keynes, Open University Press.

Leonard, P. (1984) *Personality and Ideology*, Basingstoke, Macmillan.

—— (1997) *Postmodern Welfare*, London, Sage.

Levy, A. and Kahan, B. (1991) *The Pindown Experience and the Protection of Children*, Stafford, Staffordshire County Council.

Lishman, J. (1998) 'Personal and professional development' in Adams, R., Dominelli, L. and Payne, M. (eds) *Social Work: Themes, Issues and Critical Debates*, Basingstoke, Macmillan, pp. 89–103.

Lyon, C. (1989) 'Legal developments following the Cleveland report in England – a consideration of some aspects of the children bill', *Journal of Social Welfare Law*, 4, pp. 200–206.

MacDonald, G. (2002) 'Child protection' in McNeish, D., Newman, T. and Roberts, H. (eds) *What Works for Children?* Buckingham, Open University.

Marchant, R. and Jones, M. (2000) 'Assessing the needs of disabled children and their families' in Department of Health (ed.) *Assessing Children in Need and their Families*, London, The Stationery Office, pp. 73–112.

McLeod, M. and Saraga, E. (1991) 'Child sexual abuse: challenging the ortho-doxy' in Loney, M., Bocock, R., Clarke, J., Cochrane, A., Graham, P. and Wilson, M. (eds) *The State or the Market*, London, Sage, pp. 94–136.

McNeish, D. Newman, T. and Roberts, H. (eds) What Works for Children? Buckingham, Open University.

Melhuish, E. (2003) 'The national evaluation of Sure Start in England', conference speech, Montreal, 9–10 May.

Middleton, S. (1999) *Disabled Children: Challenging Social Exclusion*, Oxford, Blackwell.

Milham, S., Bullock, R., Hosie, K. and Haak, M. (1986) *Lost in Care*, Aldershot, Gower.

Minford, P. (1991) 'The role of the social services: a view from the New Right' in Loney, M., Bocock, R., Clarke, J., Cochrane, A., Graham, P. and Wilson, M. (eds) *The State or the Market*, London, Sage, pp. 70–82.

Monaghan, M. and Broad, B. (2003) *Talking Sense*, London, The Children's Society.

Morgan, P. (1992) *The Hidden Costs of Childcare*, Milton Keynes, Family Education Trust.

—— (1995) *Farewell to the Family?* London, IEA Health and Welfare Unit.

Morris, A. and Giller, H. (1983) *Providing Criminal Justice for Children*, London, Edward Arnold.

Morris, A., Giller, H., Szwed, E. and Geach, H. (1980) *Justice for Children*, London, Macmillan.

Morris, K. (2002) 'Family-based social work' in Adams, R., Dominelli, L. and Payne, M. (eds) *Critical Practice in Social Work*, Basingstoke, Palgrave, pp. 126–136.

Moss, P. and Petrie, P. (2002) *From Children's Services to Children's Spaces*, London, Routledge.

Mount, F. (1982) *The Subversive Family*, London, Jonathan Cape.

Moyers, S. and Mason, A. (1995) 'Identifying standards of parenting' in Ward, H. (ed.) *Looking After Children: Research into Practice*, London, HMSO, pp. 67–87.

Mullender, A., Hague, G., Imam, U., Kelly, L., Malos, E. and Regan, L. (2002) *Children's Perspectives on Domestic Violence*, London, Sage.

Murray, C. (1994) 'What to do about welfare', Commentary, Volume 98, 12 Feb.

—— (1996a) 'The emerging British underclass' in Lister, R. (ed.) *Charles Murray and the Underclass: The Developing Debate*, London, IEA Health and Welfare Unit, pp. 23–54.

—— (1996b) 'Underclass: the crisis deepens' in Lister, R. (ed.) *Charles Murray and the Underclass: The Developing Debate*, London, IEA Health and Welfare Unit, pp. 100–136.

National Care Standards Commission (2003) *Protecting People Improving Lives*, London, The Stationery Office.

National Society for the Prevention of Cruelty to Children (NSPCC) (2000) *A History of the NSPCC*, London, NSPCC.

National Society for the Prevention of Cruelty to Children (NSPCC) (2002) *NSPCC – About Us*, www.nspcc.org.uk/html/Home/Aboutus/aboutus.htm.

Newman, J. (2001) *Modernising Governance*, London, Sage.

Noyes, P. (1991) *Child Abuse: A Study of Inquiry Reports 1980–1989*, London, HMSO.

Oliver, M. (1990) *The Politics of Disablement*, Basingstoke, Macmillan.

O'Kane, C. (2000) 'The development of participatory techniques: facilitating children's views about decisions which affect them' in Christensen, P. and James, A. (eds) *Research with Children: Perspectives and Practices*, London, Falmer Press, pp. 136–159.

O'Neill, T. (2001) *Children in Secure Accommodation*, London, Jessica Kingsley.

Otway, O. (1996) 'Social work with children and families: from child welfare to child protection' in Parton, N. (ed.) *Social Theory, Social Change and Social Work*, London, Routledge, pp. 152–171.

Owusu-Bempah, K. and Howitt, D. (2000) 'Socio-genealogical connectedness: on the role of gender and same gender parenting in mitigating the effects of parental divorce', *Child and Family Social Work*, 5, 2, pp. 107–116.

Packman, J. with Randall, J. and Jacques, N. (1986) *Who Needs Care?* Oxford, Basil Blackwell.

Packman, J. and Jordan, B. (1991) 'The Children Act: looking forward, looking back', *British Journal of Social Work*, 21, 4, pp. 315–327.

Page, R. (1999) 'The prospects for social welfare' in Page, R. and Silburn, R. (eds) *British Social Welfare in the Twentieth Century*, Basingstoke, Palgrave, pp. 301–314.

PAIN (Parents Against INjustice) (1993) *Statement of Purposes*, Stansted, PAIN.

PAIN (Parents Against INjustice) (2003) 'Parents Against Injustice (PAIN)', www.parentsagainstinjustice.org.uk.

Parker, R. (1990) *Away from Home*, Ilford, Barnardo's.

—— (1999) *Adoption Now: Messages from Research*, London, The Stationery Office.

Parker, R., Ward, H., Jackson, S., Aldgate, J. and Wedge, P. (eds) (1991) *Looking After Children: Assessing Outcomes in Child Care*, London, HMSO.

Parton, N. (1990) 'Taking child abuse seriously' in The Violence Against Children Study Group (eds) *Taking Child Abuse Seriously: Contemporary Issues in Child Protection Theory and Practice*, London, Unwin Hyman, pp. 7–24.

—— (1991) *Governing the Family*, Basingstoke, Macmillan.

—— (1996) 'Social theory, social change and social work: an introduction' in Parton, N. (ed.) *Social Theory, Social Change and Social Work*, London, Routledge, pp. 4–19.

—— (2002) 'Narrow, restrictive and reactive', *Community Care*, 21–27 Feb., pp. 24–25.

Parton, N. and Marshall, W. (1998) 'Postmodernism and discourse approaches to social work' in Adams, R., Dominelli, L. and Payne, M. (eds) *Social Work: Themes, Issues and Critical Debates*, Basingstoke, Macmillan, pp. 240–250.

Percy-Smith, J. (2000) 'Introduction: the contours of social exclusion' in Percy-Smith, J. (ed.) *Policy Responses to Social Exclusion*, Buckingham, Open University Press, pp. 1–21.

Petrie, P., Egharevba, I., Oliver, C. and Poland, G. (2000) *Out-of-School Lives, Out-of-School Services*, London, The Stationery Office.

Pinker, R. (1971) *Social Theory and Social Policy*, London, Heinemann.

Polnay, J. (ed.) (2001) *Child Protection in Primary Care*, Abingdon, Radcliffe Medical Press.

Powell, M. (ed.) (2000) *New Labour, New Welfare State?* Bristol, The Policy Press.

Quality Assurance Agency (2002) *Subject Benchmark Statement for Degrees in Social Work*, London, QAA.

Rawson, D. (1994) 'Models of inter-professional work: likely theories and possibilities' in Leathard, A. (ed.) *Going Inter-Professional*, London, Routledge, pp. 38–63.

Roche, J. (2002) 'The Children Act 1989 and children's rights: a critical reassessment' in Franklin, B. (ed.) *The New Handbook of Children's Rights*, London, Routledge, pp. 60–80.

Roker, D. (1998) *Worth More Than This*, London, The Children's Society.

Rowe, J. and Lambert, L. (1973) *Children Who Wait*, London, Association of British Adoption Agencies.

Runciman, W. (ed.) (1978) *Weber: Selections in Translation*, Cambridge, Cambridge University Press.

Ryburn, M. (1994) *Open Adoption: Research, Theory and Practice*, Aldershot, Avebury.

—— (1996) 'Adoption in England and Wales: current issues and future trends' in Hill, M. and Aldgate, J. (eds) *Child Welfare Services*, London, Jessica Kingsley, pp. 196–211.

Sapey, B. (2002) 'Physical disability' in Adams, R., Dominelli, L. and Payne, M. (eds) *Critical Practice in Social Work*, Basingstoke, Palgrave, pp. 181–189.

Schur, E. (1973) *Radical Non-Intervention*, Prentice-Hall, Englewood Cliffs, New Jersey.

Secretary of State for Health (1998) *The Government's Response to the Children's Safeguards Review*, London, The Stationery Office.

Secretary of State for Health, Secretary of State for the Home Department and Secretary of State for Education and Skills (2003) *Keeping Children Safe: The Government's Response to the* Victoria Climbie Inquiry Report *and Joint Chief Inspectors' Report* Safeguarding Children, London, The Stationery Office.

Secretary of State for Social Services (1974) *Report of the Committee of Inquiry into the Care and Supervision Provided in Relation to Maria Colwell*, London, HMSO.

Secretary of State for Social Services (1987) *The Law on Child Care and Family Services*, London, HMSO.

Shardlow, S. (1998) 'Values, ethics and social work' in Adams, R., Dominelli, L. and Payne, M. (eds) *Social Work: Themes, Issues and Critical Debates*, Basingstoke, Macmillan, pp. 23–33.

Sinclair, R. and Bullock, R. (2002) *Learning from Past Experience: A Review of Serious Case Reviews*, London, The Stationery Office.

Smart, C., Wade, A. and Neale, B. (1999) 'Objects of concern? – children and divorce', *Child and Family Law Quarterly*, 11, 4, pp. 365–376.

—— (2000) 'New childhoods: children and co-parenting after divorce', *ESRC Children 5–16 Research Briefing*, Swindon, Economic and Social Research Council.

Smith, R. (1990a) 'Parental responsibility and an irresponsible state?', *Childright*, 71, pp. 7–8.

—— (1990b) *Under the Breadline*, London, The Children's Society.

—— (1991) 'Child care: welfare, protection or rights?', *Journal of Social Welfare and Family Law*, 6, pp. 469–481.

—— (1995) *Values and Practice in Child Care*, University of Leicester, unpublished PhD thesis.

—— (2000a) 'Order and disorder: the contradictions of childhood', *Children & Society*, 14, 1, pp. 3–10.

—— (2000b) 'Whose childhood? the politics of homework', *Children & Society*, 14, 5, pp. 316–325.

—— (2002) 'The wrong end of the telescope: child protection or child safety?', *Journal of Social Welfare & Family Law*, 24, 3, pp. 247–261.

—— (2003) *Youth Justice: Ideas, Policy, Practice*, Cullompton, Willan.

—— (2004) 'Globalisation, individualisation and childhood: the challenge for social work', *New Global Development: Journal of International and Comparative Social Welfare*, Special 20th Anniversary Volumes, 1–2, pp. 71–78.

Smith, R., Dahme, H.-J. and Wohlfahrt, N. (2002) The Marketisation of Social Care in the UK and Germany, unpublished.

Smith, T. (1996) *Family Centres and Bringing Up Young Children*, London, HMSO.

Social Exclusion Unit (1999) *Teenage Pregnancy*, London, The Stationery Office.

Social Exclusion Unit (2001) *Preventing Social Exclusion*, London, The Stationery Office.

Social Services Inspectorate (SSI) (1995) *The Challenge of Partnership in Child Protection: Practice Guide*, London, HMSO.

Social Services Inspectorate (1998) *Someone Else's Children*, London, The Stationery Office.

Social Services Inspectorate (2002) *Coordinated Service Planning for Vulnerable Children and Young People in England*, London, Department of Health.

Standley, K. (2001) *Family Law*, Basingstoke, Palgrave.

Stanko, E., Crisp, D., Hale, C. and Lucraft, H. (1998) *Counting the Costs: Estimating the Impact of Domestic Violence in the London Borough of Hackney*, Swindon, Crime Concern.

Stein, M. and Carey, K. (1986) *Leaving Care*, Oxford, Basil Blackwell.

Stevenson, O. (1989) 'Reflections on social work practice' in Stevenson, O. (ed.) *Child Abuse: Public Policy and Professional Practice*, Hemel Hempstead, Harvester/Wheatsheaf.

Straw, J. (1998) 'Foreword' in Home Office, *Supporting Families*, London, Home Office, p. 2.

—— (1999) 'Speech to launch conference', *Supporting Families*, London, 25 Feb.

Sure Start (1999) *Sure Start for All*, London, Department for Education and Employment.

Sure Start (2003a) *Sure Start Guidance 2004–2006*, London, Sure Start.

Sure Start (2003b) 'Sure Start Principles', www.surestart.gov.uk/aboutsurestart/thesurestartprinciples2.

Taylor, C. and White, S. (2000) *Practising Reflexivity in Health and Welfare*, Buckingham, Open University Press.

Taylor, L., Lacey, R. and Bracken, D. (1979) *In Whose Best Interests?* London, The Cobden Trust/MIND.

Thoburn, J. (1991) 'The Children Act 1989: balancing child welfare with the concept of partnership with parents', *Journal of Social Welfare & Family Law*, 5, pp. 331–344.

Thoburn, J., Murdoch, A. and O'Brien, A. (1986) *Permanence in Child Care*, Oxford, Blackwell.

Thompson, N. (2001) *Anti-Discriminatory Practice* (3rd edn), Basingstoke, Palgrave.

Timmins, N. (1995) *The Five Giants*, London, HarperCollins.

Timmis, G. (2001) 'CAFCASS – a service for children or a service for the courts', *Family Law*, 31, p. 280.

Titmuss, R. (1973) *The Gift Relationship*, Harmondsworth, Pelican.

Triseliotis, J., Borland, M., Hill, M. and Lambert, L. (1995) *Teenagers and the Social Work Services*, London, HMSO.

Tunstill, J. (2000) 'Child care' in Hill, M. (ed.) *Local Authority Social Services: An Introduction*, Oxford, Blackwell, pp. 59–84.

Tunstill, J. (2003) 'Adoption and family support: two means in pursuit of the same end' in Douglas, A. and Philpot, T. (eds) *Adoption: Changing Families, Changing Times*, London, Routledge, pp. 99–105.

United Nations (1989) *United Nations Convention on the Rights of the Child*, Geneva, UN.

United Nations Committee on the Rights of the Child (UNCRC) (1995) *Concluding Observations of the Committee on the Rights of the Child: United Kingdom of Great Britain and Northern Ireland. 15/02/95*, Geneva, UN.

United Nations Committee on the Rights of the Child (UNCRC) (2002) *Concluding Observations of the Committee on the Rights of the Child: United Kingdom and Northern Ireland. 09/10/02*, Geneva, UN.

Utting, W. (1997) *People Like Us*, London, The Stationery Office.

Wallis, L. and Frost, N. (1998) *Cause for Complaint*, London, The Children's Society.

Ward, H. (ed.) (1995) *Looking After Children: Research into Practice*, London, HMSO.

Ward, H. and Rose, W. (eds) (2002) *Approaches to Needs Assessment in Children's Services*, London, Jessica Kingsley.

Waterhouse, R. (2000) *Lost in Care*, London, The Stationery Office.

Weber, M. (1957) *The Theory of Social and Economic Organisation*, Chicago, Free Press.

Williams, G. and McCreadie, J. (1992) *Ty Mawr Community Home Inquiry*, Newport, Gwent County Council.

Williams, F. (1996) 'Postmodernism, feminism and the question of difference' in Parton, N. (ed.) *Social Theory, Social Change and Social Work*, London, Routledge, pp. 61–76.

Williams, L. (1996) *Childhood Matters*, Volume 1: *The Report*, London, The Stationery Office.

Willow, C. and Dugdale, L.-M. (1999) *It's Not Fair*, London, The Children's Society.

Willow, C. and Gledhill, K. (2001) 'The Year of the Child?', *Community Care*, 4–10 Jan.

Winnicott, D. (1986) *Home is Where We Start From*, Harmondsworth, Pelican.

Wolff, R., Moore, B. and Marcuse, H. (1969) *A Critique of Pure Tolerance*, Boston, Beacon Press.

Worsley, P. (ed.) (1977) *Introducing Sociology*, Harmondsworth, Penguin.

Wyness, M. (2000) *Contesting Childhood*, London, Falmer Press.

Youth Justice Board (2000) *National Standards for Youth Justice*, London, Youth Justice Board.

INDEX